Boricua Literature

A Literary History of the Puerto Rican Diaspora

Lisa Sánchez González

NEW YORK UNIVERSITY PRESS
New York and London

For Mom, Dad, and KCK, with love and gratitude

NEW YORK UNIVERSITY PRESS
New York and London

Portions of chapter 1 were published in an earlier draft as "Luisa Capetillo: An Anarcho-feminist *Pionera* in the Mainland Puerto Rican Narrative/ Political Tradition," in the anthology entitled *Recovering the U.S. Hispanic Literary Heritage* vol. 2, ed. Erlinda González-Berry and Chuck Tatum (Houston: Arte Público Press) 1996, 148–67.

An abridged version of chapter 2 appeared as "Modernism and Boricua Literature: A Reconsideration of Arturo Schomburg and William Carlos Williams" in the journal *American Literary History* (OUP), May 2001.

Portions of chapter 6 were published in "Reclaiming Salsa," *Cultural Studies* 13 (2) 1999:237–50.

Library of Congress Cataloging-in-Publication Data
Sánchez González, Lisa, 1963–
Boricua literature : a literary history of the Puerto Rican diaspora /
Lisa Sánchez González.
p. cm.
Includes bibliographical references and index.
ISBN 0-8147-3146-5 (cloth : alk. paper) —
ISBN 0-8147-3147-3 (pbk. : alk. paper)
1. American literature—Puerto Rican authors—History and criticism.
2. Puerto Ricans—United States—Intellectual life. 3. Puerto Rican literature—History and criticism. 4. Puerto Ricans in literature. I. Title.
PS153.P83 S18 2001
810.9'97295—dc21 2001001774

New York University Press books are printed on acid-free paper, and their binding materials are chosen for strength and durability.

Manufactured in the United States of America

10 9 8 7 6 5 4 3 2 1

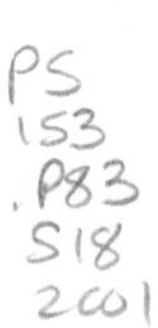

Contents

	Acknowledgments	*vii*
	Introduction	1
1	For the Sake of Love: Luisa Capetillo, Anarchy, and Boricua Literary History	16
2	Boricua Modernism: Arturo Schomburg and William Carlos Williams	42
3	A Boricua in the Stacks: An Introduction to the Life and Work of Pura Teresa Belpré	71
4	The Boricua Novel: Civil Rights and "New School" Nuyorican Narratives	102
5	"I Like to Be in America" [*sic*]: Three Women's Texts	134
6	*¡Ya Deja Eso!* Toward an Epi-*fenomenal* Approach to Boricua Cultural Studies	161
	Notes	*191*
	Bibliography	*201*
	Index	*213*
	About the Author	*216*

Acknowledgments

Alice Walker once said that she writes the books she yearns to read. Her words were a constant source of inspiration to me while I wrote my own book, the book I wanted and needed to read but never found at the library. I must thank Alice Walker, Nicholasa Mohr, Paule Marshall, Jamaica Kincaid, and all the other brave women whose books kept me company on the nearly isolated paths I took as a scholar, whose ideas revived my mind when theory numbed it, and whose graceful and powerful depictions of a familiar world reminded me to stay true to what I know.

This book is the product of a decade of study, writing, and research. That decade was a huge challenge, but in my struggle to prevail I was befriended by some amazing and gifted people. I must thank above all Katherine Callen King, my undergraduate mentor, graduate advisor, and dauntless protector at UCLA. Without her early guidance and unflinching support, I would never have realized my scholarly vocation. I thank Katherine for believing in my potential when so many others did not. Angie Chabram-Dernersesian has been an important role model for me. Her generosity of spirit, her genius, and her dedication to the life of the mind astound me, and I am honored by and grateful for her encouragement over the years. I must also thank the other senior scholars whose personal support has been an immense source of strength in my work and life as a junior scholar: Kamala Visweswaran, Frances Aparicio, Sheila Walker, Mercedes de Uriarte, and Martha Menchaca. Their friendship has meant the world to me.

A special thanks is due to my reading group colleagues at the University of Texas-Austin: Helena Woodard, Craig Watkins, Joni Jones, Ted Gordon, Liz Peña, and Robin Kilson, for striving to create a home on campus for critical race and gender studies, and to the students—Johnny Lorenz, Lisa Hernández, Maribel García, Ramón Rivera-Servera, Linta Varghese, Junaid Rana, Whitney Battle, Vincent Woodard, Eve Dunbar,

Marla Fuentes, and Jennifer Cárdenas—whose energy and intellect have also made UT a stimulating environment for the exchange of progressive and radical ideas. While I was completing this book, friends in Austin, Los Angeles, and New York kept me safe, real, and laughing. For this I am especially grateful to Julio de Souza Tavares, Sylvia Herrera, Verónica Pérez, Mary Lou Mares, Gabriel Aguirre, Gerald Thomason, Mari Infante, Bob Setty, Yonas Admassu, Ellen Healy, Victoria Santiago, Karen Wallace, John Bercovici, Genevieve Córdova, David Pendleton, Joyce Boss, Leonor Lizardo, Louie Sanchez, Rubén Lizardo, Carla Oglesby, Hunter Martin, Rose Faulborn, Heather, Chris, Cindy, and Ed Chamberlain, Ina, Pepín, and Richie Torres, Manuel Martínez, and most of all, to my best friends, Tito and Firi.

Teshome Gabriel, José Monleón, and Sam Weber gave me valuable feedback on this project at its inception. I am grateful to Brian Bremen, Ian Hancock, Wick Wadlington, Teresa Kelly, Barbara Harlow, and César Salgado for reading and commenting on chapter drafts. I would also like to thank Niko Pfund, Eric Zinner, Cecilia Feilla, Martha Kuhlman, Emily Park, and Despina Papazoglou Gimbel of New York University Press for their faith in and time on my book project, and Rosalie Morales Kearns for her meticulous edits and suggestions on the final manuscript.

The assistance I received in various libraries and collections was indispensable to my research and textual revisions. For their generous help I would like to thank Margo Gutiérrez and Jorge Salinas of the University of Texas-Austin's Benson Collection, Diana Lachatenere and the staff of the Schomburg Center for Research in Black Culture, Pedro Juan Hernández, Amílcar Tirado, and Marlon Aguilar of the Centro de Estudios Puertorriqueños library archives, and the staff of the Universidad de Puerto Rico Collección Puertorriqueña.

I am also grateful to those who helped fund the research and production of this book. I received research grants from the University of Texas Center for African and African American Studies, the University of Texas Summer Research Assignment fund, and the Recovery Project at the University of Houston, and a book subvention grant from the University of Texas-Austin's University Cooperative Society.

My parents, Miriam and Louis Sánchez, have always been my finest, most exacting teachers. My mother also proofread and commented on the entire first draft of the manuscript. I thank my mother and father for everything.

Introduction

This book is a literary history of narrative experimentation in the Puerto Rican colonial diaspora. Colonized shortly after the U.S. invasion of Puerto Rico in 1898, all Puerto Ricans are both American citizens and colonial subjects by birth according to international law. Well over a third of this population today lives in the continental United States, forming one of the nation's most significant "minority" communities. Yet despite our numbers and over a century of community building in our colonial metropole, no complete study of our literature has ever been published.[1] This book is intended to help fill this scholarly void with a series of six essays, chronologically organized, that explore representative writers, texts, and contexts of twentieth century Boricua literary history.

The title of this book, *Boricua Literature: A Literary History of the Puerto Rican Diaspora*, reflects the politics of mainland Puerto Rican group identity and marks the distinct colonial condition that has brought this community to and kept it in the States. "Boricua" is a common term of self-affirmation in the stateside community; it is an adjective that references the indigenous (Taíno) name of Puerto Rico's main island, Boriquén, as recorded by two Spanish colonial-era chroniclers, Bartolomé de las Casas and Hernando Colón (Hernández Aquino 1993: 87–90). "Nuyorican" is another important self-defining term. Initially a derisive word, popular among insular Puerto Ricans for demeaning mainland-born or -raised Puerto Ricans, "Nuyorican" was critically appropriated in the early 1970s by avant-garde poets in New York City (Algarín and Piñero 1975). Nuyorican has a specific resonance in New York, which historically has had the largest Boricua demographic in the States. For the purposes of this book, the term "Boricua" refers to the Puerto Rican diasporan community at large, and "Nuyorican" refers more specifically to the New York City community.

Throughout the twentieth century, most Puerto Ricans who moved to the mainland United States were the working poor, economic exiles of a colony devoted exclusively to serving the interests of U.S. corporations and the U.S. military (see Lewis 1963 and Maldonado-Denis 1988). Thus scholars often refer to this Puerto Rican colonial dispersion as a *diasporan*—as opposed to immigrant—experience. The term *diaspora* comes from the ancient Greek verb *diasporein,* which means to rout, to scatter, or, in the passive voice, the kind of fallout that occurs when, by irreversible force of events, natural elements are no longer contained in their usual or proper places. In contemporary social critique, diasporas refer to national, religious, or ethnic communities—such as descendants of enslaved Africans outside Africa, Jews outside Israel, or Palestinians outside Palestine—who were historically, often violently, evicted from their homelands (see Lemelle and Kelley 1994; Harris 1982; and Tölölyan 1996). Diaspora theory also helps analyze how such groups can be caught up in new patterns of community formation, new ways of being and understanding themselves in the world, and other collective responses to their eviction and to their condition as permanently dis- and relocated communities abroad (see Clifford 1994).

When I decided, many years ago, to use the term "diaspora" to describe the Boricua community, the point was to underscore the African American and Boricua experience of forced relocation to the United States and their shared contemporary condition as racial outsiders. While it is not slavery that brings the Puerto Rican diaspora to the States, it is a sadistic dynamic of eviction from a homeland, catalyzed by massive social inequalities (in part created by slavery and its effects),[2] in which the most marginalized groups on the Islands are deliberately shuttled into equally or more dire situations in the United States.[3] For these reasons, figuring Boricuas diasporically has always felt like the theoretical realization of an organic and historical affinity, and this study reads racial difference as a definitive feature for the Boricua community at large.

And in crucial ways, African American and Boricua dispersion dovetail in New York City; therefore many of the essays in this book investigate the historical overlap of Blackness and Latinidad in Boricua culture and literary history. Even though, as a politicized group identity, "Boricua" popularly recognizes the African diasporan roots of Puerto Rican social history, there are those in the Puerto Rican community who prefer to identify as "Hispanic" or "Latino" in order to cast off any suggestion of Blackness, just as there are those within other African diasporan and Latin American immigrant populations who prefer their national or regional identifications over any label that would associate them with African Americans or American Indians. My study attempts to challenge these expressions of internalized racism by attending to the Blackness of writers in Boricua literary history and analyzing the racial politics and racialized contexts that inform their lives and life's work. These essays not only recognize the African diasporan roots of Spanish Caribbean social history but also call attention to what should be recognized as a significant African diasporan legacy intrinsic to twentieth-century United States "Latino" culture.

Without question, racism has been one of the Boricua community's major obstacles in the twentieth century, and many Boricua writers have confronted and analyzed the sources, expressions, and consequences of racism as a social malaise in (and beyond) the United States. Likewise, sexism and "racism-sexism" (Nieto Gómez 1974)—or the confluences of racial and gender inequalities—are perennial thematic concerns in Boricua literature. Evaluating the development of Boricua writers' engagements with these and other collective social problems and crises across time is one of this book's major goals. Consequently, each essay helps piece together a specific *cultural intellectual* tradition that emerges from the literary and social histories of the Boricua community. Like other scholars dealing with cultural intellectual history, I often refer in this study to *discourse,* or the clusters of ideas that tend to resurface in writing and speech, clusters that are inextricably bound to their terms of expression and that form a sort of rhetorical arsenal for protecting or contesting the status quo.[4] I also examine *discursive strategies,* which, in literary studies, refer to the deliberate arrangement of such discourses in the novel, poetry, essay, and other formal genres of writing. These are particularly important when I talk of Boricuas as a *subaltern* community, or a group that has not only been invisible in national discourses of culture, but has been depicted in ways that make it impossible for the community *to render itself visible* in these discourses.[5] Since rendering a subaltern community visible in prevailing discourses is therefore, by definition, impossible, scholars in subaltern studies often analyze more symbolic (but equally sophisticated) forms of collective expression—street art, dance, stickball, or parades, for example—as vehicles of subaltern *articulation.* Appreciating subaltern articulation, in this sense, means understanding formal national languages as but one of many important and aesthetically improvised forms of human cultural communication in the public sphere.

The final chapter of this study interrogates one such form of subaltern articulation in the Boricua community—popular music. But the bulk of this study concerns explicitly literary history, and therefore might be read as an attempt to de-subalternize the Boricua community. That is, by unearthing and studying our own discursive projects, we can endeavor to make our presence tangible in the representational struggle over who and what precisely constitute *America* (i.e., the United States in the terms of its own nationalist discourse)—including its national culture and literature. In this sense, writing a Boricua literary history is, ironically perhaps, not unlike writing this community into being as legitimately American and, conversely, ensuring that the American cultural pedigree is recognized as, in part, Boricua. As I discuss in chapter 1, this kind of critical maneuver in and around America as an act of signification is indebted to a body of literary historical and cultural intellectual scholarship created in the wake of the United States civil rights movement. This scholarship is primarily preoccupied with reclaiming literatures produced by, with, and for communities of color in the United States (see Morrison 1992; Baker 1982; Kim 1982; Saldívar 1990; Sánchez 1985; and Allen 1986). Since traditional scholarly disciplines have invisibilized these communities' contributions, archives and rare book collections have become two of the most vital resources for creating new *literary canons,* or the compilation of texts considered fundamental to the development of a nation's literary tradition.

For scholars in ethnic American studies, literary canon formation is a ubiquitous but often only tacit endeavor, and finding lost or hidden texts in archives, attics, and special collections is part of this quiet but significant drama. As implicit canonical debates in African American, Asian American, and Chicano literature suggest, the stakes are high in this literary historical venture, primarily because finding new figures and texts that wedge out or critically complement the old standards can fundamentally reshape an entire generation's debates about American literary and cultural intellectual history. Insiders to the American "canon wars" (particularly archivists, I would argue) have an intimate understanding of how literary traditions are maintained, how they are built and bulwarked from start to finish. We know how precarious this process is, how figures can emerge as major writers for one generation, then languish in near total obscurity for the next. We also know that there are dangerous zones of contact with various disciplinary or even interdisciplinary establishments, that every decision we make, once published, may have an impact on the textual politics in the fields of American and ethnic studies. Archival work is therefore an important but complicated literary specialization. It is also, perforce, a holistic area of research, since archival researchers come full circle in their tasks as literary historians. These tasks are first, to find new texts; second, to analyze these texts and contextualize them as aesthetic historical artifacts; third, to survey and analyze how the existing knowledge base should accommodate the new material; and finally, to gauge the prospects of the next archival dig, if you will, making deliberate and informed decisions about where next to explore.

With careful attention to these literary historical methods and implications, this book offers readers a kind of patchwork of Boricuas in a cultural intellectual frame, analyzing the emblematic surfaces of their lives and activities captured in their writing. Much of the material I analyze here is in fact archival, and many of the figures I selected for analysis are lesser-known or neglected writers in both American and Puerto Rican literary historical scholarship. My archival and first-edition research revolves around three major collections: the Schomburg Papers, housed at the Schomburg Center for Research in Black Culture (the 135th Street branch of the New York Public Library system), the Colección Puertorriqueña at the Biblioteca Lázaro of the Universidad de Puerto Rico, Río Piedras, and Hunter College's Centro de Estudios Puertorriqueños library and archives.

My work in these special collections and archives was necessary because very little scholarly attention has been devoted to primary texts authored by Boricuas who published before the 1960s, and what little literary scholarship is in circulation generally concerns poetry. Although sociologists and anthropologists are fond of citing creative writing in this community as illustrations of bilingualism, code switching, and ethnic or class consciousness, my contribution to the field is an explicitly literary and historical analysis of an integral body of writing specific to the Boricua community.

The cultural intellectual history I uncover vis-à-vis Boricua narratives is patterned in an irregular but consistently ethically driven aesthetic, forming a poetic juxtaposition that I have learned to appreciate and even cherish on its own terms. Contemplating this aesthetic can be as involved as each person cares to make it, but my lenses and senses as a cultural and literary historian are calibrated not merely to fathom but also to *feel* the motifs and motives behind and within textual evidence. Through the fractured windows of the Boricua archive we can witness a human drama unfolding and, if we finely attune ourselves as readers, we can experience this drama in coeval empathy. This kind of mindful, embodied perception—what I would like to propose here as archival "rememory" (Morrison 1987)—is particularly available among the first generations of Boricua cultural intellectuals, whose essays are remarkably passionate. This passion has moved me—the life of my mind is also the life of my body, sentiments, and sensibilities—thus I have not only witnessed but *felt* their decided compulsion to write with exclamation marks, to polemicize, to call people (both dead and alive) and ideas out, to fight and scream in print, to blow up the metropole's postings, and I have *felt* the checking of this passion. And since this passion is righteous (ethically authentic), and since checking or repression of this sort always implies aesthetic displacement and transference, *metonymy* and *metaphor,* my study seeks this kind of sensual/literary resurfacing as an aspect of cultural intellectual writing we should dare to explore.

Luisa Capetillo (1879–1922) most profoundly calls us back to this kind of passion at the historical juncture of the working-class colonial diaspora's first settlements in the United States. As I elaborate in the first chapter, the Boricua experience of modernity at the turn of the twentieth century is brilliantly invoked in the corpus of a woman—a radical feminist, a radical anarchist—who was ignored and reviled in and after her time. Her writing presents the gorgeous and contentious relationship between her texts and contexts, suggesting that the genres of writing with which she experimented were inadequate to her visionary desires. Capetillo rode the edges of the most progressive discourses of her era, pushing further and further ahead, intimating an ideal somewhere beyond the sanctioned institutions of language and politics. Nothing is standardized (or sacred) in Capetillo's work—not Spanish, English, Church, State, Party, Marriage, Masses, Pleasure, nor Literature. Capetillo was compelled toward the most perfect expression of a quasi-metaphysical but totally human liberation, yet this desire never finds complete and utter satisfaction in her life or writing; instead, her work intimates the promise of fulfillment, just beyond reach, but close enough for the faithful to feel it coming. But unlike Glissant's (1981) diasporan "diversion" in the Caribbean—what he describes as a tendency among the colonized to look away from the domestic drama, the scene of their national bondage, searching for then idling in an elsewhere that conveniently obscures the colonial fact—Capetillo always bring us back to the scene of the wreckage in vivid detail. Capetillo thus represents, for me, the most appropriate foundational figure for our narrative history. Chapter 1, "For the Sake of Love: Luisa Capetillo, Anarchy, and Boricua Literary History," discusses how Capetillo opened a space in literature for the performance of a radical desire that fulfills itself somewhere beyond the text, one that yearns for a utopia while scribing and grieving the actual state of things; a desire whose projection, however, is not a luxury, but rather a necessity for survival in present and precise context.

As chapter 2 intimates, an archive is a curious notion, a kind of virtual deep freezer for papers and the affairs they represent; archives hold secrets we must all agree to tuck away, catalogued and put on ice for a posterity that is not necessarily supposed to care. The archival researcher moves in this frozen discursive realm, gloved and silent like a thief, looking for scandal, shivering and scribbling (only pencils are allowed in library archives) when s/he finds it. Archival documents are valuable precisely because they are obsolete, because they are illegitimate in the circuitry of capital exchange; they are priceless shares because they are authentic originals, and therefore it seems we must hide and treasure them in dry, chilly places. But when we find the inscription of lost voices in the archives and bring them back into the sun (thawing and massaging them by citation), it is a scandalous resurrection, a passionate revival. This is the hidden drama of Arturo Schomburg (1874–1938) and William Carlos Williams (1888–1963).

"Boricua Modernism: Arturo Schomburg and William Carlos Williams," the second chapter, dwells on what modernism means for Boricua literary and social history, analyzing Williams's and Schomburg's archival inventions and reinventions during the 1920s. Since both men are conventionally read as foundational figures for American modernism (the twentieth century's first major literary movement), I explain how Williams's and Schomburg's interpellation by academic discourses as "(white) American" and "Black (immigrant)" men (respectively positioned as intellectuals within the American "high" modernist and Harlem Renaissance contexts) belies the complications of their work as Boricua literature. Examining Schomburg's and Williams' poetics in colonial and African diasporan context forms the chapter's main priority. I analyze how both writers remaster the historical essay in efforts to seize the English language, turn it upside down, empty it of its usual meanings and refill it with new meanings—that is, their efforts to *Calibanize* narratives and genres of the Americas' colonization. I read Williams's *In the American Grain* (1925) in tandem with a selection of Schomburg's essays and private papers as texts that challenge, complement, or revise the discursive aspirations of their Anglo-American and African American contemporaries. Beyond the revelation of their significance as emblematic Boricua writers for their generation, this chapter explores the vicissitudes of Boricuas as a nationless nation coping with nationalist constructions of racial identity. Though they have different critiques of these constructions, they both express their critiques through texts stylized aesthetically and ethically in defiant counterpoint to prevailing notions of modernity, American culture, and national canon formation in the United States. The second chapter thus deals with the continuity of ethical/aesthetic enjambment in a unique modernist literary project that responds to *the* narrative predicament of the Puerto Rican diaspora: *paperlessness*.

While we revel in rescuing our paperwork, we must realize that what literacy and papers signify cannot and should not stand in for people themselves. The elitist underpinnings of traditional canon formation are subjects of critique throughout this book, a critique readied and launched in the first two chapters. In chapter 1 it should become clear that Luisa Capetillo was utterly disinterested in being a "great American writer," and this disinterest is one of the major reasons I recuperate her work as the most appropriate corpus for analyzing Boricua narrative experimentation at the turn of the century and, furthermore, as the most appropriate corpus for inaugurating Boricua cultural intellectual history. Chapter 2 explores both Schomburg's and Williams's preoccupation with rescuing lost testimony to the subaltern experience of American history (the *Americas*' history), and their efforts to refill evacuated archives reads in many ways as the guiding metaphor of my own project. Coursing between archives and the contemporary scene of warring cultural and racial imaginaries, between the past as a reservoir of feelings and the present as piles of antagonizing or vindicating books and documents, begets a literary historical method that necessarily fails when it relaxes its own motion between texts, contexts, and the affective legacies they represent.

Chapter 2 ends with a discussion of the significance of Boricua writing in comparison with other American literatures, leading into an exploration in chapter 3 of Pura Belpré's (1902–1982) collected papers. The first Afro-Latina librarian in the New York Public Library system (NYPL), hired and trained at the 135th Street branch (where Schomburg's archives became an institutional wedge for retaining and promoting Black librarians), Belpré, like Schomburg, strategized around bibliographical politics and policy initiatives affecting public library acquisitions and community service programs. Belpré's main concern was giving children access to and enthusiasm for books; she created the first multicultural, transracial, and bilingual children's reading room in the NYPL, and her efforts have yet to be fully explored and acknowledged in Puerto Rican studies and other relevant disciplines.

Chapter 3, "A Boricua in the Stacks: An Introduction to the Life and Work of Pura Teresa Belpré," examines how Belpré's contributions helped humanize the public library for its Harlem constituency, reshaping its character as an inviting, warm, and friendly environment for children, young adults, and their parents. Evidently, this was not a simple task: given the disarray that characterizes her papers, Belpré must have been one of the busiest women in Manhattan. One can easily imagine that her desk was a familiar mess, and yet, despite her hectic schedule and multiple responsibilities, Belpré managed not only to institute significant changes in New York City's public libraries and schools but to write fiction as well. Along with translating many Spanish-language Puerto Rican folktales into English and committing the orature she heard at home to paper, Belpré also authored a number of highly sensitive tales about Boricua and other children of color growing up and confronting complex prejudices in New York's urban neighborhoods. The poetics of place, gender, race, and cultural difference in Belpré's fiction create a nonexclusionary "home" for children of color in books, which complements the institutional programs she designed and implemented at the public library itself.

To foreground the complex engagement with institutions and self-representational interventions occurring during this period in the Nuyorican community, chapter 3 begins with a perusal of Pura Belpré's early and largely unpublished essays. Her archival essays provide a rare source of information about the earliest decades of Boricua history in Harlem. These essays not only help track Nuyorican settlement patterns and organizational politics, but also offer us invaluable insight into the everyday life of the community. In search of her public intellectual motivations as an activist and advocate, I pay special attention to Belpré's often digressive narration of her work, as I do in my reading of Luisa Capetillo's prose. Evaluating Belpré's literary and library work together also helps document alternative Boricua librarianship in Harlem, Brooklyn, and the Bronx throughout much of the twentieth century.

While the few articles in print on Belpré's life and work concentrate on constructing her biography, to date there has been no critical discussion of Belpré's fiction. To help fill this literary critical gap, I devote a substantial portion of chapter 3 to analyzing three of her published manuscripts: *Perez and Martina* (1932), *The Tiger and the Rabbit and Other Tales* (1946), and *Once in Puerto Rico* (1973). My focus in evaluating her fiction is the subtle allegorical maneuvers she executes as a children's folklorist, maneuvers that suggest a pedagogy concerned with Puerto Rican history. In particular, I prioritize allusions to the colonial experience of slavery, poverty, and sexual violence for women in Puerto Rican social history, which I trace in her recuperation of Puerto Rican orature. Pedagogically oriented allegorical signification is pervasive in Belpré's published work, and my analyses chart the shift in her work from the African and Spanish traditions she privileged in her earlier texts—a largely oral-based cache of tales—to the more cultural nationalist tradition that informs her later versions and translations of anthologized insular Puerto Rican folktales.

The following chapter, "The Boricua Novel: Civil Rights and 'New School' Nuyorican Narratives," moves into the generation of writers who began to explore the Puerto Rican colonial diaspora during the late 1960s as a community entangled, with other (internally) colonized peoples, in complicated webs of sociohistorical inequalities. The work of the civil rights generation spans roughly from the 1960s to the mid-1970s, although Nicholasa Mohr (b. 1935) and Piri Thomas (b. 1928), the main novelists under consideration, are still vital contributors to American letters. Their early work represents the ways Boricua writers of this period, in tandem with authors from other subaltern communities, contrived a "novel of becoming" (Bakhtin 1986) to illustrate and explicate complicated matrices of racialized and gendered oppression in national contexts. Once seized, the novel is turned into a literature of access, popular in its trappings, targeting communities of color in the United States and abroad as its primary audiences. I analyze this appropriation and literary communication among Nuyorican novelists as an effort to forge a sense of Boricua cultural citizenship as an organic—and organically resistant—North American formation. These texts revise the novel's generic conventions, using a specifically Boricua idiom of the English language while narrating the emergence of critical consciousness in stories that revolve around adolescent Nuyorican protagonists. Given the hostile social and discursive context people of color confronted during the civil rights movement, I explain how fictional modes of self-representation became one of the few alternatives for voicing public dissent. This quasi-autobiographical genre enabled writers to challenge the literal and figurative attacks on communities of color that characterized popular, postwar imperial fictions in the United States. These imperial fictions informed the propaganda that helped spawn a huge migration to the States of Puerto Ricans in search of good jobs and other economic opportunities that really existed only in government-sponsored science fiction (like the story cycle of "development" in Puerto Rico entitled Operation Bootstrap). This chapter also situates the literary movements across United States communities of color (Black, American Indian, Boricua) within the larger movements of anticolonial writing in Africa and the Caribbean of the period, which had a profound but rarely discussed impact on this generation's cultural intellectual agendas. All told, the renaissance of the sixties and seventies is a paperback challenge to the fantastic fictions of post–World War II American imperialism.

Chapter 5, "'I Like to Be in America' [*sic*]: Three Women's Texts," moves into contemporary fiction within the Puerto Rican colonial diaspora. The three writers analyzed here are Carmen de Monteflores (b. 1933), Judith Ortiz Cofer (b. 1952), and Esmeralda Santiago (b. 1950), whose work forms part of a small "boom" in ethnic American literature during the late 1980s and early 1990s. In these authors' fictionalized memoirs I trace the emergence of perhaps the most intriguing aspect of the publishing industry's commodification of ethnic market niche writers: the socially upward bound, "white," and ethnically glossed feminist allegories that, as allegories, seem to have found a comfortable space in contemporary publishing and academic milieus despite the worsening poverty among Boricua women and children, collectively, in the United States. Although the intensity of this sensibility varies significantly between the three novels analyzed, covering the range of elite (Monteflores), middle-class (Ortiz Cofer), and working-class (Santiago) feminist narratives, this chapter is a critical intervention into contemporary Boricua feminist discourse.

Literary critics in the United States tend to read all ethnic and "third world" literature, including autobiographical novels, as communal or national allegory (see Jameson 1986). While this approach may have its limitations when non-Western literary traditions are at issue (see Ahmad 1992), contemporary American authors from communities of color who aspire to represent their cultural difference for general consumption are without question involved in an allegorical enterprise, regardless of their texts' generic trappings. My reading of Boricua autobiography does not criticize the facts of the authors' lives but rather interrogates the deliberate stylization of these lives in the novel. Autobiography is no alibi for fiction: the stylization of memoir is all about literary artifice, and artifice involves not only the aesthetic dimensions of elements such as tone, pace, personification, setting, and dialogue, but also the construction of a plot—the calculated emphasis, understatement, or omission of the multiple possibilities intrinsic to any life story.

Paramount in my critique is the allegorical impact of these novels in the United States, where, for the past four decades, the most intimate details of Boricua private life have been perennial topics in public policy debates about culture and poverty. As more than mere coincidence or biographical detail, each of the authors I discuss in chapter 5 explicitly invokes her "minority female" condition in the United States as legitimation for her writing. And since the author's individual experiences in these texts are based in her cultural condition, and since this cultural condition in these texts is based in the author's narration of her individual experiences, allegory becomes the only way for the reader to sort out the two. Consequently, chapter 5's meditation on "Latina" feminism should not be read as merely a dismissal or indictment of the narrative gender politics expressed in these fictions. Instead, I attempt to capture for critique precisely how these particular texts perform as self-consciously ill-begotten allegories. I elaborate how these texts undermine their own narrative authority and thus suggest to me a triangulated set of impossibilities inherent to contemporary debates about "Third Worlded" feminism in a First World context: the impossibility of writing Latina feminism, the impossibility of not writing Latina feminism, and the impossibility of not writing. Similar to certain strains of insular Puerto Rican literary experimentation, allegory in these fictions functions not in spite, but *because,* of its generic failure.

Since Boricua literary production, in the most contemporary instance, has become such a paradoxical venture, an approximation to other social texts as fulcrums of passionate engagement, self-representation, and subaltern articulation winds this study up with a look beyond exclusively literary texts. Chapter 6, "*¡Ya Deja Eso!* Toward an Epi-*fenomenal* Approach to Boricua Cultural Studies," concludes with an exploration of how to read salsa music as a living aesthetic legacy. The artists discussed in this analysis—Juan Luis Guerra, Willie Colón, and Rubén Blades—are Dominican, Boricua, and Panamanian respectively, but all three performers have built on a musical tradition founded and fomented within the Boricua community. Their music expresses a certain co-motion within the diaspora as it approaches the millennium, reflecting the dynamic interplay between "Latinoamerican" communities and bi/trilingual/-cultural communities of color in the United States and elsewhere for whom salsa has become a shared socio-rhythmic expression. Here there are clear tensions between subaltern musical traditions and the commodification of popular music, not merely in the marketing of compact discs and cassettes, but also in how these CDs and cassettes are used by artists and audiences. This chapter represents my effort to capture the *vaivén* of this syncopated production of meaning in subaltern American context. And in many, multiply valenced ways, this musical culture can be read as a poetic realization in sync with Boricua cultural intellectual history—Capetillo's insurgent anarchism, Williams's reinvention of the Americas' history as a living legacy, Schomburg's call for African diasporan collaboration, Belpré's preoccupation with allegory and orature, Thomas's Afro-Rican quandaries, and Mohr's crosshatching of different art forms—all of which mutually inform the lyrical inventions and rhythmic signification of *the* twentieth-century Boricua social text par excellence: salsa.

My intention in publishing this study is to reach the largest audience interested in Boricua literary and cultural intellectual history, including other researchers in American, ethnic, Caribbean, Latin American, gender, and critical race studies. For the academic audience, I position my ideas in current debates relevant to the research and analysis I undertake in each chapter. But since I also want to reach a less specialized audience, including high school teachers and college students, I have attempted to write as clearly and understandably as possible despite my academic orientation. Thus, my introduction to this study deliberately avoids the kinds of protracted, erudite, academic discussions that tend to mystify literary history. Wherever possible, I also clarify critical terms or concepts that might boggle the general or interdisciplinary reader. To make the study more engaging, I have strived to bring my readers into the scenes of my research, to give extensive examples of the texts under scrutiny, and to provide biographical information on many of the lesser-known authors I examine.

When I began this project I envisioned a more encyclopedic recuperation and consideration of Boricua literature, but, happily, I encountered more material than a single text could responsibly cover. Since this study focuses on narratives (novels, essays, and prose experimentation) rather than poetry and other genres (which have already garnered a relatively large amount of critical attention), important figures like Julia de Burgos, Miguel Piñero, Tato Laviera, Sandra María Esteves, Martín Espada, and others are not within the scope of this study. For each chapter I analyze the work of a single writer or group of writers whom I consider emblematic of their respective generation, and each chapter elaborates my motivations for privileging the writer(s) I selected. In some cases, particularly the earliest chapters, my efforts to present figures otherwise absent in Puerto Rican studies scholarship also meant that the work of more celebrated and generally recognized authors, such as Jesús Colón and Bernardo Vega, have been referenced largely outside my primary textual analyses. Some may argue that Vega is more important than Luisa Capetillo, that Colón is more important than Pura Belpré, and so forth, and I am looking forward to these and the other scholarly debates that this text will hopefully kindle.

Above all else, my hope is that this book will help introduce twentieth-century Boricua literary and cultural intellectual history to a wide audience while facilitating more detailed and substantive scholarship in the near future. Throughout the study I have deliberately made my priorities as a researcher and cultural critic clear so that the reader may have an idea of my own motives and limits. I also hope that further archival research will uncover even more Boricua texts and, with this in mind, that my self-conscious discussions of journeying to and through archival papers will motivate others to do the same.

To some extent, I am troubled by my audacity in writing such a book; my youth does not entitle me to assume the wisdom and circumspection required for any authoritative treatise on such a vast human drama. In this, I often think of my parents, grandparents, and other elders, whose knowledge and experience far outreach my own, but who are busy making sense of this legacy in loving ways that continue to preclude writing a book. Thus I submit this book to my readers with a dose of humility, hoping that my enthusiasm and ambition will not overrun my capacities.

1

For the Sake of Love

Luisa Capetillo, Anarchy, and Boricua Literary History

La instrucción se adaptará sin banderas ni en
determinado estado o nación; el respecto absurdo
e idolátrico de los gobiernos será abolido, . . .
La fraternidad como ley suprema, sin fronteras
ni divisiones de razas, color e idiomas,
será el ideal religioso. . . .
El interés común como divisa, y como lema la verdad.
—Luisa Capetillo

love
knows
no
compromise
—Tato Laviera

The very notion of Boricua literature is indebted to a body of scholarship in American literary history that has emerged in the past thirty years, one engaged in a recuperation of literature by and about people of color in tandem with a critique of elitist tenets tacitly at work in the formation of the United States' literary canon, a canon that has, until recently, all but excluded nonwhite writers. This new scholarship, which includes the work of critics such as Toni Morrison, Elaine Kim, Ramón Saldívar, Houston Baker, Lisa Lowe, Paula Gunn Allen, and Clara Lomas, illustrates what Baker (1995: 35) terms a "contiguity" of dissent, that is, the way demands for radical institutional change in the States, historically articulated by communities of color in popular political mobilizations, should translate into parallel agendas in scholarship concerning these communities.

Yet Boricua literary studies has been slow to realize its potential in this new academic milieu; with a few notable exceptions, like the recovery work of the historian Virginia Sánchez Korrol, scholarship on Boricua cultural intellectual history simply has not enjoyed the same kind of critical momentum that has fostered the development of African American and other U.S.-based critical race and gender studies in the late twentieth century.

Why this lag? Certainly the difficulties of garnering mainstream institutional support is a substantial part of the problem, as well as the obstacles that effectively bar the vast majority of Boricuas—a full 99 percent of the Nuyorican population and 88 percent of Boricuas nationally (Navarro 2000)—from access to or success in higher education.

However, there is a related difficulty within university-based Puerto Rican studies itself: the reluctance to deal with the diaspora as a distinct constituency in the United States, one that has self-consciously *produced its own body of knowledge, based in its own specific assessment of its own unique predicament as a U.S. community of color*. In lieu of recuperating a cultural intellectual tradition organic to the Boricua experience, Puerto Rican studies in the States (as its name clearly implies) has pivoted around insular Puerto Rican disciplinary canons, especially the social sciences, and the concerns raised in the consolidation of these canons. This orientation makes it virtually impossible for critics to systematically explore the diaspora as an integral community with its own political, aesthetic, and philosophical agency and agendas. Although at moments the existing scholarship may express an idealistic desire to bridge the divide between the colonial diaspora and Puerto Rico, it can ultimately function to displace the diaspora's self-articulation in an important realm of representational struggle in the U.S. public sphere—academia—with Puerto Rico's nationalist imaginary and the institutions that shore up this imaginary.

Though the humanities constitute a relatively minor area of mainland Puerto Rican studies, still the priorities of Boricua literary scholarship, which is almost entirely authored by scholars trained and/or teaching outside literary disciplines, tend to follow the lead of the social sciences. A prime example of this tendency is a set of essays included in the 1985 bulletin of the American Departments of English (ADE). As the first and, to date, last extended scholarly discussion of

"Puerto Rican" literature in English published by a major U.S. academic journal, this special issue of the *ADE Bulletin* is as much a milestone as it is a touchstone for illustrating how Boricua literary history can be introduced as a topic only, in the final instance, to be supplanted by insular canonical concerns.

Indeed, according to one of this issue's contributing authors, Yanis Gordils, the "literature of the United States Puerto Rican communities, whether in English or Spanish, never totally detaches itself from the national literature of Puerto Rico" (1985: 52). This argument deploys rhetorical devices common in Puerto Rican studies concerning the diaspora, devices that appear to broach but overlook the particular cultural intellectual tradition organic to this community in its most precise U.S. contexts. Gordils contends that "any serious consideration of United States Puerto Rican literature requires extrapolations, sociohistorical contextualizations, and intertextual analyses" (52), ostensibly in exclusive concert with insular Puerto Rican literary history. Yet, in her discussion of these imbrications, the supposed literary dialogue between the Islands and the diaspora never surfaces; while she can cite a number of Island-based authors who have appropriated the Nuyorican experience as subject matter for their fiction—often in highly problematic ways—Gordils does not offer evidence of any sustained and substantive Boricua engagement with the insular experience.

Furthermore, though Gordils argues that a certain intertextual relationship obtains between these distinct literary traditions, two of the texts she cites to corroborate this claim, Tato Laviera's chapbook of poetry, *La Carreta Made a U-Turn* (1979) and Sandra María Esteves's poem "A Julia de Burgos" (1980), both subtly censure the Islands' canonical project. The first is a satiric response to a modern work of Puerto Rican dialect literature; the second is a poetic expression of empathy with a woman poet who, though posthumously reclaimed by the insular canon, exiled herself from Puerto Rico and died friendless, broke, and drunk on a New York City street corner. While Gordils duly notes that insular Puerto Rican literary scholars by and large simply ignore Boricua literature, and that many Boricua authors have absolutely no interest in the insular literary tradition, she still insists that it is "extremely difficult, if not impossible, to draw a clear-cut line between" Boricua literature and "the national literature of Puerto Rico" (1985: 52).

Gordils's desire to append the diaspora's literature to the Puerto Rican canon resembles another article in this special ADE issue, Juan

Flores's "Puerto Rican Literature in the United States: Stages and Perspectives." This essay opens with a polemic about why U.S. students and scholars should read the Puerto Rican canon, then eventually segues into a discussion of Nuyorican writing as a liminal creature, one that "retains its association to Puerto Rico's national literature and, by extension, to Latin American literary concerns, . . . In fact, it is Nuyorican literature's position straddling two national literatures and hemispheric perspectives that most significantly distinguishes it among the American minority literatures" (1985: 39). Yet, like Gordils, Flores offers evidence of this "straddling" effect that is primarily the work of insular authors who have, again, exploited the Boricua experience as thematic material. While Flores is highly critical of this insular appropriation, and distinguishes it as "a literature *about* Puerto Ricans in the United States rather than *of* that community" (42), still the bulk of his article concerns these and other outsider perspectives.

Flores and Gordils both intimate that there is a distinct body of mainland Puerto Rican literature, produced under a unique set of colonial diasporan circumstances and absent in or marginalized by both the Puerto Rican and the U.S. literary canons. Thus the question arises: should the field of Boricua literature be annexed by the Puerto Rican canon and, if so, why this colonization in reverse? In this, Flores's closing argument may offer some hints. Coming full circle to his opening polemic, Flores's conclusion articulates what seems to be less a concern with the diaspora's literary "stages" and "perspectives" than an explicit anxiety over protecting the status of Puerto Rico's national canon:

> Despite the sharp disconnections between Island- and United States–based traditions, and between stages of the literary history here, it is still necessary to talk about modern Puerto Rican literature as a whole and of the emigrant literature—including the Nuyorican—as an extension or manifestation of that national literature. . . . After all, if Tato Laviera and Nicholasa Mohr are eligible for canonical status [in the States], why not José Luis González or Julia de Burgos, or, for that matter, Manuel Zeno Gandía, the author of the great Puerto Rican novel *La charca*? (44)

Thus expressing solidarity with the Islands' national literary project by proposing its inclusion in the U.S. canon is the article's ultimate, if paradoxical, concern. This also entails narrating Boricua literature as a mere "extension or manifestation" of the Puerto Rican canon, despite the obvious and profound differences between these two literary histories.

But why is the anxiety over the Puerto Rican canon's relative obscurity triggered by the fact that Black and women writers from the diaspora's working class, such as Laviera and Mohr, are garnering a legitimate place, albeit in the wings, on the stage of American letters? Flores's rationale for including insular "greats" like Manuel Zeno Gandía in the American canon is that their work would serve to mitigate the narrow nationalist and ethnocentric tendencies of this canon. Yet, if the goal is genuine sensitivity to and appreciation of writers from marginalized communities, would merging Boricua literature into the Puerto Rican national canon, then merging this canon into the U.S. national canon really level the playing field for those from underrepresented groups in *either* national context? This is an especially pressing question where Boricua authors are concerned, since, as Flores and Gordils agree, they constitute one of the most under- and misrepresented groups in *both* the Puerto Rican *and* the U.S. literary traditions.

Given the neglect of Boricua literature in both national canons, alongside the habitual expulsion of Boricuas from both national identities, we might well argue that tethering Boricua literature to either "Puerto Rico" or "America" as acts of nationalist signification simply does not serve the best interests of Boricua literary scholarship. Clearly the work of Boricua writers and cultural intellectuals is an equally valuable and vulnerable legacy that is routinely hijacked and/or disappeared on either side of the San Juan–New York divide. Reclaiming Boricua literature therefore means attending to this perpetual sequestration and invisibility in a context of forced exile from *dual* national identities and nationalist intellectual traditions. More important, however, it also means tracking and analyzing the diaspora's unique tradition of contiguous dissent and self-articulation, speaking not only of or about but *with* a community facing its own specific challenges in its own creatively stylized and politicized ways. For Boricua literary historians, this further entails the invention of a preliminary frame of reference, one that helps historicize Boricua narrative experimentation in its unique moments and milieus.

Flores's article proposes that the mainland Puerto Rican community's oldest extant literature will be found among an early migratory circuit of Island-based intellectuals agitating for independence, such as Ramón Emeterio Betances and Eugenio María de Hostos, who spent time in New York as political exiles in the mid- to late nineteenth century. But while the travel writings of these figures may be extremely important for Puerto Rican literary and social historians, *Boricua* cultural intellectual history does not begin with these bourgeois revolutionaries' intellectual activities and sojourns in the United States. Rather, the first chapter of Boricua social and literary history begins at the turn of the twentieth century with the nomadic trek of humble exiles and activists jettisoned to New York after their involvement in Puerto Rico's more popular social movements of the 1890s. Many of these migrants were fairly young (in their late teens, twenties, or early thirties), highly politicized, usually underemployed, and keenly autodidactic; among them were Bernardo Vega, Jesús Colón, Arturo Schomburg, and Luisa Capetillo. All four of these figures left behind significant bodies of published work and archival materials attesting to the specific struggles and achievements of the first working-class emigrant enclave in New York City, a community defined in its literature by radical and mutually implicated aesthetic and political agendas. But while Vega's *Memorias* (1988) and Colón's *A Puerto Rican in New York* (1961) have been reclaimed, republished, and taught by Puerto Rican scholars and educators as the pioneer emigrant generation's most representative texts, Schomburg and Capetillo have been all but completely ignored.[1]

No doubt this elision is related to how both Schomburg and Capetillo struggled *within* the Puerto Rican and Cuban nationalist organizations of their time.[2] In this political engagement, Schomburg refused the tendency to put aside questions of internalized and structural racism in the Caribbean and its diasporas, and Capetillo insisted on the eradication of sexism as the sine qua non of genuinely revolutionary praxis. Their work consequently attests to inner contradictions that would mitigate the arguably heroic masculinist-nationalist fabrication of Boricua social and literary history as an insular postscript.[3] And it is precisely this mitigation, this elaborate and elaborated threat *from below* to sacrosanct narratives of national and nationalist signification—not only Puerto Rico's, but the United States' as well—that distinguishes their work as the earliest extant corpus to critically speak from, with, and of the Boricua community. The fin-de-siècle working-class migrant generation's most avant-garde texts, therefore, in this critic's assessment, comprise the foundational narrative enterprise of Boricua literary history.

Schomburg's legacy is one of chapter 2's primary concerns. This chapter proposes Luisa Capetillo, an anarcho-feminist effectively exiled to the New York Boricua community, as one of the earliest and most pivotal Boricua literary figures. The works Capetillo produced as an exile from Puerto Rico during a time of tremendous political upheaval, along with the work of this entire pioneer generation, should be read in light of the Islands' pre-and post-1898 military regimes—first the Spanish, then, with the support of the insular elite, the U.S.—under which the very act of writing for working-class women and men of color was a highly subversive tactic. Describing this repressive ambient in Puerto Rico at the turn of the century, Julio Ramos explains that

> la escritura—en el sentido amplio, que incluye, más allá de la literatura, la administración misma de las leyes y los discursos estatales—era un dispositivo de control y subordinación social. . . . la escritura—más que un simple marcador del prestigio de los sujetos—era una tecnología . . . que posibilitaba la administración de la vida pública y que decidía, en el campo de la producción "simbólica" y cultural, la legitimidad de cualquier discurso con expectativas de representatividad y hegemonía. (1992: 15–16)
>
> [writing—in the broadest sense of the word, which in addition to literature includes the administration of state laws and discourses—was a mechanism of social control and subordination. . . . writing—more than a simple marker of subjects' prestige—was a technology . . . that made it possible to administer public life and, in the field of "symbolic" and cultural production, to decide the legitimacy of any and all discourses that aspired to be representative and hegemonic.][4]

Ramos adds that the "entry" of Capetillo and other voices into the "technology" of Puerto Rican writing was difficult and usually dangerous. These subjects, who were part of a constituency that had never enjoyed any self-representational power in Puerto Rican history, forced themselves into the socio-symbolic fray, one of the "most jealously protected realms," where "power produced the fictions of its law." Consequently these discursive agitators often suffered reciprocal—though usually more literal—violence at the hands of both Spanish and American colonial authorities and their agents.

Ramos portrays Capetillo as a radicalized product of the period's anarchist movement in Puerto Rico, Cuba, and Ybor City, and his introduction to her work offers a sketch of the more specific movement among tobacco workers, focusing on their workshops' unique political and intellectual culture. But what are we to make of Capetillo's specific role as an anarcho-*feminist,* as a working-class woman vying for a position as a "new discursant" in this transnational context, and in what she and her anarchist colleagues considered a *supra*national movment? As an audacious and committed woman activist and writer, Capetillo ultimately found herself in the most peripheral and clearly dangerous discursive and physical spaces allotted her within the marginalized and imperiled workers' movement. This plight ultimately compelled her to leave the Islands, after being harassed by both colonial regimes she had experienced in Puerto Rico and becoming discontented with the workers' movement, which quickly transformed into a quasi-nationalist mobilization after 1898. Capetillo, with her demonstrated commitment to radical anarchist and feminist ideals, did not fit the part scripted for her in this emergent nationalist drama; or perhaps more accurately, despite proving the strength of her convictions in Puerto Rico's highly politicized field of discursive and institutional struggle, she was exploited then ejected by the Islands' hegemonic and counterhegemonic technologies, which were owned and operated by opposing groups of men whose exclusive interests, she argued, were negotiated vis-à-vis these technologies. And as she moved farther away from this dangerous locus of utter discomfiture and contradiction, her life and work became more and more emblematic of the working-class experience of exile and political reengagement in the United States.

Capetillo was scandalously anomalous for her times, not merely as an anarchist but as a very well educated working-class Puerto Rican woman. Luisa Capetillo Perón was born in 1879 in Arecibo, Puerto Rico.[5] Her mother, Margarita Perón—a French national, probably from another Caribbean colony—apparently migrated to Puerto Rico as a young woman. Perón worked for one of Arecibo's wealthier families, first as a governess and later as a laundress. Capetillo's father, Luis Capetillo, was a Spanish immigrant worker who also settled in Arecibo. According to Capetillo's biographer, Perón frequented a neighborhood café called *La Misisipí* (The Mississippi) and was the only female participant in the *tertulias* (group discussions) that were regularly held there. Margarita Perón had a reputation for her liberal views and congenial temperament, characteristics that Capetillo eulogized in the dedication to her penultimate text.

Capetillo's parents were autodidacts whose education was stimulated within the progressive circles of Puerto Rico's fledgling socialist movement. Luisa was their only child and although education was scarcely available at that time to women—and even less readily available to working-class children—her parents gave her a rather extensive education, primarily at home.

Luis and Margarita were determined to nurture their daughter's intellectual growth. While it seems that insular Puerto Rican literature was not part of this project, they had a library that included texts of literary vanguards in Russia, France, England, and the United States. Capetillo read the work of Tolstoy, Hugo, Zola, Turgenev, Kropotkin, and Mill, among others. She learned French from her mother, while her father taught her the basics of reading, writing, and mathematics in Spanish.

Beyond this rather rough sketch, we know very little about Capetillo's childhood and adolescence. By her eighteenth birthday in 1897, Capetillo's father had apparently abandoned the family, and she had become involved in an amorous relationship with the son of her mother's employers; between 1898 and 1900 Capetillo gave birth to two children, and soon afterwards the couple separated (Valle Ferrer 1990: 54).

To support herself and her children, Capetillo became a garment worker in 1905. As early as 1904 she was writing newspaper articles in Arecibo (Ramos 1992: 65). In 1906 she began her post as a *lectora* (reader) in one of Arecibo's tobacco workshops. These kinds of "readings" were not an uncommon practice in Puerto Rico, particularly among tobacco workers. For a minimal fee, designated readers would provide workers with the latest news and fiction in circulation—usually materials related to current events and socialist politics—by reading out loud and facilitating discussions while the rest of the employees had their hands and eyes occupied with the day's labor.[6] Finally, according to her biographer, Capetillo formally joined the Federación Libre de Trabajadores' Arecibo organization in 1907 (Valle Ferrer 1990: 131).

For women workers at the turn of the twentieth century, both on the Islands and in the States, the practice of reading aloud in workshops provided a rare educational opportunity. Only a few critics have discussed the ways Puerto Rican women, who were also a significant part of the tobacco industry's workforce (not to mention the workers' movement overall), took advantage of this type of education (Azize Vargas 1987; Ostolazo Bey 1989; Romero-Cesareo 1994). Although Capetillo's early and extremely liberal studies at home certainly set her apart from most working-class women of her time, her coming to consciousness as a political activist and her subsequent literary contributions began with her post as a workshop reader. Her contributions therefore provide an important inroad for understanding the specifically feminine concerns of her epoch.

My primary interest here is to analyze Capetillo's last surviving collection, *Influencias de las ideas modernas* (The influences of modern ideas), published in 1916, which includes most of her fiction and experimental prose. This text also contains her ultimate thoughts on feminism, anarchism, and other related topics, and was written primarily during her stays in the United States, beginning around 1912. But in order to make sense of her work at that juncture, I will begin with her literary career in Puerto Rico.

All of Capetillo's earlier texts reflect her formative involvement as an anarchist organizer and agitator. These texts, published between 1907 and 1911, pivot around three major issues: an outline of daily practice for women; the course of current politics, primarily the socialist agenda in Puerto Rico; and the development of a global workers' social movement. Her early work demonstrates how Capetillo analyzed and promoted the anarchist project in light of Puerto Rico's specific structures of social inequalities, especially those that contravened working-class Puerto Rican women's basic human dignity and rights. While crafting her ideas in these texts, Capetillo critiques a number of deeply entrenched institutions, especially the Catholic Church and, more emphatically, what she argues is the morally corrupt dogma promulgated by Christian institutions. She also offers numerous critical examples of the corruption of the elite classes and works through the complexities of working-class oppression and resistance, all the while critically engaging the political discourses of her time.

In her earlier texts, Capetillo's explication of a liberatory daily practice for women is like a spider's web; her diverse observations, commentaries, and polemics concerning the plight of working-class Puerto Rican women take irregular shape, but as she weaves them together, a single overall pattern becomes clear. Within this web, Capetillo captures for critique the most emblematic scenes of women's everyday life. We have no record of how she engaged her audience in her public speeches, but we can assume that the performative moment would have added even more sprawling dimension to her analytical method.

The stylization of this method, which evolves in her later writing, is rudimentary in her first collection, *Ensayos libertarios* (Libertarian essays) (1904–7). At this early moment in her development as a social critic, Capetillo insists that people are good by nature, but that this goodness is slowly but surely tainted by the imposition of nationalist and other bourgeois- or elite-identified structures of thought. Long before Althusser would garner credit for calling our attention to "ideological state apparatuses" (1971: 127–86), Capetillo, in solid anarchist form, was already interpreting the maintenance of state-sponsored ideologies in commonsense attitudes and daily practices. Progressive education, in Capetillo's analysis, provides the best antidote to this manipulation of human will, since it can help working-class women identify and evaluate for themselves the belief systems and everyday customs that can otherwise coerce them into compliance with an oppressive social order and sexist culture. For Capetillo, the basis of this education should be philosophically grounded in liberatory Christianity—her rendition of an alternative conceptual space for elaborating a new feminist theory—which she references in exhorting even privileged women to change their ways:

> [El bien] no consiste en . . . dar ropa gastada, teniendo escaparates repletos de lujosos trajes, como si hubieran algunos con más derechos a usar trajes nuevos y lujosos. Se me dirá: que los trabajen si los desean iguales. Continuamente están trabajando y continúan rotos, descalzos y hambrientos. ¿Y acaso trabajan las esposas e hijos de los explotadores? ¿Se llaman cristianos? ¿Dónde están las prácticas? hechos y no fórmulas. ¿Dónde el desinterés y abnegación por el prójimo? entonces ¿qué derecho tienen a llamarse cristianos, si son vanidosos, indolentes, egoístas, indiferentes y soberbios? Son vanidosos, porque nada hacen oculto; todo con la trompeta del anuncio y el halago; por eso hacen caridad o algún bien mal hecho al prójimo.
>
> Son indolentes, porque para todo tienen un ser humano para todos sus caprichos y no la hacen por sí mismos.
>
> Egoístas e indiferentes, porque luego de cubrir sus necesidades y vicios, no creen a los demás con derecho para hacerlo y tratan de mermar el mezquino salario de sus sirvientes, y guardan todas las monedas que pueden, siéndole indiferente que sus hermanos, sirvientes, estén descalzos y duerman en el suelo; y se llaman cristianos. (1904–7: 6–7)[7]
>
> [[Goodness] does not consist . . . of giving away worn-out clothes, while keeping closets full of extravagant outfits, as if some people were more entitled to wear new and luxurious clothes. You will tell me, "Let them work for it if they want such nice clothes." But they are continually working and yet continue to dress in torn clothes, to go barefoot and

hungry. And do you think that the exploiters' wives and children work? And they call themselves Christians? Where are the daily practices, in deeds not formulas? Where's their selflessness and abnegation when their fellow human beings are concerned? By what right do they call themselves Christians, if they are vain, lazy, selfish, indifferent, and arrogant? They are vain, because they do nothing [good] in secret; everything they do is heralded with announcements and self-flattery—that's why they do charity work or some good deed, poorly, for their fellow humanity.

They are lazy, because they keep other human beings around for their caprices, and don't do a thing for themselves.

They are egotistical and indifferent, because after taking care of their own needs and vices, they don't believe that others have the right to do the same thing, and they try to lower their servants' measly salaries, and they hoard all the coins they can, feeling indifferent to the fact that their brothers and sisters, their servants, are barefoot and sleep on the floor; and they call themselves Christians.]

Not uncoincidentally, Puerto Rico's first published working-class feminist is also the first to insist on elaborating class divisions between women, which she argues are habitually rationalized in Puerto Rican culture. Capetillo was especially intolerant of those women who feel entitled to their relative luxury while seeing others in their immediate vicinity—even women working long hours in their own homes—suffer for lack of the most basic necessities. It is likely that her childhood experiences growing up as the daughter of a domestic servant of one of Arecibo's wealthiest families galvanized the indignation of her first published text. In this passage, Capetillo analyzes emblematic, everyday signs of more general inequalities between women. Shuttling between ruling-class privilege and working-class deprivations, while analyzing the most basic material and communicative contradictions they entail, Capetillo depicts the broad outlines of social stratification without ever losing sight of everyday reality. And like prose poetry, her clauses test and transgress the limits of standard grammar and syntax. Yet her paragraphs are forged together with a liturgical urgency that makes each idea and phrase move confidently and logically into the next.

Ensayos libertarios, published in 1907, marks Capetillo's entry into the public scene of politics, and includes work she wrote between 1904 and the date of publication. Her next text, *La humanidad en el futuro* (Humanity's future), published in 1910, is a hastily prepared monograph exploring an ideal society. Her third work, *Mi opinión: Sobre las libertades, derechos y deberes de la mujer como compañera, madre y ser independiente* (My opinion: Concerning women's liberties, rights, and duties as partners, mothers, and independent beings), published on the eve of her exile to the United States in 1911, is a wide-ranging exploration of the female condition.

Mi opinión is introduced in the preface as a humble effort to illustrate how, in Capetillo's words, "¡Querer es poder!" (Desire is power!) (vii). The preface concludes with the premise that "the present social system, with all of its errors, is sustained by ignorance and the enslavement of women" (El actual sistema social, con todos sus errores, se sostiene por la ignorancia y la esclavitud de la mujer) (viii). Capetillo furthers this compelling argument in the opening selection, "La mujer en el hogar, en la familia, en el gobierno" (Women in the home, in the family, in the government). This essay proclaims marriage the most culpable ritual in the perpetuation of women's bondage, and urges women to reconceptualize love in ways that make desire a productive force in their lives rather than a naturalized obligation—sanctioned, codified, and enforced by the institutions of formal and common-law marriage—that reduces them to objects of exchange between men.

Subsequent pieces in *Mi opinión* include an edited translation of the French anarchist Madeleine Vernet's essay "L'amour libre" (Free love). One of the segments Capetillo emphasized in her representation of Vernet's original argues that depriving a woman of sexual pleasure is a deformation of her spiritual, physical, mental, and moral well-being; in fact, it means robbing her of a full fourth of her very existence, and can actually kill her (43–44). In tandem with this proposal of the quintessential necessity for women's sexual liberation *and* satisfaction, "Free love" also avers that women must learn to make the necessary distinctions between marriage, love, and sexual desire:

> He dicho al principio que no debe confundirse el amor con el matrimonio. Pues bien; antes de salir del terreno fisiológico iré más lejos, y diré que no debe confundirse el amor con el deseo.
>
> El amor es la comunión completa de dos cerebros, de dos corazones, de dos sensualidades. El deseo no es más que el capricho de dos seres que una misma voluptuosidad reune. Nada es tan pasajero que o poco estable como el deseo; no obstante, ninguno de nosotros se escapa de él. . . .
>
> Nosotros no podemos ser dueños del deseo carnal, como tampoco lo podemos ser de la tiranía de nuestro estómago. Los dos son inherentes a

nuestro ser físico; ellos son el resultado de dos necesitades naturales y también legítimas así la una como la otra. (44–45)

[At the beginning I said that love shouldn't be confused with marriage. Well, enough said; but before I finish with the topic of physiology, I'll take it one step further and say that love and desire should not be confused either.

Love is the complete communion of two minds, of two hearts, of two sensualities. Desire is nothing more than the whim of two beings united by the same voluptuousness. Nothing is as ephemeral or as unstable as desire; yet no one can escape it. . . .

We cannot control carnal desire, just as we cannot control the tyranny of our stomachs. Both are inherent to our physical being; they are the result of natural necessities, and one is as legitimate as the other.]

Furthermore, it seems that anarcho-feminists were pressed not only to insist on sexual equality among their male peers, but also to quell fears that it would foster some sort of hedonistic epidemic among women. In response to these fears, this article proposes that more sexually active women *should* be able to explore their pleasure without social censure, while the less erotically inclined should likewise be free to remain abstinent when and if they like:

La libertad en amor así para la mujer como para el hombre, no es más que una gran justicia. Eso no forzará nunca a las "frías" a ser apasionadas, pero permitirá a las apasionadas no sufrir más la cautividad de leyes convencionales y sociales. (44)

[Free love for women as well as men is simply and purely justice. It would never force "frigid" women to be passionate, but it would free passionate women from their suffering under conventional and social laws.]

Thus the anarcho-feminist agenda promoted freedom of choice for women in the most intimate aspect of their lives, though, in a sort of playful and sarcastic tone, the article also contends that "there is absolutely no doubt that if woman lived normally, if she weren't deformed by the physical and moral contract, the number of 'frigid' women would be greatly reduced" (no hay ninguna duda que si la mujer viviese normalmente, que si no hubiese sido también deformada por la contrata física y moral, el número de mujeres "frías" sería muy reducido) (43–44).

Other pieces Capetillo included in this collection contest the common contradictions bearing on women's lives and urge women to take control of their public and domestic situations by exhorting them to demand their "natural" rights in everyday life as well as the socio-symbolic order. Building from the basic premise that the oppression of women is the root of all oppressions, the individual pieces that Capetillo published in *Mi opinión* elaborate the more general argument that sexual sovereignty for both women and men is the necessary first step for any genuine social revolution.

For Capetillo, the anarcho-syndicalist agenda seemed to offer the best blueprint for revolutionary action, and we see in her first texts a tremendous faith in the ideals of Puerto Rico's anarchist movement and the Federación Libre de Trabajadores (FLT) in particular. Yet her work suggests that she was under constant attack for her radical anarcho-feminist perspective. Already in *Mi opinión,* Capetillo is speaking as if she assumes her audience will be skeptical and outright dismissive of her ideas. She directly confronts her detractors in the opening lines of the book's preface:

> Al publicar estas opiniones, lo hago sin pretender, recojer elogios, ni glorias, ni aplausos. Sin preocuparme de la crítica de los escritores de experiencia.
>
> El único móvil que me impulsa a dar a la publicidad este tomo, es decir la verdad; la cual, aún aquellos que están en mejores condiciones y con más talento para decirlo no lo hacen. ¿Por qué? Por susceptibilidades de opinión, por no apoyar conceptos de una idea, cuya doctrina, la consideran utópica. Ese modo de juzgar no es suficiente para no publicar las verdades que encierra. (v)
>
> [I publish these opinions without expecting to receive praise, glory, or applause. Without worrying myself about the criticisms of experienced writers.
>
> The only motive compelling me to promote this book is to tell the truth, which others with more resources and talent do not tell. Why? Because they are sensitive to public opinion, because they won't support the concepts of an idea whose doctrine they consider utopian. This kind of judgmental thinking is hardly grounds for not publishing the truth all around us.]

She argues that these so-called utopian projects are, in her opinion, as realistic as any nascent venture. She also condemns the politicos of her time as a self-interested and unenlightened bunch. In her words:

> Los que vivían y viven de la ignorancia del pueblo trabajador. ¿Dijeron la verdad? No, falsearon los hechos, calumniaron a sus apóstoles! ¿Qué conceptos tenemos de los que se oponen a todas las ideas de igualdad y libertad humana? . . . Todos los que juzgan una idea llevada a la práctica, utópica, son obstáculos, y los obstáculos deben empujarse a un lado. Son los que entorpecen las grandes iniciativas, las obras de bien.
>
> Y aun así, se llaman patriotas y padres de la patria.
>
> ¿Qué concepto de la patria tendrán? Un concepto egoísta, que empieza en ellos y termina en ellos. Ellos lo son todos. (vi)
>
> [Those who lived and live off the ignorance of the working-class community, have they ever told the truth? No, they lied about events, and slandered the community's apostles! What concept should we have of those who oppose every idea of equality and human liberty? . . . All those who pass judgment against putting a utopian idea into practice are obstacles, and obstacles should be shoved aside. Such men obstruct the great initiatives, the works toward the common good.
>
> And still, these men call themselves patriots and the nation's fathers.
>
> What conception will they have of the nation? A conceited conception, that begins and ends in them. All of them are like this.]

From around 1910 on, Capetillo perpetually argued that Puerto Rico's self-appointed "patriots" were frauds, and she never ceased to condemn what she considered the opportunistic and misinformed maneuvers of both Puerto Rico's political elite and the socialist leadership. We do not have a clear idea of how her polemics were received, or who precisely posed as her antagonists. Perhaps comments such as the above would have resonated with men like Manuel Zeno Gandía, who was elected legislative representative of Arecibo, Luisa's hometown, shortly after he helped negotiate the U.S. invasion. Or perhaps she was alluding to Santiago Iglesias and his retinue, the exclusively male leadership of the FLT. Bernardo Vega (1988: 134–35) reports a heated debate in the New York community, spurred by a polemic in which Luisa Capetillo participated, citing her argument that "la tiranía, como la libertad, no tiene patria, como tampoco la tienen los explotadores ni los trabajadores" (tyranny, like liberty, has no fatherland, just as workers and exploiters have none).

What we do know is that Capetillo was clearly under attack in all these circles simultaneously because of her public, anarcho-feminist critique of nationalism. Politically, it seems she was caught between the proverbial rock and a hard place. To the right, many of those within

Puerto Rico's propertied and professional classes were actively supporting U.S. rule on the Islands. To the left, the anarchist leadership made a series of concessions after the U.S. invasion, particularly with the various national parties that were preparing themselves for the autonomy promised but never granted by the U.S. government. They also negotiated formal ties with the American Federation of Labor (AFL), under the leadership of Samuel Gompers.[8] All of these gestures toward becoming part of the insular institutional apparatus and the most centrist U.S. labor union of the time arguably compromised the anarchist tenets that had once made the Federación Libre de Trabajadores so appealing to Puerto Rican workers. The significance of these maneuvers was not lost on Capetillo and the organization's membership at large,[9] and also ignited the major debate among Boricua workers in New York City in which Capetillo participated.[10]

Like the other figures of the *pionero* generation, Capetillo never lost faith in Puerto Rico's working-class causes, despite the far Left's political mistakes and compromises in the wake of the Spanish American War. She continued her work with the FLT, however, amid a serious crisis in the anarchist movement.

Under pressure, the FLT leadership justified its bids to form official ties with the Islands' paranational political parties and the AFL as inevitable steps, given what they assumed was Puerto Rico's imminent independence. But by 1908, two local elections had been held on the Islands affirming the populace's desire for national sovereignty, and neither was recognized by the U.S. Congress as a legitimate "democratic"vote. Finally aware that the Puerto Rican people had been duped by the empty promises of the U.S. government, the FLT leadership decided to redefine the organization's platform in an effort to reconcile its original anarchist program of action with its new syndicalist agenda, targeting two internal priorities: (1) propagating union organization; and (2) promoting working-class solidarity via the development of an alternative proletarian culture (García and Quintero Rivera 1982: 59). The new platform's second project reaffirmed the early anarchist program, which fully rejected party politics and institutional reform, and opted instead for educating and supporting workers in projects they designed and implemented for themselves, especially cooperatives and mutual aid societies. As part of the new program of action, the FLT launched the "Cruzada del Ideal" (Crusade of the Ideal), delegating worker "crusaders" to agitate and educate other workers on the concepts of a new, socialist world order where, in the words of a writer well-circulated among Puerto Rican anarchists, "each individual is a producer of both manual and intellectual work" (Kropotkin 1912: 23). In what seemed a perfect project for her at the time, Capetillo joined the ranks of the Crusaders in 1909.

Working in the Cruzada should have been invigorating for Capetillo, whose education and idealism, after all, resonated with the program's timbre. The authors, texts, and ideas in circulation that were read, discussed, and evaluated by Puerto Rican workers in their workshops and during the events sponsored by the Crusaders and the FLT came from all over the world. Anarchist newspapers and pamphlets arrived from places like Brazil, Panama, Argentina, and of course Spain, while some of the most popular polemics and novels were translations from Russian and French, such as the work of Tolstoy, Bakunin, Chernyshevsky, Zola, Diderot, and Balzac, with which Capetillo was already familiar. But despite this seemingly perfect match between her personal philosophies and political activities, Capetillo, again, was disillusioned and critical. Like so many of her contemporaries, she decided to leave Puerto Rico in hope of finding better situations for her life and life's work in the United States.

This turning point in Capetillo's life—her disappointment with the vagaries of insular politics and politicos, her feeling of solitude as a working-class activist, and her self-imposed yet still politically forced exile—is what makes Capetillo such an important figure for understanding the dilemmas that the first avant-garde of Boricua writers and activists faced in their lives and explored in their work. Her engagements with broad revolutionary concepts like anarchism, socialism, and feminism had been, by this juncture in her life, tempered by her very personal recognition of their limits; not as discourses in and of themselves, but rather as ideals that, in the translation into practice, were bogged down by too many real-life, real-time complications.

Capetillo's earlier published collections are self-conscious meditations focused primarily on the predicament of working-class women during the latest stage of Spanish colonialism and the earliest stage of U.S. colonialism and imperialism in the Caribbean. Her later narrative experiments, which she wrote mainly in the United States, evince her effort to elaborate in fiction her vision of the trajectories of her life and work as a political activist and theorist. In both phases of her writing, narrative devices of various genres provide her with a wide range of tools that she unapologetically manipulates (regardless of their conventional uses) to craft provocative new images, ideas, and social identities. Although Capetillo recognized the formidable challenge of constructing a conceptual landscape uninterrupted by sexual, class, and geopolitical borders, she never gave up hope of making this ideal a reality. In her last text, hope and love are foremost in her thought as she reaffirms the imperative of social revolution in the fullest and necessarily *creative* sense.

If we strictly use the standard Euro-American literary historical categories, we can only describe Capetillo's final work, *Influencias de las ideas modernas* (1916), as a naively postmodern piece, anachronistically published during Latin and North America's modernist periods. But although her experimental prose challenges the limits of traditional generic structure and metanarrative conventions—two of the commonly definitive characteristics of postmodern literary expression—the postmodern label does not really fit the context or content of Capetillo's work. Fredric Jameson's reading of postmodern pastiche, for example, as "blank parody, a statue with blind eyeballs," converts it into a "neutral practice" of parody, a "blank irony" that is "devoid of laughter and of any conviction" (1992: 17). But the pastiche effect of Capetillo's final text is not an experiment in emptying aesthetic form of life and humor, nor is her tone plagued with the exasperated despair or cynical pleasure of finding the parts not fitting the whole. Rather, her writing is inspired by, and saturated with, a political and philosophical conviction that serves as its textual and extratextual logic. Furthermore, though we might read Capetillo's work as a particular type of poetic *bricolage* or rearrangement, the fragmentation and disjuncture of her text may also be simply due to the fact that a working-class woman of her times may not have had the luxury of revising and editing, of composing longer, more integrated narratives, or the resources (including editorial support) for publishing more extensive and polished volumes of prose.

Influencias de las ideas modernas, which includes plays, letters, journal entries, short stories, and a number of genre-defying fictional and quasi-fictional pieces, was composed primarily in New York City and Ybor City, Florida, during 1912–1916, although the title play was composed in Puerto Rico in 1907. Three years after beginning her work in the Cruzada and in the magazine *Unión Obrera* (Workers' Union), and founding a feminist magazine, Capetillo traveled to the continental

United States in 1912 to continue her work within the *colonias* or settlements of the Puerto Rican diaspora. Like Lola Rodríguez de Tío, who traveled to New York City in 1903 despairing over the situation in Puerto Rico (Vega 1988: 119–20), Capetillo arrived in New York despondent but hopeful of gathering new strength and support in the Puerto Rican communities stateside. But it seems Capetillo was confronted with a whole new set of challenges to her radical beliefs and agenda among her peers in the United States. And as the situation became more hostile, Capetillo's anarcho-feminism became more adamant.

As all her work insists, the status quo in *Influencias* is an intolerably backwards affair. Appearances almost always mask an ugly truth, and unequal relations of power are both source and symptom of this masquerade. A decade before Gramsci would compose his prison notebooks, Capetillo is already writing of the inversion of reality via discourses that continually reproduce themselves in everyday life. In *Influencias* she applies this analysis of language and hegemony to the issue of political opportunism; crucially, the budding socialist organizations of her time were not immune to this critique.

Moreover, Capetillo's reading of power relations is vehemently positivist, which, in the best of the humanist tradition, often appears as the most natural expression of common sense. Words and concepts have essential meanings, according to Capetillo, and human usage of language—not language itself—is imprecise. We see this taken to near neo-Platonic proportions in *Influencias*. For example, Capetillo avers that a corrupt politician is an oxymoron, because politicians by definition should be naturally disinclined to corruption (1916: 54–55). The established codes of licit and illicit behavior in this text are also suspect. In Capetillo's reading, the only differences between an entrepreneur and a petty thief are the scenes of their crimes and the clothes they wear; the petty thief being, by all rights, the more socially acceptable of the two (54). In a similar semantic twist, the term "civilization" is convoluted in its popular usage; Capetillo argues that the adjective "civilized" in reality signifies the ways Westerners use fashion to mask their inattention to hygiene, while the so-called barbarian races do not need hats, breath mints, and fancy overclothes, for their hair is habitually clean, they consume healthy food, and they need not hide dirty underclothes beneath expensive suits (96). Finally, what passes as "humanitarianism" in North America, it turns out, is not really so humane: Capetillo calls our attention to the fact that while there were organizations to protect the rights of animals, no one seemed to have an interest in the welfare of the most vulnerable constituencies of human society, such as children, the elderly, and the sick (60).

This method of essentializing concepts, which Capetillo grounds in poetic renditions of "Nature" as the originary and benevolent referent, is a common device in nineteenth-century Euro-American romantic realism and certain strains of modernism. But the crucial difference in Capetillo's narratives, which she perhaps shares with some Latin American and Iberian modernist tendencies, is the constant imperative of literally returning to some semblance of the "natural order" by explicitly calling for revolutionary practice. And it is here precisely, as she narrates an anarcho-feminist outline for the practice of everyday life, that her writing undoes the binary logic that her essentialist method implies, because she derives her theory from the scene of practice, despite her positivist impulses. She cannot help but de-essentialize and de-romanticize social constructs, because her feminist and anarchist convictions require that she dwell on the very seams of the binary split between theory and practice; as she dwells on these overlapping edges, the contradictions, ambiguities, and other complications become apparent, even glaring. In fact, in Capetillo's daily life, every choice—from what she ate to what she wore—was loaded with political significance. Like her suits, the trappings Capetillo borrows from the Occidental tradition do not quite fit; the gendered politics of Capetillo's cross-dressing strategy—wearing clothes cut for men over a woman's body—might also be a useful metaphor for describing her scandalously inappropriate appropriation of patriarchal structures of thought and modes of writing. What may seem awkward at first glance may instead suggest a specifically feminine *escritura,* a highly complex articulation of gendered ambivalence that questions the very concept of male/female polarities and, with it, the binary logic endemic to the positivist tradition.

This cross-dressing effect is most clearly marked in her discussion of feminist practice in *Influencias*. Here, Capetillo clearly wants to base her ideas about gender in biology, or the most natural of the natural sciences, but her analyses ultimately overflow the biological concepts she borrows or invents. For example, in a fascinating section entitled "Cartas interesantes de un ácrata de Panama" (Interesting letters from a Panamanian anarchist), Capetillo includes a series of letters written to her from a Panamanian admirer, omitting her side of the correspondence. The anarchist's letters are reprinted in chronological order, and it is clear that Capetillo's side of the correspondence was friendly but contestatory. Yet since her letters are absent, the reader must guess what Luisa's responses entailed. The Panamanian's letters subtly suggest Capetillo's critique of his positions, particularly his cynicism and his varied but problematic takes on feminism. One of his letters, for example, states that women should always be gently treated, because tension causes their chest muscles to contract, which can damage their ability to lactate properly (149). Judging by his next letter, Capetillo had written him to say how bitter she had become, because no one seemed to understand what she really meant to say; presumably, as his opinions in the previous letter insinuate, her Panamanian comrade was not much of an exception (149–50).

Capetillo's positions on feminism likewise begin to unfix themselves from their essentialist underpinnings in her final text. Sexuality in *Influencias* is no longer represented as a specifically male/female concern; she now characterizes love with terms that are not gender-specific, such as the union of "beings" (seres), "souls" (almas), and "bodies" (cuerpos) (65–67). Likewise, the almost constant conflation of womanhood with motherhood in her earlier work begins to subside in *Influencias*. Capetillo argues at one point that to be "complete" (mujer completa) a woman must have children, but then undercuts this claim by stating that all women are mothers, regardless of whether they literally bear children (65, 86).

Overall, *Influencias* tests the limits of romantic and modernist discourses of nature, finding them inadequate to the task of revolutionary feminist theory, fiction, and practice. When Capetillo returns to the issue of feminism, she does so by rejecting any and all formulas for behavior, dress, sexual practice, and love. Midway through the text, for example, she includes a dialogue on the *qué dirán* syndrome, exploring what others say about Elena, a woman they see getting into a car with a man named Andrés.[11] Elena and Andrés are attracted to each other, and rather rationally decide to spend an afternoon together exploring the options of carnal desire and romance. A pair of *curiosos* (busybodies) are watching the action, and discuss the implications of Elena's behavior. One of these voices keeps complaining that a woman should "belong" to one man only, while men have the right—indeed the natural instinct—to pursue as many women as possible. The other busybody critiques this double standard, and they engage in a long, somewhat pedantic but amusing stichomythia. In the end, the *machista* (male supremacist) refuses to concede any ground in the argument, so he is dismissed by his friend with the words: "You are the representation of tyranny against women. See you later, liberator" (Ud. es la representación de la tiranía contra la mujer. Hasta otro día—Adiós libertador) (93). Meanwhile Elena and Andrés drive off and make love in the open air, forging a lasting relationship free of coercion and matrimony, creating a happy ending to the story of Elena, who did what she thoughtfully pleased with her own body (94).

This freedom of form and movement, in terms of plot, generic experimentation, and political subtext, mirrors the significance of fiction itself in Capetillo's final work. *Influencias*' textual logic suggests that fiction became her last resort for exploring the revolutionary ideal, an ideal that her nonfictional writing and other projects had not apparently managed to articulate to her own satisfaction.

A certain innocent, sensuous desire is Capetillo's key vehicle for depicting this ideal in action. In *Influencias,* all of her stories' protagonists contest and transgress the social norms and mores that inhibit their most pristine filial, romantic, and erotic yearnings. Her first story, entitled "The Cashier," revises the usual nineteenth-century romantic realism of authors such as Charles Dickens, Charlotte Brontë, and Emile Zola, by appropriating and critically reinventing the trope of the orphaned youth (105–13). This character, Ricardo, receives the disinterested help of a kind benefactor, who, pitying his plight, arranges and pays for his education. But unlike Jane Eyre, for example, who uses her mysteriously granted fortune to establish a bourgeois paradise, Ricardo is disgusted with his middle-class lifestyle and, successfully robbing a huge sum of money from his employers, runs off with the cash—and his beloved—to St. Petersburg. Another piece, a play aptly titled *The Corruption of the Rich and the Poor, or How to Prostitute a Rich and a Poor Woman,* opens with a young noblewoman engaged to a rich suitor against her emotional inclinations (167–96). On the eve of her marriage, she decides to elope with her true love, and in a very crafty way, sneaks off with the title to the land her mother left her as a dowry. In yet another play, *A Marriage without Love: Consequence—Adultery,* the heroine, Esmeralda, like Elena in the piece mentioned above, meets a handsome youth on the street while out shopping (171–78). Esmeralda's husband is a boring businessman who takes his young wife for granted. Rather than tolerate her loveless marriage, Esmeralda runs off with her lover. The adulterous consequence here is perfect happiness. In Esmeralda's terms, she needed "to feel that natural and spontaneous feeling that makes you feel delirious, that makes you commit the grandest insanities" (sentir ese natural y expontáneo sentimiento que hace sentir el delirio, cometer las mayores locuras), all of which her husband cannot inspire (173). Unlike Tolstoy's hapless Anna Karenina, as well as many other tragic heroines in nineteenth- and even twentieth-century literature, Capetillo's adulteresses live happily ever after.

In all of these stories, Capetillo devises ways for the revolutionary desires of women and men to break free from socially enforced psychological constraints and the miserable entailments of capital accumulation. In the pursuit of love and the fulfillment of sexual desire, Capetillo's characters literally run off from the scenes of their oppression, and her stories close with the blurring trails of their escape.

Unfortunately, Capetillo's literary career came to an end soon after she published her first collection of fiction in 1916. Just six years later, Luisa died of tuberculosis. Unlike her characters, whose self-imposed exiles seem destined to end in bliss, Capetillo's new life in the United States caused her more trials, alienation, and disillusionment, and ultimately exposed her to an incurable disease. She never ceased to struggle within and for the anarchist and socialist organizations of her time, but the tragic end to her own story forms a telling contrast to her literary characters'. She was buried in Río Piedras's municipal cemetery, after a humble service attended by a small group of her family and friends from the FLT, just a few miles away from the Ateneo Puertorriqueño, where eight years later the body of Manuel Zeno Gandía would lie in state, amid the glory of honor guards and an extravagant public funeral.[12]

In critical response to her experiences in and between two national contexts, Capetillo wrote a wide spectrum of analyses of Puerto Rican women's oppressions, which ultimately called for them to win, protect, and enjoy, for themselves, in public and in private, what she considered their natural civil and sexual rights. Her legacy thus offers both testimony to the Boricua predicament at the initial moment of this community's formation in the wake of 1898, and a serious corpus of Boricua feminist public intellectual work extant among a small group of predominantly male peers. Like the work of Zora Neale Hurston or Phillis Wheatley, whose contributions to African American cultural intellectual history have been recuperated and duly appreciated, Luisa Capetillo's work is a major legacy, ripe for further study. Yet none of the four books Capetillo published has ever been reissued in its original Spanish or translated into English, few scholars have seriously broached her work in either Puerto Rican or American studies, and as a result her intellectual and literary legacies have languished in near total obscurity.

A radical anarcho-feminist may be the most apt foundational figure for a colonial diaspora's literary history. Indeed, Capetillo's intransigent rejection of geopolitical, gendered, erotic, philosophical, and generic borders as obsolete concepts suggests the kind of socially, ethically, sensually, and aesthetically engaged hermeneutics relevant to a community barred wealth and socio-symbolic status, in transit, from one stifling national context to another. In this project, Capetillo was not alone. The entire first generation of Boricua writers were actively and consciously writing against the grain of what national literary canons conventionally imply as a concerted, celebratory expression of bourgeois sensibilities. These men and women were transnationalist agitators who labored in print and public to incite what they audaciously imagined as an impending social revolution and, in this, the very least of their concerns was writing the "Great American Novel." Recuperating Capetillo's *Influencias de las ideas modernas* as the first major Boricua literary text thus points toward a politically contiguous recovery and analysis of Boricua cultural intellectual history.

The Boricua authors under consideration in the next chapter, William Carlos Williams and Arturo Alfonso Schomburg, build on and, in significant ways, transform this hermeneutical project into a more literary historical enterprise. Like Capetillo, Williams and Schomburg seized and sabotaged a number of core concepts intrinsic to national canon formation in the Americas, among them the notion of "America" as a stable, exclusively United Statesian or Euro-American signifier. Schomburg's legacy attests to his lifelong commitment to reclaim, appreciate, and historicize the aesthetic and political contributions of African descendants to transamerican and transatlantic civilization. His collected papers contain a wealth of information about his work as an archivist, including essays, letters, notes, and position papers that suggest an Afro-Boricua narrative and institutional politics at work within the Harlem Renaissance. And though William Carlos Williams did compose *The Great American Novel* (1923), this text aspired to put under question, through a provocative modernist literary experiment, the very terms of its own entitlement. Beyond recuperating their work as Boricua cultural intellectuals, the comparison of Schomburg and Williams as Boricua modernist writers in chapter 2 opens a number of questions about the predicament of Boricua literature in the context of contemporary critical race scholarship in American literary history.

2

Boricua Modernism

Arturo Schomburg and William Carlos Williams

And if the world will not have it—
if the world will not have her—
then I will turn the world to my way.
—William Carlos Williams (of his mother)

Although many would like to claim otherwise, William Carlos Williams (1888–1963) and Arturo Alfonso Schomburg (1874–1938) were, in point of fact, Boricuas, as the evidence surrounding both their families' histories makes clear. William Carlos Williams's mother, Elena Hoheb Williams, was born in Mayagüez, a city on Puerto Rico's western coast, sometime during the mid-nineteenth century. Her mother's family had been in Puerto Rico for countless generations, while her father's family were apparently emigrants from the West Indies (possibly of Dutch extraction). Elena's brother Carlos introduced her to her future husband, William George Williams, and after they married, the couple moved to the United States, ultimately settling in a New Jersey suburb. Although Williams's father may have been born in England, he was culturally shaped by the Caribbean as well; raised from a very young age in the Dominican Republic (Puerto Plata), William George Williams was most comfortable speaking Spanish, which was the primary language spoken in the Williamses' New Jersey household. Without question, William Carlos Williams, who was raised in this home, was born into the diasporan Puerto Rican, Dominican, and West Indian history he publicly claimed as the context of his family's history in both his *Autobiography* (1951) and, more emphatically, in his biography of his mother, *Yes, Mrs. Williams* (1959).

Williams's migratory family history in the Caribbean, as well as his bilingual, bicultural formation in the States, fits a common profile in the Boricua community during the first half of the twentieth century.

Likewise, Arturo Schomburg publicly claimed his Puerto Rican heritage, and his apparently complicated background and family history are *not* anomalous within the Boricua community during the late nineteenth and early twentieth centuries. Like others in his birthplace—Cangrejos, which was historically a free Black community near the port of San Juan where many worked in the shipping industries—Schomburg had relatives in other Caribbean port communities. Looking for more opportunities, Schomburg spent some time (apparently with his maternal great-uncle) in St. Croix while he was still a teenager, then soon after joined the Puerto Rican working-class migration of the period to New York City.[1] When he arrived in the States his life also resembled common Boricua experiences: he became an expatriate activist for Puerto Rican independence, then married, established a career, started a family, and settled in Brooklyn for the rest of his life.

Williams and Schomburg are conventionally read as foundational figures for U.S. modernisms, respectively defined in academic discourse as "white" American and "Black" immigrant men, and thus easily categorized as writers in the high modernist and Harlem Renaissance canons. This essay moves beyond these conventional canons and analyzes Schomburg and Williams as Boricua modernists whose legacies contradict prevailing North American assumptions about modernist poetics and early twentieth century racial politics. By examining how their historical contexts as members of the Puerto Rican colonial diaspora inform their lives and lives' work, my analysis illustrates how these two figures have been assimilated by a dichotomous and naturalized racial allegory that belies the socio-poetic complications of their work as Boricua narrative. The juxtaposition of these two figures as Boricua modernists challenges the segregated critical milieus that have claimed them, and posits a more precise reading of their transnational and anticolonial registers as American writers.

My aim in this chapter is to center Schomburg and Williams as representative figures of Boricua cultural intellectual history, focusing on both writers' critical appropriations of historical documentation in essays that revise the master narratives of colonization in the Americas' history. Racism, genocide, and colonialism are core thematics in both Schomburg's and Williams's transamerican inventions and interventions. Since both men were radically racialized as U.S. citizens (consensually, at certain junctures, and against their will at others), my argument is that their narrative strategies for dealing with these core thematics and processes of racialization must be analyzed in closer cultural, historical, and discursive context. Strategies, in this sense, involve Michel Foucault's theorization of discourse, "truth effects," and knowledge, or the implication of language itself as the mediating ground for both maintaining and countering existing relations of power (1972–77). Complicating this Foucaultian reading of discursive strategies are Schomburg's and Williams's multiple racial and cultural backgrounds as well as the transnational dimensions of their intellectual formations, literary interests, political motivations, and lived experiences as members of the Puerto Rican colonial diaspora. The explicitly literary aspects of Williams's prose experimentation and the explicitly polemical aspects of Schomburg's work as an essayist and archivist further compound the hermeneutical crisis I identify for early-twentieth-century Boricua narrative. In this crisis—in the eternal scripting of Boricuas as culturally alien and racially illegitimate in U.S. nationalist imaginaries—both Schomburg and Williams attempt to overcome paperlessness, the deliberate exclusion of not only Boricua but also African and other subaltern constituencies in the annals of transamerican history. My feminist reading of gender and nation in their work—one that, akin to Michelle Wallace's (1992) prescription, must insist on a simultaneous analysis of race and class—also reveals a masculinist bias in their new conceptualizations of transamerican civilization and recuperations of transamerican history.

Williams's literary strategy involves a new mode of narrating history. Rather than subscribing to the teleological North American notion of the nation-state, which assigns normative cultural citizenship to certain essentialized racial identities, Williams approximates transnational American history as a transtemporal "plateau" of meanings; that is, as an impassioned flux of American signification, "a flow of desire and sexuality, . . . a collective assemblage of enunciation, a machinic assemblage of desire, one inside the other and both plugged into an immense outside that is the multiplicity" of American subjectivity, rather than any singular racial American subject per se (Deleuze and Guattari 1972–80: 23). Conjuring it as a vexed and hexed reservoir of desires, Williams attempts to write and read transamerican history as a sensual and living—as opposed to an essentialized and deadened—experience. At its finest moments, Williams's poetics provoke us not merely to witness the violence of the Americas' colonization in his prose, but to *feel* this history, to assimilate the past as a contiguous experience.

However, as I argue, Williams's project ultimately fails to transcend the racial essentialism and genocidal apologetics he poetically condemns in U.S. (literary) history when he resorts to the Latin American paradigm of *mestizaje* (racial miscegenation), a paradigm that simultaneously celebrates Eurocentricity and whiteness (veiled in claims to voluntary cultural syncretism) and metaphorically exploits—even rapes—the engendering significance of the dead, anonymous indigenous woman. This nameless, faceless, ungrieved yet definitive American woman, whom Williams alternately reduces to the earth's sex, functions in his rhetorical economy as an authenticating, fecund trope that valorizes a certain fictional exposition of *mestizo* (male bi- or triracial) historical consciousness. The violence of colonial American history thus melts away into mestizo consensual pleasure, and mestizo consciousness becomes the glorious result of men who learned to seduce and therefore love her—América/the earth/dead Indian/woman—properly. My argument is that as radical as this experiment may read in Anglo-American modernist context, Williams's reliance on mestizaje discourse, which also informs his nearly complete elision of Africans and slavery in the exposition of colonial transamerican history, not merely limits his aesthetic experiment but undermines the ethical imperative that underscores what I describe as its metonymic provocations and evocations.

Schomburg's strategy, on the other hand, is to recuperate the papers necessary for constituting historical archives in the most literal sense. His goals in this archival project are to identify and celebrate Black contributions to transamerican civilization, and he was particularly (though not exclusively) prone to research concerning men of African descent. In these lifelong pursuits, Schomburg was extremely successful; the papers and artifacts he gathered became the world's first major collection of transamerican and transatlantic Africana, which is today the African diaspora's largest combined archives. Yet while Schomburg's accomplishments as an archivist have been duly recognized, there is important evidence in his private papers suggesting that he himself was considered a racial outsider among some of his most influential African American peers. Furthermore, over the past twenty years Schomburg's biography has been reinvented by North American scholars interested in reclaiming him and his legacy as West Indian American. My argument is that Schomburg, whose library work was essential to establishing twentieth-century African American and African diasporan research, and who considered himself Black (racially) and Puerto Rican (culturally), has been narrated in the United States as Black and not Black according to various generations' political convenience and ethnocentric biases. In this, as I explain, the scholarly stories spun from Schomburg's life and life's work form some of his legacy's most fascinating and relevant fictions for contemporary American studies.

In effect, Schomburg's and Williams's work and figurative significance perform a specific type of Boricua modernism that simultaneously spins *and* reinvents the wheel, so to speak, of American literary history. And though both writers have been posthumously hailed by white and Black literary traditions in the United States, during their lifetimes their peers contested Williams's and Schomburg's legitimacy as white and Black cultural intellectuals. Taken together, both figures thus help us analyze the manner in which the Boricua community fractures the North American color line and has consequently disappeared in U.S. literary history. This eternally contingent dis/placement on the U.S. white/Black social grid reveals the ethnocentric biases of many commonsense notions of race endemic to mainstream twentieth-century American studies and also illustrates the need for a new, transnationally attuned dialogue on race and American modernism. My interest here is not to contest the fact of Blackness in the United States, nor to add a new racial category to the debate, but rather to complicate our readings of modernism in ways that recognize and analyze Boricua cultural intellectual contributions in the overlap of African diasporan and U.S. literary history.

William Carlos Williams's *In the American Grain* (1925) is an experimental prose meditation on the confluences of post-Columbian social histories in the Americas. Each of his chapter-length essays exaggerates or critically elaborates on the ways these confluences are captured in colonial American literatures and archival documentation. In her 1987 study of Williams, Jay Wright, and Nicolás Guillén, Vera Kutzinski analyzes this prose experiment as an articulation of a "New World" aesthetic Williams shares with Wright and Guillén, one that counters the conventions of their North American contemporaries. Kutzinski writes, "[t]o unsettle the myth of America, New World writing has to begin by subverting the traditional concept of Literature as a mythical system that pretends either to transcend itself into a factual system (as in the case of the novel or other prose) or to contract itself into an essential one (as in the case of poetry)" (10). In contrast with this conventional literary divide, Kutzinski reads *In the American Grain* as a willfully "illegitimate" counter-canonical "archive" that, citing a line from Williams's *Paterson* (1946–58), offers a "relief from meaning" in its usual moral and religious trappings (Kutzinski 1987: 28–29).

Indeed, representing Williams's innovations in this text as an archive prompts a highly suggestive reading. What this archival-esque reading underestimates, however, is the significance of Williams's appropriation of fiction for his colonial-imperial critique. This core element of his literary strategy resonates with a number of his Latin American contemporaries' modernist poetics, or what Iris Zavala identifies as the "anatropic" lenses of postcolonial Latin American literature. Zavala's anatropia characterizes what she terms "inversions of the cognitive eye," that is, "upside-down" epistemic perceptions of colonial "mechanisms of oppression," perceptions that Latin American modernist writers characteristically relied on fiction to elaborate. Across the Americas modernist literature thus became the prime technology for both inventing and contesting pre- and post-national cultures and identities in the late nineteenth and early twentieth centuries (Zavala 1992: 1–3). Zavala's analysis of how national formation and culture in transamerican colonial context are encoded and contested in literary movements adds more historical dimension to Kutzinski's comparison of twentieth-century Cuban, Puerto Rican, and African American literature.

Williams shares this anatropia with Hispanic Caribbean and other Latin American modernists, although the contours of his literary experiments are arguably unique in this transamerican milieu. In *In the American Grain,* Williams molds language into a project that self-consciously "plugs" itself into an "assemblage" of historical meanings that are contiguous with, rather than anterior to, the present. This contiguity infests the present with violent feelings and attitudes, in particular what he narrates as the emotional residue of Anglo-European racism, moral righteousness, and the childish colonialist impulse to destroy what cannot be assimilated to a very narrow worldview, all of which Williams narrates as inversions of love in documents of the Americas' history. Eschewing the "propagandistic" tendencies of historical critique, as Brian Bremen argues, Williams fashions instead a critical reappraisal of historicity in his work.

Citing Fredric Jameson's notion of "existential historicism," Bremen calls attention to Williams's syncretization of literary tradition and modernist consciousness in the "moral ideals of mutuality and intersubjectivity" at the root of his poetics (Bremen 1993: 121–59). Building on this schema, I would argue that Williams experiments with metonymic devices that reclaim history as a troubling and tangible presence. Rather than narrating the past as a temporally discrete and distant—and therefore hermeneutically sealed—realm of anterior signification, Williams approaches history as a mélange of affective correlatives that he culls from extant and imaginary historical sources, which together in this text represent the possibility of a sort of coeval empathy in fiction. Therefore what "was" (signified) in history enters what "is" (the text's signifiers) on paper. Following Jacques Lacan's reading of language, the unconscious, and Sigmund Freud's notion of displacement, we could say that this aspect of Williams's poetics is metonymic (rather than metaphoric) signification (Lacan 1966: 160). Crucially, however, Williams reverses the psychological impulses Freud assigns to displacement: for Freud, displacement is one of the unconscious mind's devices for *forgetting* something shocking or uncomfortable, while for Wil-liams such metonymic displacement in literature is a shocking and uncomfortable way to *remember*. In simpler terms, the safely contained words Williams commits to paper—words that explain what the past means—these words actually give way to how the past, in all its dangerous and gruesome detail, feels. In historiography, this metonymic method could also intimate a new category of narrative approaches to the past, one that moves beyond the conventional scripting of history (White 1973).

In the American Grain is thus less concerned with righting the historical record or literally countering its supremacist postures than with making history "show itself" (116), as Williams puts it, and narrating a transamerican archive of *feelings* (rather than any discretely national American archive of books and papers) in literature to testify to the subaltern experience of the Americas' history. In this sense, perhaps despite himself, Williams writes like a protofeminist of color, because of his sustained concern with collective subjectivity as a baseline textual logic, shaped as an intergenerational reservoir of intimacies that are shaded by affective forces ranging from joy to brutality. This collapsing of time and ethos might also be read as a sort of diasporan literary juju, or "conjure"—Houston Baker's term for certain African diasporan sensibilities—by which an author "causes definitions of 'form' as fixed and comprehensible 'thing' to dissolve" (Baker 1987: 43–44). This narrative ethics is likewise akin to what Jacques Derrida terms a "hauntology"—the literary resurrection of the dead as spectral beings caught between the absence of history and the presence of the living, invoking a certain, definitively disturbing clan of transtemporal *zeitgeister* (time-ghosts), if you will, who vandalize European languages and aesthetic processes within (and because of) the new world order (Derrida 1994: 10).

In this reservoir of intimacies certain images surface, sink, and resurface as emblems of desire, images that are more often than not capsized by the sadistic conjuring of colonial and imperial powers. Williams's clearly gendered images of the blossoming "white flower" (7), for example, embody the possibility of European man's sexual and symbiotic—or "stemenotic"—engagement with the land, respect for the original population's autochthonous wisdom, and the genuine humility necessary for comprehending the New World as the yearning body of a unique spiritual lover. But in this we might think of *In the American Grain* as an anti-foundational fiction for the United States, to borrow from Doris Sommer (1991), since the consummation between the male European lovers and the feminized colonial territory is almost always thwarted. That is, in Williams's treatment of Columbus, Ponce de León, Champlain, Cortés, and other historical figures, the Americas' process of becoming—that sensualized motion toward being, toward coming, or, in his vocabulary, toward "flowering"—is perpetually doomed by ignorance, fear, arrogance, and otherwise violent psychological responses and projections characteristic, to varying degrees, of Spanish, British, and French colonization of the Americas.

Williams does show us how these lovers, nevertheless, attempted to finesse the bud—or the earth's sex—into opening herself to them, by fleshing out a continuum of organic and inorganic affections in his character sketches. At the puritanical extreme, "Cotton Mather's Wonders of the Invisible World" represents what Williams terms the pathetic "tight tied littleness" (110) of spirit and understanding among the United States' founding settler colonists, their crude superstitions, their witch-hunts, and their bad spelling posing as a moral grammar for the nation's political imaginary. The backward, ugly, messianic impotence Williams sees fueling this "contemporary Puritan imagination" (113) is vehemently criticized in "Père Sebastian Rasles," the central chapter of the text, which narrates a conversation in Paris between Williams and a French Americanist who is an avid admirer of American colonial literature. Here Williams, as an exasperated character in his own text, proclaims the "immorality that IS America," the "white savagery" of British colonists, their "abortion of the mind," their absence of love—their inhumanity—still haunting us as a perverse and "stinking" presence on the world stage (112–17). What Williams calls this "ghostly miasm" [*sic*], in fact, is revealed as the very "thing" he attempts to rarefy as the book's prime "object"; the "thing" being, of course, Williams's catchword for the ontology of the poetic act itself. In his words, this thing, this haunting miasma, America (the United States), is

> an atrocious thing, a kind of mermaid with a corpse for a tail. Or it remains, a bad breath in the room. This THING, strange, inhuman, powerful, is like the relic of some died out tribe whose practices were revolting, . . . [It is a presence that] lives and there [in Cotton Mather's books] hides, as in a lair from whence it sallies now and then to strike terror through the land. (115)

The theme of the United States as a vile spiritual "THING"-in-the-world, jettisoned by British colonial terror, is elaborated further in the chapter "Jacataqua," in which Williams portrays the United States as an avaricious and shrewd monstrosity, a fearsome "Titan" spawned by wealth and nourished, again, by sense-less puritanical fervor. Like José Enrique Rodó's (1900) Caliban figure, Williams's monster represents the United States as an uncultured, ineducable, and violent imperial beast whose hyperbolic wealth only serves to indulge its pathological desires. Lurking in books and archives, the U.S. presence on the world stage performs its pragmatic rhetoric, its paranoid aversion to others, and its incapacity to love fully, that is, for Williams, to love *sensually*:

> [North American] wealth, all that is not pure accident—is the growth of fear.
>
> It is this which makes us the flaming terror of the world, a Titan, stupid (as were all the giants), great, to be tricked or tripped (from terror of us) with hatred barking at us by every sea—and by those most to whom we give the most. In the midst of wealth, riches, we have the inevitable Coolidge platform: "poorstateish"—meek. This is his cure before the world: our goodness and industry. THIS will convince the world that we are

> RIGHT. It will not. Make a small mouth. It is the acme of shrewdness, of policy. It will work. We shall have more to give. Logical reasoning it is: generous to save and give. It is bred of fear. It is as impossible for a rich nation to convince any one of its generosity as for a camel to pass through the eye of a needle. Puritanical; pioneer; "out of the small white farm-house"—the product of delay. The characteristic of American life is that it holds off from embraces, from impacts, gaining, by fear, safety and time in which to fortify its prolific carcass—while the spirit, with tongue hanging out, bites at its bars—its object just out of reach. (174–75)

The sensual depravation of the North American stock personality is a profound conceptual key for *In the American Grain*. The basic incapacity to touch, tenderly, the Other is for Williams the definitive tragic flaw of Anglo-American cultural history. The juxtaposition of the United States' unparalleled power as a nation and its poverty of aesthetic-ethical (read sensual) grace is also an obvious thematic legacy of Walt Whitman's *Leaves of Grass* (1855). While Williams may seem less than generous in diagnosing the United States' spiritual malaise, he is still cautiously optimistic à la Whitman that the most plausible cure is obtainable in ethically inflected poetics. Beyond their obvious differences, the most pronounced disparity between Whitman's and Williams's poetics is their mode of narrating the North American spiritual character. For Whitman, the "cosmic" poet's task is to name and cherish for posterity the finest and most beautiful national spirit as it emerges, naïvely (and voluptuously), from the proletarian masses, whom he suggests as the varied "leaves" of his text's title. But for Williams, the quintessential American poet is less sovereign as a narrator, since he represents historical violence and its emotional residue as if it were externally shaping the "American grain" on its own (metaphysical) volition.[2]

To foil the United States' repressed and therefore violently enacted sexuality, Williams celebrates the more catholic colonial desire of the French, which finds its most triumphant "blossoming, thriving, opening, reviving" expression in the figure of Sebastian Rasles, a physically handicapped Jesuit missionary whose "tenderness, devotion, insight and detail of apprehension" bore the American colonies' most "luscious fruit" (121). And here we discover the gendered paradox of Williams's anti-imperial poetics: the colonial lover can indeed prevail over America, but only if he can seduce her properly. As an emblem of this organically cultivated seduction, laced with institutional authority,

Rasles represents a sort of "sensitive mind" and sensual lover for her, for the New World:

> Already the flower is turning up its petals. It is *this* to be *moral*: to be *positive,* to be peculiar, to be sure, generous, brave—TO MARRY, to *touch*—to *give* because one HAS, not because one has nothing. And to give to him [that is the Indian] who HAS, who will join, who will make, who will fertilize, who will be like you yourself: to create, to hybridize, to crosspollenize, [*sic*]—not to sterilize, to draw back, to fear, to dry up, to rot. It is the sun. (121)

This affirmation, for me, marks the critical limit of Williams's experiment. Like other Hispanic American modernists, Williams presents seduction here as the con/sensual consummation of a sort of mutual and liberatory desire between the European (men) and the indigenous (wo/men); he erupts in a panegyric tone that clearly inscribes the authenticity of mestizo consciousness as *the* American consciousness. Celebrating hybridity, in this instance, is a conceptual trap, since such discourses of mestizaje in the Americas tend to gloss over actual caste and gendered inequalities with myths of racial democracy.

Yet—just to ride the edges of this a bit—considering that Williams himself had been accused by Ezra Pound of being a "bastard of the Caribbean" and that, in part, *In the American Grain* was a response to Pound's essentialist taunt that Williams could, as a Caribbean bastard, know nothing about American literature or culture, this celebration of hybridity and "cross-pollination" specifies a certain polemical function in a North American context.[3] At the risk of waxing functionalist, we could say that compared with the wild primitivism of some of his modernist contemporaries—Gertrude Stein's "Melanctha" (1909), for example, or just about anything by D. H. Lawrence—Williams's argument here is also less jarring in its own literary historical context than it might appear in light of more contemporary racial and gender critique.[4]

Ultimately, however, there is no alibi for this ethical slippage in Williams's text. Given the catastrophic fact of indigenous genocide in the Americas' colonial history, Williams's mestizo polemic is deflated by a central, arguably anthropophagic paradox: the desire for a romantically construed "Indian" as the prototype of organic New World subjectivity (particularly evident in his chapter on Daniel Boone) alongside the desire to represent this prototype's social death as that which enables European colonists who truly "cross-pollinize"—that is, mestizos—to engender a modern, more salutary quasi-"Indian" New World subjectivity. In effect, this poses a clash between metaphor and metonymy in the text; Williams wants to have his authentic American Indian (as a metaphor for America) and to eat her/him too (as a sign irrevocably split and supplanted by a solipsistic Euro-American racial fantasy). Indeed, for Williams the most meaningful Indian is the dead Indian who can serve his hauntological needs. Of the Taíno genocide, Williams writes: "In the heart there are living Indians once slaughtered and defrauded—Indians that live also in subtler ways" (42). How subtle? Very, for Williams understands history as "a tyranny over the souls of the dead" (189) and thus the only hope of liberation for the living resides in the resurrection of these dead subjects as food for thought or—as he explains in his chapter "On the Virtue of History"—the resurrection of the dead in literature.

Furthermore, this kind of rhetorical inversion of genocide and erasure of slavery, this reliance on an alternative yet crucially limited Latin American model of cultural and social history, is seminal for twentieth-century U.S. Latino poetics. That Williams privileges this paradigm marks his legacy in a distinctively masculinist Boricua fashion; caught between complex North and Latin American rhetorical structures that rationalize white privilege and ethnicize his experiences and understandings of historical subjectivity and, at the same time, exoticized and ostracized by the racism endemic to U.S. imperialism and colonialism in Puerto Rico, Williams opted to poeticize the model of history and cultural identity that served to legitimate (his) Latin American whiteness and Otherness simultaneously. Like the Boricua community as it entered into the twentieth century, Williams was a figure forced into the U.S. binarism of racial identifications that ironically made him the (nonwhite male) Other of the (Black male) Other. But instead of unraveling these contradictory subjective dialectics, Williams sublimates them by exploiting the (nonwhite female) Other of the (nonwhite male) Other of the (Black male) Other, creating a subjective syntax that confounds rather than compounds the now commonsense Hegelian approach to subjectivity. By relying on the notion of the nonwhite woman's death—literal, figurative, and subjective, both the primordial American lover and mother—as the grounding, procreative, and (sexually) satisfying referent for mestizo consciousness, Williams deadens and deforms the very trope that would otherwise ensure that this consciousness will not be haunted by its own violent foundational episteme.

Another blind alley in this text (also characteristic of the mestizo theoretical milieu) is how Williams almost entirely elides the African presence in the Americas' history. In fact, Lola Ridge, who reviewed *In the American Grain* in the *New Republic* (March 24, 1926), comments on this elision, stating that Williams's

> treatment of the Negroes, a people who have given so much to America's spiritual and aesthetic life, is singularly inadequate. He is not unsympathetic—far from it. But he approaches them as a spectator and seems to watch, fascinated, a single gesture that, in all its variations, becomes *his* beauty—to be segregated and kept pure for his perpetual enjoyment. He is grateful for their joy, the "quality" they brought to America—and of which they had so much that all their giving has not left them bankrupt. But [she cites] "all the rest is to keep from having to say anything more . . . it is their beauty." (149)

Despite her own critical limits, Ridge's main point is well taken: why is it that Williams neglects to include the African diaspora as an integral part of the New World's human drama? To make sense of slavery, survival, and involuntary cultural syncretism as core elements in his poetic reinvention of transamerican history? To elaborate on the affective contribution of Africa to what he otherwise defines as the racially, culturally, and ethnically pluralistic Americas?

Since I am reading Williams as a Boricua writer, this elision deserves close consideration. As a Boricua, Williams himself was a member of a multiracial community. Although he was born and raised in New Jersey long before Boricuas settled there in any large numbers, Williams's medical internship was in a New York City public hospital, where he most likely was one of a few bilingual doctors (1951: 93–105).[5] Thus Williams must have had some personal experience with the Boricua community at large, which was substantial in New York City at the time. As interested as he was in the Americas' racial histories, it seems impossible that his own community's multiracial composition (particularly among his less affluent female patients) escaped the characteristic acumen of this observer of the human condition. Indeed, in his biography of his mother he calls clear attention to his awareness of Caribbean racial miscegenation. "In the West Indies, in St. Thomas, Puerto Rico, Santo Domingo—the races of the earth mingled and intermarried," Williams writes, adding an awkward anthropological comment, "imparting their traits one to another and forgetting the orthodoxy of their ancient and medieval view" (1959: 135–36). Closer to home, he also volunteers his own possibly multiracial background in this text, carefully scripted in a somewhat confused sentence: "Nothing is known of our family beyond the last three generations and not all of that—other than vague rumors, enticing, irritating, scandalous—racially doubtful in certain cases" (132).[6] Furthermore, he was well-read in Latin American history, so he should have known about the significant (and, in many regions, majority) African demographic across the Americas during the colonial era. For these reasons, Williams's all but complete disregard of the African presence in transamerican colonial history is troubling.

Perhaps a pragmatic reason for this elision is that Williams's main resource for writing *In the American Grain* was the American History Room of the New York Public Library (NYPL), which did not have "the original records" of African diasporan history across the Americas that he required for his project (1925: second title page; 1951: 183–84). Granted, the Schomburg collection was purchased by the Carnegie Corporation and donated to the NYPL during 1926, a year after *In the American Grain* was published, so it stands to reason that Williams did not have access to Schomburg's archives, which, again, constituted the world's first major African diasporan public collection. Yet people traveled from all over the globe to visit Schomburg in Brooklyn, where over ten thousand documents and artifacts were stored in his famous, cluttered apartment on Kosciusko Street, and other writers, like W. E. B. Du Bois, Paul Lawrence Dunbar, Claude McKay, and Pura Belpré, knew how to find him. Dr. Julio Henna, a mutual acquaintance of Williams and Schomburg, could have certainly introduced them had either one requested a meeting. Yet it seems neither was inclined to strike up a relationship with the other, even though both apparently crossed the color line, as it were, in their professional and personal lives.

It is tempting to read the fact that Schomburg and Williams never met as a consequence of racial segregation, plain and simple. And, in fact, the ways they adopted "white" and "Black" U.S.-based racial identities are, to a great extent, responsible for their distance. Indeed, Puerto Rico has never been the racial democracy that many of its cultural historians would like it to be, and as figures caught up in the racial and class interpellation of their times in New York, New Jersey, and sometimes Paris, Schomburg and Williams would have been actors in a social dynamic that exacerbated insular Puerto Rican and Dominican brands of racism, brands that Schomburg himself had experienced and of which Williams was well aware.[7]

What Schomburg and Williams do have in common is their attempts to reject U.S. and Puerto Rican nationalist identities in their respective archival (re)inventions and, within this, any simplistic evocations of race. These attempts match their experiences in the United States as Boricuas who could not quite fit on either side of the color line. Although in their daily lives they both, perforce, attempted—sometimes successfully—to situate themselves on either side of this color line, in the process they were both habitually checked or embraced as useful outsiders. This definitive dilemma of Boricua social history during most of the twentieth century further complicates aesthetic and ethical tensions that are usually narrated as a racial divide—white versus Black—in U.S. modernist scholarship (Hutchinson 1995). Perhaps one of the greatest (and most underexplored) contributions of Boricua writers to American literature is precisely this complication of the color line, a thematic that perpetually surfaces in Boricua narrative and other literary and artistic genres. Given their pivotal roles for American modernism and the Harlem Renaissance, it is time we critically explore and accept Schomburg and Williams as figures who contest the Manichean white/Black allegories of U.S. subjectivity, literary history, and modernist poetics.

Schomburg's conceptual contribution to the African diaspora's cultural intellectual tradition was, as he defined it, shaping a "republic of arts and letters" from an encyclopedic recuperation of the African diaspora's documentary history in Spain and the New World (Schomburg 1927b: 154). His definition of diasporan subjectivity was clearly irreverent toward nationally normed identities (his ideal "republic" being, after all, bibliographically constituted), and he elaborated this racial constituency along a broad spectrum beyond whiteness and Blackness as they have been legislated, lived, and, consequently, assumed in the United States. In ways that resonate later in the work of Edouard Glissant (1981), Schomburg suggests a mobilization that invites variously termed Caribbean and Latin American communities to the table of an insurgent, African diasporan collectivity. This conceptual scope attended to the complexities of the Americas at large, precisely calibrated to account for not only U.S. institutions of slavery but also Luso-Iberian caste systems as they were legislated and lived during the Caribbean and Latin American colonial and slavery eras. Unlike African diasporan theorists who only research and analyze documents produced in the English language (Gilroy 1993a; James 1998)—a bias that arguably responds to a demographic minority in the Americas that is bolstered by a language privilege based in U.S. imperial prerogatives—Schomburg's interests comprehended much more than the United States and the Anglophone West Indies. Unlike most of his Anglo-/Afrocentric and monolingual peers (then and now), Schomburg understood—through research, political and personal experience, and expertise as a man of color fluent in more than one language—that racialization throughout the Americas involves diverse experiences of slavery, miscegenation, cultural syncretism, and racial politics, experiences that inform the inclusionary historical rubric in which he situated the African diaspora's transatlantic and transamerican archives.

Questioning fractured color lines is one of Schomburg's implicit preoccupations, and his archival papers suggest that he was habitually suspicious of cultural discourses that denied the Africanity of Hispanic Caribbean social history. As my reading of the limits of Williams's experiment avers, fractured color lines are often glazed over by cultural politics in the Americas at large, in particular popular and state-sponsored articulations of mestizaje and *criollo*-isms that erase African diasporan and indigenous contributions and demographics in nationalist discourses of identity. With color reduced to national culture in these discourses, and national culture reinvented as a white-ish formation, people of color in the Americas have been historically tossed out of the nationalist discursive loop, even (or especially) where they are or have been the nation's demographic majority. These identity politics might be explained as a discursive inversion of U.S. segregation; in the context of Latin American and Caribbean independence projects, elites composed new languages for non-European white national identities, in which tinge (never taint) lent enough local "color" to define the emerging American nations' cultural (*never* racial) difference without guaranteeing explicit Black or Indian inclusion.

Frustrated by these deeply seeded manipulations, Schomburg contested those who invoked *criollo* identity as a white racial legacy. Schomburg reappropriated "creole/criollo" as a Black moniker with the following argument, published in the journal *Light* in 1927:

> [T]he name Creole applies to the Negro born in America in contradistinction to the one brought from Africa. So the fair damsel who goes the round trying to make people believe that the word Creole has a charm to make people think it stands for a person descended purely from white stock, is nothing short of nonsense. Cervantes, the author of *Don Quixote,* is clear, and Tirso de Molina is unequivocable in his explanation. So that the fellow who goes the round of society trying to make people believe that the soft word of being a creole puts him across the bar will have henceforth to dig up his family tree for, like old words, it is getting obsolete.

Clearly, Schomburg was persistently perturbed by claims to "white purity" he encountered among people of Caribbean backgrounds in general, as this and other documents attest. His early critique of this mode of passing is relevant to contemporary insular Puerto Rican nationalist discourses as well, since *criollo* has indeed been appropriated as a nostalgic, nineteenth-century "white" cultural formation, precisely in the ways Schomburg hoped to curtail with this and other polemics.

An undated article among Schomburg's collected papers outlines the multiracial layering of his version of *creolité.* Schomburg's article launches a diatribe against John Crosby Gordon, whom Schomburg accused of publishing a letter that "obscure[d] the issue of Black and White, *and the various degrees of shade of color*" in transamerican context (Schomburg Papers, my emphasis). Apparently Gordon argued in his letter that, due to miscegenation, racism had become a nonissue in the Caribbean, and that consequently the only authentically Black experience was exclusively U.S.-based, to which Schomburg replied with the following:

> No people can brush away with an article, sp[e]cious in its construction, three hundred years of an awful oppression as suffered by men of African descent. We know that in nearly all parts of the British West Indies the practice, rather than the exception, is for members of the household as soon as they come up to the point or degree of light hued color—coffee and milk—where they can pass muster, are gone over to the other side and live in a pseudo-atmosphere of being classed as nearly white, they generally form a society based on their light-hued skin. At which time they look down on the poor black with disdain [who,] unless he can return home from Cambridge or Edinburgh with his parchment attesting to his superiority to his fellow native and his pseudo-equality with the unlettered white, is relegated to the Limbo of uncertainty.

Schomburg continues with a litany of social conflicts based in intraracial hostility—Haiti comes first to his mind, then Cuba, then, ultimately, Washington, D.C., where the "nearly white" brigades fight their own "sable brothers." Schomburg's preoccupation with analyzing the creases of the color line has a double valence, extending the creole net to include all peoples of African descent in the Americas at large, according to the complexities of places as diverse in their racial histories as Haiti and Puerto Rico, and simultaneously criticizing the U.S.-centric understandings of African diasporan history in the Americas. This, I would argue, is a quintessentially Boricua doubly bound racial articulation, in which blackness is not necessarily Black by U.S. standards, and what appears white is not necessarily white by U.S. standards, but race and racism are nevertheless *the* definitive concerns. Nowhere is this clearer than among the faces of people Schomburg claimed as distinguished members of the African diaspora—such as Anita Otero, Juan de Pareja, and Antonio Maceo—who look more "Latina/o" than "Black" according to the usual U.S. racial/ethnic stereotypes.

Since he lived in Brooklyn, scholars commonly assert that Schomburg exiled himself from the Boricua community because he felt more at home among African Americans (James 1998; Sinnette 1989). However, a study of Puerto Rican settlement in the New York City area documents the fact that Brooklyn, where Schomburg lived, also had a Puerto Rican enclave, one as significant at the time as the East Harlem community (Sánchez Korrol 1994: chap. 3), so evidently Schomburg was not a marginal member of the Boricua community in his daily life. Likewise, much has been made of his dissociation with the Cuban and Puerto Rican expatriate activist community. What few mention about this community, however, is that its political organizations basically disbanded after the 1898 U.S. invasion of Cuba and Puerto Rico, its members moving on to activities in various socialist and nationalist projects for which the islands themselves became the organizational seats.[8] Even if Schomburg had been inclined to continue the struggle for Puerto Rican independence, he would have probably had to go it alone. Because the premise of the U.S. invasion was decolonization (obviously a ruse, but at the time, political activists believed the United States was not interested in colonizing Puerto Rico), the *independentista* agenda in New York was effectively dissolved shortly after 1898 and only resurged decades later when Schomburg, no longer as interested in activist leadership, had already defined his life's work as a full-time archivist and librarian.[9]

The representation of Schomburg's seamless entry into U.S. Afrocentric activities is flawed by a predictable enthusiasm among scholars who want to claim him as a West Indian American radical. Their reinventions of Schomburg's biography are impressive efforts to fathom something that defies the tacit boundaries between Boricua and African American studies.[10] In this sense, Afro–West Indian American scholarship on Schomburg is an invaluable resource for meeting the challenge of understanding intraracial cross-cultural relations in U.S. context, particularly the rift between insular Puerto Rican and African American academic understandings of Caribbean-U.S. radicalism.

But we should also keep in mind that Schomburg faced resistance among some African Americans who doubted his Black identity, a painful issue that Schomburg allusively discussed in his private letters.[11] As an oft-cited passage by Claude McKay proposes, Schomburg's apparent resemblance to the popular "Gypsy" stereotype—his locks of curls, his olive skin tone, his clear brown eyes, and so forth—gave some African Americans the idea that he might easily pass as "nearly white":

> In appearance [Schomburg] was like an Andalusian gypsy, olive-complexioned and curly-haired, and he might easily have become merged in that considerable class of foreigners who exist on the fringe of the white world. But because of his African blood, he chose to identify himself with the Aframerican [*sic*] group. (McKay 1940: 140)

Being identified as a "Gypsy" in the United States, of course, hardly guarantees social mobility.[12] Given the utterly maligned status of Romani peoples in North America, and the exclusionary and punitive laws still in effect against this community in the United States, this misidentification could only worsen a person's social and legal alienation; in fact, the Romani are probably the racialized ethnic group least likely to enjoy white privilege (Hancock 1987). The Gypsy metaphor is an exotically constructed stereotype designed to romanticize and criminalize another diasporan community; that McKay chose precisely this metaphor to describe Boricua phenotype is as telling as it seems to be common among African Americans. In a joking tone, Toni Cade Bambara recollects that, as a child, she shared this mispersuasion:

> I remember when *you people* moved on *my* block. I was in the fourth grade. Some new people moved into the apartment building. Big family; babies, school children our age, some teenagers, married couples, maybe two or three sets of elders. They didn't speak much English, but that didn't strike us as strange; this was New York. What did strike us as strange was that the new people wore a lot of jewelry. The little girls, they had pierced ears, and they wore bangles and very bright clothing. *And so we thought they were gypsies, a new kind of gypsy; the kind that intended to stick around for a while.* One of the boys was in my class for about a minute. . . . what we found strange about the new boy and his family was some of his relatives looked like gypsies, but some of his relatives looked just like us. Who were these people? (Interview in Negrón-Muntaner 1994; my emphases)[13]

Bambara's childhood recollection of her understanding of Puerto Ricans as interloping, exotic, and sedentary foreigners in predominantly Black New York neighborhoods attests to both the de facto racial segregation of the Boricua community and a certain curious ignorance about a community that had been a significant presence in New York (particularly Harlem and Brooklyn) since at least the 1890s.

In similar fashion, rendering his Puerto Rican and Dominican background as the "dark," exotic, and mysterious side of William Carlos Williams is a perennial device among Williams scholars, usually couched in flourishes on his middle name. As late as 1994, we are still finding allusions to Williams's full name "as a vehicle for publishing his 'dark' side" or his "alien Spanish heritage," a certain "wildness" suggested by "Carlos" firmly checked and tamed by his "Anglo-Saxon" first and last names (Ahearn 1994: 2). Even Julio Marzán's study of Williams's "Spanish American roots" relies on bifurcating his Anglo and Latin consciousness, drawing what Marzán deems an analytically relevant distinction between "Bill" and "Carlos" as alter egos; Bill being an "exterior" Americanized mask that "camouflaged" Carlos, his "inner self" (1994: 2). While Marzán's framing of Williams's narrative voice as the manifestation of a split personality is not unproblematic, his attention to the Espanglish nuances of Williams's poetry and his explicit engagement with his Puerto Rican heritage add an important set of issues to Williams scholarship—issues, it is worth noting, that have been attacked in print as Marzán's articulation of "nationalistic propaganda" (Oliphant 1995: 71). Furthermore, despite Williams's quite direct explication of his mother's birth into a typical middle-class Puerto Rican family, as well as her typically Puerto Rican claims to a generationally distant European heritage (via undocumented family ties to the Dutch and French West Indies), scholars still seem reluctant to relinquish their attachment to the portrayal of Williams's mother as a Franco-Caribbean woman. But his mother's Francophilic tendencies evince a pattern consistent with nineteenth-century Puerto Rican bourgeois sensibilities, and thus hardly establish anything more than a willful (and often playful) Eurocentric affinity; in fact, although he may have romanticized French colonialism in *In the American Grain,* Williams gently parodied his mother's self-stylized French mannerisms in both his *Autobiography* and *Yes, Mrs. Williams.*

Like others in their community, Schomburg and Williams were forced into a characteristic bind of being racially "suspicious" on all fronts in a national context of routinely legislated and policed racial borders, in which communal belonging is guarded from the inside as well as the outside. Hence the amnesia, even among prominent cultural critics like James Clifford (1988), concerning Williams's Puerto Rican heritage. Hence too the propensity for African American and, more recently, West Indian appropriations of Schomburg's institutional and archival work, which is arguably the most significant legacy of Black cultural intellectual research in the twentieth century, and the simultaneous disregard of his own writing, which is obviously inflected by his Puerto Rican background and research interests.

The most illustrative example of this disregard among the African American intelligentsia during Schomburg's lifetime is an episode never discussed by his biographers. In January 1932, Schomburg was asked to take a leave of absence from his post as curator at Fisk University's library to tend to his collection in Harlem. But when news hit the surrounding community that Schomburg would replace the African American woman then in charge of the collection, Catherine Allen Latimer, Schomburg met organized resistance, apparently mobilized by W. E. B. Du Bois. This controversy was first covered in a Harlem newspaper called the *Defender* (January 23, 1932), worth quoting at length:

> NEW YORK—That all Harlem isn't homeless and destitute is attested by the tempest that is now brewing over personnel changes in the 135th Street branch of the New York Public Library.
>
> The library powers that be have designated Arthur A. Schomberg [*sic*] "curator pro tem" at the 135th Street branch, thus superseding Miss La-

> timer of Brooklyn, much to the discomfiture of friends of Dr. W. E. B. Dubois [*sic*], editor of the Crisis and an associated Harlem colored group, it has been reliably reported. . . .
>
> A few years ago Schomberg accepted a nominal price of $10,000 for his collection of historical and literary data on colored people, including the works and writings of colored authors. It is on file at the 135th Street branch and formally labelled "The Schomberg Collection." This exhibit has come within the jurisdiction of Miss Latimer, and it is Schomberg's supersession of her for a year by orders of "downtown" that has sent the Du Bois group on the war path, it is said.
>
> It is reported that friends of Dr. Du Bois and a committee of Harlemites made a formal protest at the main library located at Fifth Avenue and Forty-second Street against the change and even went so far as to demand the ousting of Schomberg.
>
> The protestors were informed, so the story goes, that Mr. Schomberg would remain for at least a year for the purpose of affording a real bibliophile's attention to his own collection, in the paramount interest of those who rely on the New York Public Library for authentic information, so that in so far as the Schomberg Collection goes such may be got with the least reasonable confusion, not now possible.

Thus, eight years after he sold (for a fraction of its worth) his archives and artifacts to the Carnegie Corporation, Schomburg's collection seems to have become an institutional wedge for hiring and promoting African American librarians at the 135th Street branch. His entitlement, as its founding curator, to spend time organizing and supplementing his archives as a temporary paid employee of the library system was apparently subordinated to this agenda by one of the era's most influential African American intellectual groups.

In my research I did not find any correspondence between Du Bois and Schomburg that would indicate the two had discussed Schomburg's proposed appointment in 1932, although documentation does show that Schomburg eventually accepted this post as an "unpaid consultant" (Ortiz 1986: 79). Thus, despite his reputation as the premier African diaspora archivist, Schomburg was still deemed an outsider when public maneuvers in the name of African American intellectual consensus and institutional politics were at stake in Harlem. An article that appeared the next week in the *AfroAmerican* (January 30, 1932) clarified Du Bois's position on the issue. Here the journalist claims that the point was not the group's opposition to Schomburg per se, but rather a long-standing effort to hire and promote Black librarians in the NYPL, a politicized priority to which, it seems, Schomburg's temporary appointment was deemed a threat:

> NEW YORK—Charges that W. E. B. Du Bois, editor of The Crisis, was bitterly opposed to the appointment of Arthur Schomberg [*sic*] as temporary curator of the 135th Street branch library, were denied by friends close to the editor, this week. . . .
>
> From persons familiar with the part played by Dr. Du Bois in the controversy it is said that the fact of the matter is that for years the group has been trying to get colored library assistants into the public library, meeting a great deal of difficulty. . . .
>
> Two years ago Dr. Du Bois is said to have taken up the matter of one appointee who was not getting promotion as she deserved. A quiet, but insistent conference resulted in her appointment as first assistant librarian, the highest appointment that we have had. . . .
>
> "Many of us," representatives said, "immediately protested, not against Mr. Schomberg, but against the demotion of Mrs. Latimer. We all expressed together with Mrs. Latimer the highest respect for Mr. Schomberg and rejoiced at his connection with the library, but we insisted that this was no excuse for demoting or changing the work of Mrs. Latimer.
>
> "As a result of our protest, Mrs. Latimer retains her third grade position and remains as reference librarian of the Schomberg Collection."

Clearly, Schomburg's (brief) appointment at Fisk University disqualified him as an underemployed Black librarian. Yet, while the framing of this story by local papers would have us believe that hiring, promoting, and retaining African Americans in the NYPL was the prime objective of Du Bois's mobilization, it also seems evident that Latimer's authority over the collection itself was a major concern, as the second article suggests in its closing lines. As the reference librarian, she would have had the everyday run of the collection, as well as the power to catalogue the collection's items as she deemed fit and probably no small say in further decisions about acquisitions. Thus, beyond the surface concern with employment, the controversy signals a struggle over representation as well. We do not have further documentary evidence of any power struggle between Schomburg, Du Bois, and Latimer; however, we can infer that part of this negotiation had to do with Spanish-language text acquisitions. In a letter dated November 5, 1933 (corrected to read 1934), written by Schomburg to Joaquín Becerril, editor of the San Juan paper *La Voz del Obrero* (The Worker's Voice), Schomburg explains that he is eager to acquire more Puerto Rican texts to augment the collection at the 135th Street branch, expressing his desire to provide Spanish-speaking readers and researchers access to books that document Black contributions to the full spectrum of the Americas' arts and letters, particularly in Puerto Rico:

> Se[ñ]or Editor:
> . . . En esta biblioteca, una de las cuarenta y cinco que dotan la ciudad de Nueva York, regalo del millonario Andrés Carnegie, existe el departamento de referencia y estudio donde tenemos más de diez mil libros sobre la raza negra desde Africa hasta América. Libros sobre el descubrimiento, colonización y exploración por los [e]spañoles y despues por las otras naciones de Europa. Aquí tenemos el folleto de Salvador Brau sobre Rafael Cordero como también datos sobre Campeche. Tenemos un buen número de libros en el idioma de Cervantes y Calderón de la Barca, pero *estamos ansioso que figure[n] en este establecimiento los libros de los [*sic*] puertorriqueños* como Eleuterio Derkes [y] Tomás Carrión; solamente tenemos un libro de Gonzalo Marín y P. C. Timothee.
>
> Nosotros estamos dispuestos a pagarle por conseguirnos estas obras o indicarnos dónde se pueden conseguir. Yo tengo la seguridad que [a] Usted y otros amigos muy bien pueden interesarles que las obras de los Riqueños se conserven en este sucursal donde vienen muchos de habla Español [*sic*] a estudiar. Por acá no hay una copia del libro de Sotero Figueroa "Ensayo Biográfico" que fue publicado en Ponce [en] 1888.
>
> Con la esperanza que esta nota encuentre eco por las praderas o montes de mi país, le ruego en la primera tertulia nombre al amigo Timothee como miembro del comité *para poner en las vitrinas de este establecimiento una docena de libros pro o que se refieren a las personas de color*. Entonces pídame algo. Por ejemplo no tenemos la obra de Tomás Carrión titulada "Ten con Ten."

> Mr. Editor:
> . . . In our library, one of the forty-five funded by the City of New York, is a reference department and study area (a gift from the millionaire Andrew Carnegie) where we have more than ten thousand books concerning the Black race from Africa to America. These are books about the discovery, colonization, and exploration by the Spanish and, later, by other European nations. We have Salvador Brau's pamphlet on Rafael Cordero here as well as information on Campeche. We have a great number of books in the language of Cervantes and Calderón de la Barca, but *we are anxious that books by Puerto Ricans* like Eleuterio Derkes and Tomás Carrión *have a place in this establishment*; we have only a single book by Gonzalo Marín and P. C. Timothee.

> We are prepared to pay you to obtain these works for us, or pay you to let us know where we might find them. I am certain that you and other friends may very well be interested in making sure that Puerto Rican texts are conserved in this library branch, where many Spanish speakers come to study. We have no copy here of Sotero Figueroa's "Biographical Essay," published in Ponce in 1888.
>
> With the hope that this note finds an echo in the meadows or mountains of my country, I implore you, during the first study group meeting appoint Timothee as a member of a committee *dedicated to filling a display case in this establishment with a dozen books in support of, or that refer to, people of color.* And charge me something for it. For example, we do not have the work of Tomás Carrión entitled "Ten con Ten."[14]

There is no return correspondence from Becerril in Schomburg's private papers and none of the titles he requested in this letter were ever acquired by the 135th Street branch library. Whether or not the problem remained the apparent indifference of his insular colleagues to his acquisitions project at the NYPL or, after his departure, later administrative indifference toward shoring up the 135th Street branch's tiny collection of Puerto Rican authors of color, we will probably never know. What this does indicate is that Schomburg felt a compelling interest in maintaining the representational scope of the collection he founded, inclusive of Spanish language texts, as well as his more specific personal and political interest in providing Harlem's Spanish-speaking community with books by or about people of color in Puerto Rico. It also displays both insular Puerto Rican disrespect for him as a Black researcher and his African American colleagues' disrespect for him as a Puerto Rican researcher.

Both Arturo Schomburg and William Carlos Williams were motivated to recuperate, reorganize, and reconceptualize documentary evidence, and each crafted distinctive critical agendas alternately aligned and at odds with the modernist impulses of their contemporaries. To elaborate these agendas, Williams resorted to a deconstructive mode of literary historical recuperation, while Schomburg devoted his life to a literally constructive one. Aesthetically, Schomburg and Williams have virtually nothing in common, except perhaps their problematic takes on sensuality and gender. In his effort to capture history as a sensual plateau, Williams radically engenders the land and essentializes seduction, deadening into motifs the very feminine and indigenous presences he attempts to conjure back to life in his text. In his effort to elaborate the Africanity of the Americas, Schomburg represses the sensual and feminine entailments of social history, opting instead for a masculinist polemical recuperation in the name of "men of African descent." More poetically construed, it seems that while Williams was trying to find a palimpsest of genuine love on archival documents of transamerican history, Schomburg was busy building and filling his own shelves with actual documents, often exploited, unloved, and summarily dismissed on every side for his efforts.

Yet, as disparate as their aesthetic projects were, both Schomburg's legacy and Williams's *In the American Grain* attest to a singular Boricua predicament of Americanization: subalternization situated in the nation's sociohistorical divide between Blackness, rooted in a specific struggle to mend the human devastation of U.S. slavery, and whiteness, rooted in what Williams poses as a coeval and sadistic colonial desire to torture and consume the racial Other. Crucially, neither figure read or wrote this predicament in isolation from other analogously dispossessed and dispersed supranational or internally colonized ethnic communities, whose histories and cultures informed their historical memory. In Boricua modernist narrative, the shared condition of subalterity in the Americas' history drives an explicit ethical commitment to social justice in literature.

This reconsideration of Schomburg and Williams as Boricua modernists therefore suggests some provocative questions about contemporary American studies and American literary history. My framing of these inquiries runs in tension and tandem with alternative formulations of American subjectivity emerging in American Indian and African diasporan literary and cultural criticism, scholarship that often revolves around what critics read as culturally specific ethical and aesthetic motivations in nineteenth- and twentieth-century literatures and cultural intellectual histories (Baker 1987; Gates 1988; Harjo and Bird 1997; Allen 1986; Deloria 1969).

If, for example, as Henry Louis Gates asserts, African Americans in the United States faced the challenge to "write themselves into being" as the prime criterion for establishing their humanity, their reason, and, ultimately, their American subjecthood in the New World, or if, as Vine Deloria argues, the members of North America's first nations were ironically forced into the human category by colonists whose only motive was to entitle them, literally, to sell their land, then what can

Boricua critics cite as our foundational episteme as dis- and rearticulated subjects in the continental United States (Gates 1992: 57; Deloria 1969: 172–73)? If for Blacks the key issue in struggling for human legitimacy can be historically traced in and around U.S. slavery, and if for American Indians this same struggle revolves around alien codes, bureaucracies, and documents violently imposed on them only because of their preexistence on and relationship with the living earth and her landscapes, then how, again, do we cast Puerto Rican diasporan subjectivity as an Othered discursive formation negotiated under the Manichean colonial and imperial allegories of Blackness and whiteness, of savagery and civilization, of literal or cultural citizenship and "alienized" alterity?

Answering this theoretical challenge begins with finding the paperwork—the essays, novels, position papers, and other primary documents of the Puerto Rican diaspora's literary history—a corpus that, according to the Library of Congress catalog, does not exist (there is no such index as "Boricua—" or "Puerto Rican colonial diaspora—literature"). Searching for Boricuas in the available anthologies of American literature also reveals no clearly discernible trail of clues. In fact, judging by the constitution of the twentieth-century American canon, it would seem that Boricuas simply did not write (or publish) until the civil rights movement, and even then, all one finds is poetry. Thus, at the highest ordering strategies of paperwork in our metropolitan archives, our folders, it would seem, are virtually empty. Our chapters have not been, because they cannot be, written; we are instead, it appears, a lyrical but paperless community.

So many of the usual terms will not suffice for this predicament. "Erasure" of Boricua specificities in American cultural history is a too facile complaint, for it does not capture for critique the complicated processes involved in subjugating knowledge. "Marginality" implies an acknowledged presence, off-center, but nonetheless articulated. Even cognitive mapping will not do, because it suggests some semblance of sovereign terrain, and we have no such literal or figurative territory. As a nation and a Nation, as a topos and trope, Puerto Rico is a colonial territory of the United States, and both our insular and mainland communities' documents (including, in point of fact, Puerto Rico's national archives) have been disappeared by colonial allegories as well as administrators.[15] In response to this paperlessness, to this representational void imposed by these official allegories and administrators,

Boricua modernist writers contrived pragmatic and poetic solutions, stocking the cultural imaginary and the public library with printed antidotes to our paperless malaise.

By committing this paperless metaphor to paper and outlining our subjectivity as such, I do not mean to play hopscotch, gingerly, over the violence of history. *Paperlessness* is a serious metaphor, it is a metaphor that frowns, yet it is *the* Boricua dilemma implicitly broached in our authors' early twentieth-century narratives. Paperlessness denotes a chronically alienated subjectivity, a hermeneutical crisis based in an endless cycle of deferral in U.S. national imaginaries, a cycle that perpetuates Boricua alterity despite documents that should guarantee a legitimate referent (citizenship) and an enunciative center (literature). Unpredicated by literacy, land, or immigrant trauma, our first generations on the mainland were wo/men denied not just citizenship and passport papers but a legitimate existential pedigree in our colonial metropole's socio-symbolic order. Countering this alienation is, I submit, Boricua modernism's prime motivation. Conscious of and conscientious about this alienation in the United States, Boricua modernist writers proposed more inclusionary genres of fiction and public intellectual advocacy. As a creative (perforce) challenge to paperlessness and bastardization, Boricua modernist narratives authorize themselves to trespass generic, cultural, and national boundaries at will, and constitute a corpus of writing in which transracial, translingual, and transcultural legacies radically reshape the substance of and standards for archival recovery and literary experimentation. Their audacious recuperation of desire and documentation—the ironic legitimization of illegitimacy, however incomplete or problematic as it may ultimately read in the present—counter an antinomical experience of the early twentieth century on the U.S. mainland and intimate a uniquely diasporan yet definitively American modernist poetics.

Constructing a legitimizing Boricua literary and cultural intellectual history, or a metanarrative of this scribing of our paperless condition, requires new paradigms and research methods that are sensitive to the institutional, political, and narrative tendencies of figures like Schomburg and Williams. In this project there is still a wealth of material waiting to be explored. The next chapter, which analyzes the life's work of Pura Belpré, takes the archival project a step further by recuperating another extraordinary Black contributor to Boricua literary history.

Sadly, if predictably, all of the work Belpré published during her lifetime has gone out of print. Like Arturo Schomburg, Belpré has enjoyed a reputation for her commitment to alternative librarianship, but her writing has been relegated to the Centro de Estudios Puertorriqueños' archives and a few holdings in U.S. libraries of her first- and second-edition texts. To my knowledge, there is not a single article, let alone a more extended study, devoted to a critical consideration of Belpré's essays and fiction. That both Schomburg and Belpré were Black Boricuas whose work reflected antiracist agendas suggests that the critical amnesia concerning their legacies is a racist symptom of not only American studies but of Puerto Rican studies as well.

Like my work on Williams, Schomburg, and Capetillo, my research on Belpré, which began with heavy intuitive hints while visiting New York City's public libraries, is an effort to recuperate an emblematic figure of Boricua cultural intellectual history. Belpré began her career at what is today called the Schomburg Center for Research in Black Culture, and her life's work offers invaluable leads for recuperating and analyzing the Nuyorican experience in Harlem during the Depression, through the post–World War II period, and into the era of the civil rights movement.

3

A Boricua in the Stacks

An Introduction to the Life and Work of Pura Teresa Belpré

At the start of the research and development of this study, I realized that one of the prime locations for materials on the Puerto Rican colonial diaspora is the Centro de Estudios Puertorriqueños archives at Hunter College in Manhattan. Early on, I had the opportunity to explore the Colección Puertorriqueña at the University of Puerto Rico, Río Piedras, which initially seemed the most likely site to search for the diaspora's earliest texts and contextual documentary evidence, and this is where, ultimately, I found the original publications of Luisa Capetillo's work. However, generally speaking, there was not much more material on or about the Boricua community in Puerto Rico's premier research library's special collections. After thirteen months in Puerto Rico I returned home to California, where I had access to a fabulous library system at UCLA, and I managed slowly but surely to find more material. Arturo Schomburg's papers are available on microfilm through interlibrary loan in the University of California system, for example, and while the quality of the reproductions on these reels fell short of what I ultimately required, the microfilm was an important research entry. Later, at the University of Texas at Austin, I had the Ransom Center for first editions of William Carlos Williams's work, and the Benson Collection, which is an invaluable resource for both U.S. Latina/o and Latin American studies. Yet, all the while, I knew that New York would be the archival mecca for my study. The problem was how to finance the trip and stay there long enough to do the research properly.

My previous research on Boricua literary history informed the decision to search for new voices on the East Coast, and therefore focusing on New York City's archives was a choice organic to the holistic process of literary historical recuperation discussed in the introduction. At different junctions I had to make similar decisions. I wanted to find a voice that I thought spoke for the generation of working-class men and women who had made that first trek to New York City after the U.S. colonization of Puerto Rico, and Luisa Capetillo had been the perfect candidate. I gathered that modernism is a touchstone for contemporary debates about literary history and racial politics in the United States and, since I also wanted to unravel and document for my peers the racial complexities of Boricua social and literary history, comparing Schomburg and Williams became a priority. Each essay in this study evolved in a like manner, and though I eagerly gathered pounds of paper in the process, I learned to be patient with myself as the appropriate choices emerged.

Once I had the opportunity for an extended stay in New York, the guiding concerns for my research were multiple and complex, but I knew that I had a conspicuous lacuna between the modernists and the civil rights generation that needed to be addressed. My time in New York City was limited, so I was forced to strategize, and filling this lacuna became the primary goal, while the relatively smaller gaps in my Schomburg research became the secondary concern. Since my radar for selecting representative figures scanned for those whose writing complemented their institutional politics, the Centro's archives were the obvious first choice, a choice that necessarily excluded a number of other places, such as various New York Public Library (NYPL) branches with texts difficult to find elsewhere, or the Smithsonian (only a train ride away in Washington, D.C.), not to mention the art spaces, such as the Museo del Barrio, or the curious pilgrimage I wanted to make to William Carlos Williams's haunts in New Jersey.

For a month I spent a good portion of every morning and early afternoon at Hunter College, then I traveled to the Schomburg Center, often walking the distance via Fifth Avenue and feeling the immense difference between these two locations. In the morning, once I got past the guards at Hunter College's general library entrance, who often hassled me about my identification and business there before reluctantly letting me through the turnstile, I took a quick left to enter the Centro's Puerto Rican library (which, by the way, is supposed to be open to the general public). The Centro library has a wonderful reading room, and the librarians there were extremely helpful and generous with their time. However, it was almost entirely empty that summer.

The Schomburg Center, on the other hand, was much more inviting. The guards posted at the door were friendly to everyone who came in, and (without exception) they graciously opened the heavy glass doors to the building and kindly offered to store visitors' personal items. And unlike the rather lonesome library at Hunter College, the Schomburg Center was teeming with activity every day. When I signed in, I could see the names of people who had traveled from many other states and countries to visit the library, which made me feel so proud of this man and his work, and seeing the local children doing their homework in the reading room, I felt even prouder of his legacy. There were also young men and women working at the request desk in the basement where I spent most of my time, and hearing them laughing and joking with each other as they managed their tasks made me feel at home. When I needed a break, Malcolm X Boulevard was also an inspiring experience. Just standing there in front of the library, taking in the commotion, or strolling to the independent bookstore down the street, or eating a late lunch at the diner across the way where, no matter how much my mind was spinning in its own little sphere, I was always caught up in some lively and friendly conversation.

Soon I began hoping that I would find some legitimate reason to spend more time at the Schomburg Center, but there really was not much for me in the collections to pursue, given my research priorities, and given my time limitations, just hanging out (no matter how inspiring) was not an option. At first I was saddened to think that, despite Schomburg's commitment to the Puerto Rican section of his collection, the current holdings had few texts by or about Nuyoricans for me to spend time reading. Then I reasoned with myself that his vision had been African diasporan, his collection indeed followed that foundational vision, and AfroRicans form only a relatively small part of the larger diaspora. Still, whenever I saw the children doing their homework, I felt an acute sadness that more young Boricuas were not there too, thinking hard and feeling the immense pride the building inspired in me. After all, I thought, the Schomburg Center is a public library that services Harlem as its immediate constituency, and Boricuas are one of Harlem's largest and longest-standing communities. Spanish Harlem may have a closer library, but the Schomburg Center is only about ten or fifteen minutes away on foot. Outside, no one batted an eye when I passed, because I looked like part of the scenery: a young Nuyorican woman, tall and thick in most of the usual places, sporting a bad perm, gold hoops, old Nikes, and snug designer jeans, just walking down the street. Why then, I wondered, was I apparently a rarity in the library itself?

Introducing the Work of Pura Teresa Belpré

My experiences in and shuttling between the Schomburg Center and the Center for Puerto Rican Studies library influenced my research in both locations, and my walks, thoughts, and impressions between these two collections also provided important hints for this chapter's interventions. Once in New York I really wanted to know more about Boricuas who, like me, had explored this city in search of a comfortable and inviting place to read, to think, and, ideally, to feel part of a dynamic and intellectually engaged group of peers. And since the character of the public libraries was such a pronounced concern in my thoughts about New York City, I felt compelled to pursue the legacy of Pura Teresa Belpré (1902–1982), the first Boricua and Afro-Latina librarian in the NYPL system, who was hired and trained in the 1920s at the 135th Street branch library (which eventually became the Schomburg Center). My archival intuition led to a woman who was not merely a librarian, but a *children's* librarian whose life's work revolved around narrative and public institutional interventions vis-à-vis the libraries in which she worked, the communities she traversed in her daily life, and her vision of precisely the kind of mutual understanding between people of all backgrounds that can be inspired by books, a vision whose praxis always started first, quite wisely, with children.

In an uncanny revelation, I found out years later that one of the most important moments for Belpré occurred just before she began her career, sometime around 1920, when she saw Catherine Allen Latimer assisting teenagers at the Schomburg Center, then known as the Countee Cullen branch.[1] Watching Latimer inspired Belpré in much the same way a similar scene had provoked me. Belpré recounts,

> It was at the Countee Cullen Branch of the New York Public Library where I found my profession. We had recently arrived in New York. One day my younger sister and I set out to find a library where she could find material for a book report she had to do for her English class at Julia Richman High School. A policeman pointed the way to us. As we entered the reading room, I noticed the librarian, Miss Allen, later

> Mrs. Latimer, moving slowly among the crowded room, helping teenagers. As I watched them the thoughts of my friends in the island made me feel lonely for the first time. I thought, "If I could do what this lady is doing for the rest of my life, I would be the happiest person on earth." (López and Belpré 1974: 88)

According to Belpré's account of how her "wish" to work with the children at the library became a reality, the first step in her career as a librarian occurred through politicized collaboration among women in 1921 (and her brother-in-law's sexist outburst, which she perhaps slyly includes in her account):

> That wish was granted through the vision of Ernestine Rose, the [135th Street] branch librarian who, noticing a "Bodega" (grocery store) and a "Barberia" (barber shop) suddenly appearing in the community, thought that the best thing to do was to secure the services of a Spanish-speaking assistant. One of the readers at the branch was a Puerto Rican teacher. To him she confided her thoughts. He said, "I have just the person you need." So home he came to offer the job to my recently married sister. "No," said her husband, "My wife is not going to work." My sister said to me, "Why don't you go and try it. You might like it." So I did, liked it, and a wonderful new world opened for me. (López and Belpré 1974: 88–89)

From this position Belpré launched a career that took her to a number of NYPL branches over the course of her life, usually in the tracks of the Nuyorican community's shifting settlement.[2] For the purpose of outlining her life's work, we can divide Belpré's career into three phases: first, between 1921 and 1943, when she did the pioneering work that established her international reputation for bilingual children's librarianship; second, between 1943 and the early 1960s, during her time traveling with her husband, when she concentrated on her writing and did occasional public performances and lectures; and third, from around 1962 to 1982, when Belpré reentered the NYPL to work for systemic renovations in services to communities of color during the civil rights era. Although she published two major works earlier in her career, it is not until the final decades of her life that Belpré more firmly established herself as an author. Her later texts are collections of many of the stories on which she had worked throughout her life, along with various essays, two bibliographies of children's literature, and a number of books about child protagonists and contemporary urban life.

Belpré in the NYPL: 1921–1943

Belpré's archival collection is imperative to understanding the first phase of her career in the NYPL, because during this period she was extremely productive yet published very little; her archival papers offer a wealth of information about her projects and the community's settlement patterns, but the majority of these papers were written as lectures, notes, and speeches. In Belpré's accounts of her first twenty-odd years working in the NYPL, the most prevalent theme is her commitment to inspiring all children to read and to take advantage of the public libraries' resources. Reading, as she understood it, galvanized children's imaginations, improved their self-esteem, and could even make them feel loved. Furthermore, she felt the libraries had a public trust, and she made herself responsible to this trust in dynamic ways.

This commitment forms the baseline of Belpré's entire career. And as she elaborated her vision of the libraries' public service responsibilities, she also habitually commented on the misperceptions adults may have of children living below the poverty line. Many of the essays included in her archival papers contain a running commentary on negative adult perceptions of lower-income children, usually couched in a valorization of every child's basic humanity. In an undated essay titled "The Reluctant Reader: What Makes Him?" Belpré explains,

> There is a mistaken idea that the reluctant reader is mainly a product of poverty and disadvantaged areas. Nothing can be further from the truth. These children share the universality of childhood, that is theirs regardless of their status in life. They have their hopes, dreams and little joys. They need a little more individual care, a feeling, perhaps, of love, to fill the vacuum of so many empty hours alone. They respond quickly and naturally to attentions for they are sensitive children.
>
> They have a great sense of humor and curiosity which shows in the kind of books they like to see or be read. They enjoy books that deal with different ethnic groups and familiar situations. They like to identify themselves with them. Animal folktales are a popular subject with them. . . .
>
> The bilingual child is often considered as a reluctant reader, mainly because he is just beginning to learn English as a second language. Here the problem is mainly one of a lack of understanding on the part of the teacher. All these children need special care. They [more specifically, Puerto Rican children] are the latest immigrants to create a new foreign speaking community. They differ from all the other migrants in that they are American

> citizens and in their tendency to cling to their native language and traditions even through their process of assimilation. (Belpré Papers)

The "universality of childhood" is a persistent topic and subtext in Belpré's essays, as are the "hopes, dreams and little joys" each and every child is naturally predisposed to feel, which she suggests are often misunderstood or ignored in less affluent areas by teachers, librarians, and other authority figures who have racist and otherwise "mistaken ideas" about poverty and its effects on children. Belpré argues that such adults, who are simply uneducated about children of color's cultural backgrounds, cannot comprehend the particular needs and aptitudes of bilingual children. (These are themes that we shall see are also pervasive in the work of later Nuyorican writers, like Nicholasa Mohr.) Puerto Rican children are born, Belpré reminds us, not only into the "universality of childhood," but also as U.S. citizens, and learning Spanish as a first language is common in this community, even stateside. But rather than seeing bilingualism as a kind of deficit that somehow automatically results from their lack of access to material resources, Belpré prefers to call attention to the unique cultural and linguistic syncretism that Boricuas experience in the States, a syncretism that does not preclude "assimilation," but rather nurtures a child's development in unique ways, with its own built-in rhythms and tendencies. Importantly, being a "reluctant reader" is not the bilingual child's fault, but "mainly" a result of her or his teacher's "lack of understanding."

In her 1968 essay "Library Work with Bilingual Children" (Belpré Papers), Belpré further discusses the issue of mean-spirited attitudes toward Boricua and other lower-income children. Her message here is that, despite their limited material resources, children living below the poverty line inherit rich cultural legacies:

> Often the term "culturally deprived" is used with bilingual children, as it is also used for all children residing in sections of the city considered "underprivileged." One can't call a culture that is 400 [years] old, culturally deprived. The fault of the term lies with those who lack the knowledge of the background, and the respect for the culture of these children. It is the knowing and understanding of it, that uplifts the child and gives him pride in himself. No one can give it or help to preserve what one does not know. A child will be better prepared to understand the value of another culture when he knows the value of his own. Once out of a home in one of the poorest sections of the city, came the most perfect Peruvian exhibit the branch library had ever had. Books, crafts, music and

> a program of folk dances that took the neighborhood by surprise. Poor, yes, the family was that, but not culturally deprived. This family was preserving a culture centuries old. To be able to look past these social expressions, and consider the families as individuals, provides many surprises. One of them was provided by a family considered "underprivileged," who provided the making of an exhibit of native crafts of their country. The exhibit cases became the center of admiration for the priceless collection they displayed. These are two examples of the wonderful finds one comes across in sections of a city where blind eyes see only poverty and miss the inner beauty of its people. (6–7)

Again, Belpré calls attention to adults who presume to pronounce cultural deficiencies among children of the inner city, adults "who lack the knowledge" of these children's cultural backgrounds, and thus develop an egotistical defense mechanism that converts this ignorance into malicious condescension. Even today, most low-income graduates of public school districts could narrate any number of episodes that would corroborate Belpré's assessment here. Importantly, however, Belpré does not dwell on racism and adults who project their insecurities onto children. Instead, she focuses on the children involved and the value of cross-cultural understanding for everyone. The argument here is familiar: "A child will be better prepared to understand the value of another culture when he knows the value of his own," and being open to "surprises" is an important aspect of this cross-cultural understanding. Children, of course, adore surprises, and are therefore predisposed to enjoy them. The implicit message is not only that educators should appreciate and foster children's natural propensities, but that if adults gather the courage to look beyond the stereotypical labels, to unlearn their fearful and condescending reactions to the "social expressions" of poverty, then they might learn to appreciate the cultures of the so-called underprivileged, cultures, Belpré reminds us, that are often ancient, and that can be a source of "priceless" aesthetic legacies. Comprehending the "inner beauty" of people in these communities can inspire "admiration," which in turn can foster self-respect, for both adults and children, in tandem with respect for others.

Like Luisa Capetillo's narrative approach, Belpré's theorization of culture always returns to lived experience, and her essays tend to weave between her observations in daily life and her ideas for improving the quality of this daily life for children. And like Capetillo, Belpré approached her community in a grassroots style. During the first two decades of her career, Belpré was directly involved with thousands of children, hundreds of parents (especially mothers and grandmothers), and dozens of community service organizations. In her essays she details her strategy for bringing children into the library: entrenching herself in the community's everyday life, assessing the needs and desires of the community from that vantage point, and organizing events that respond to these needs and desires in convenient locations and in creative ways that are both entertaining and educational. She also mentions that attracting mothers to the libraries was an extremely successful tactic.

Soon after her training at the 135th Street branch and course work at the NYPL library school, Belpré was transferred to the Seward Park branch, where there were a variety of successful children's programs already in place, and where she developed community partnerships with the Union Settlement, the Madison House, the Henry Street Settlement, and the Educational Alliance. She tells us that she began planning some of her first bilingual story hours by keeping close tabs on those from the Boricua community who frequented the Seward Park branch, whom she discovered were generally grandmothers looking for *cartillas* (Spanish ABC's books for children). Many of these elder women were involved in church organizations, so Belpré began collaborating with the first Spanish-language church in the Harlem community, an Evangelical church called La Milagrosa, located on Seventh Avenue between 114th and 115th Streets in a building that previously housed a synagogue. Belpré tapped into the church's bilingual projects for children and young adults, and made sure that the library's resources were made available. Consequently, a group of mothers and grandmothers started a Spanish story hour at La Milagrosa, and a group of young adults formed a teen reading club that regularly used the library. In a similar fashion, Belpré organized her first bilingual picture book hours with children from an East Harlem day care program that used the roof of what was then known as the "Jewish YMCA" (at 110th Street and Fifth Avenue) overlooking Central Park (Belpré Papers, "Bilingual Story Telling" n.d.: 1). A few years later, Belpré was transferred again, this time to the 115th Street branch, in the center of a Jewish community, she alludes, in the process of "white flight," as Puerto Ricans and African Americans moved into this neighborhood during the 1920s. In the 1930s Belpré was transferred yet again, this time to the Aguilar branch in El Barrio (East Harlem), a historically Italian neighborhood that became at that time (and is to this day) a predominantly Nuyorican enclave. Her work at the Aguilar branch, particularly the puppet shows and Día de los Reyes (Epiphany) celebrations, made her a familiar and admired figure in the East Harlem community during the Great Depression.

Wherever Belpré was transferred following the shifting trail of Puerto Rican settlement in Harlem in the 1920s and 1930s, she was quick to make connections with the most important community-based service organizations in the vicinity, including the Porto Rican Brotherhood, La Liga Puertorriqueña e Hispánica, Casita María (the first Puerto Rican Catholic center), and the Shelter—a housing/detention complex for children, mostly "older girls" she recounts, who were court-appointed wards of the state (Belpré Papers, "Library Work with Bilingual Children" 1968: 4). Her grassroots approach to community library services was a significant part of her success as an advocate. Belpré built new links between the community and the public libraries, and because she forged these links in strong, definite patterns, Puerto Rican children and young adults—along with their parents and other relatives—felt welcome to avail themselves of the resources the libraries had to offer them. Furthermore, as Belpré carefully and tactfully implies in a number of her essays, her promotions were more often than not catalyzed by coincidence rather than recognition of her important work in the community. It seems that it was only when her colleagues—many of whom apparently had the advanced degrees she lacked, and who often had much less practical experience in libraries than she had—left their positions to travel, marry, or work elsewhere, that Belpré received the promotions she deserved.

Another important aspect of Belpré's success was her engagement with people, not only through her storytelling performances (by all accounts brilliant), but also through her public service, which for her was born from a genuine love for her work *and* for the people she encountered through her work. I came to her material prepared to find a rather bookish and shy librarian, but all the evidence points to the absolute contrary. Pura Belpré had a stunning effect on people, a warm and pleasing effect, and she infected all who crossed her path with her contagious enthusiasm. Her vibrancy as a person was matched by her seemingly tireless devotion to her work; she inspired not merely admiration but a profound trust, and this is the source of her genius as a public intellectual. Community activists and advocates of all ages would do well to take serious note of Belpré's style and commitment, her joyful dedication not merely to her agenda but to people as well, and the smooth, artful, and powerful ways she realized this dedication in her work.

The joy Belpré shared with children and adults through books and stories is a continual source of some of the most effective autobiographical digressions in her archival papers. These digressions, again, form an important experiential syncopation to her thoughts on the larger issues she broaches in her writings, such as these recollections in the context of her essay "Bilingual Story Telling" (Belpré Papers):

> The most gratifying phase of this work has been the storytelling conducted in Spanish and English. It was interesting to arrive at a branch and be greeted by a group of children who still remember the stories you told. To have a child ask you to repeat a story he missed, because his friend had told him it was "super." Or, overhear a Jewish boy plead with his mother to let him stay for the story hour instead of going, just this once, to Hebrew class. Or, to meet six children who missed a Spanish story session at their school, because it was given to a special class and members from the Board of Education. I was hurrying to the library to phone my report. We were in the neighborhood of the Fordham branch. The children followed me. So up we went. After explaining the situation to the children's librarian, the rolling door[s] of the story hour room were set in motion, and six children had their wish. A Spanish story hour, the first in that branch. Before they left the children joined the library. Or, perhaps, the small child at a Halloween story hour at the Columbus branch in Manhattan, who on her way out after the story, pulled my hand and gave me a kiss. (14–15)

The trail of Belpré's recollections here matches the narrative style of Luisa Capetillo, the meandering and forceful rush of images and ideas that are not containable by the syntactical precision of written language, and the desire to represent on paper the feelings that writing can mask or smother. This kind of immediacy moves the reader, places her in the moment through a kind of micro-storytelling within another genre of writing. The imagery of these miniature stories is vivid and effective, bringing the reader or listener into the emblematic scenes of her daily life. After mentioning the Board of Education, Belpré's narrative quickly shifts, prompting us to imagine her on the way to making a phone call. Then a group of children who were excluded from the "command performance" start following her as if she were the Pied Piper, and she happily fulfills their wish to be a part of the storytelling too. Or the depiction of Belpré listening in on a Jewish boy pleading with his mother to remain a little while longer so he can hear children's stories from other cultures, to miss his Hebrew class "just this once," he says, suggesting he craves other cultural experiences to complement his own, and that Belpré was pleased to have inspired this craving. And Belpré saves the most compact image for the final moment of the paragraph, in the affective force and simplicity of a child's grateful kiss.

Although Belpré's work was primarily with and for children and young adults, she was also very popular among mothers, grandmothers, and other adult women. Given her grassroots connections to the community and her reputation for the Christmas holiday events at the Aguilar branch, it is not surprising that older women would gravitate to her performances via the children. A later recollection in "Bilingual Story Telling" (Belpré Papers) captures this charm, Belpré's personal *imán,* even on the streets:

> Have you ever heard of storytelling between two parked cars in the South Bronx? Listen: After a visit to a school where the librarian had asked me to tell Puerto Rican folktales to a fourth grade class, as I was leaving the school—a young girl passed me running downstairs. Outside her grandmother was patiently waiting for her. "Grandma, she told us stories from Puerto Rico. One was '*La Matita de Albahaca*'" (The Albahaca Plant). "Oh," said grandmother, "how I loved that story. What memories! Will you please tell it to me." So, there, between two cars, with trucks whizzing by, the grandmother had her wish. (17)

Belpré often related her pleasure telling stories on the spot for audiences of any age. This particular recollection is a story within a story within a story, thrice removed from the actual event recounted in her essay, yet the reader can still feel the immediacy of the "trucks whizzing by" in the South Bronx. This is a sophisticated oral storytelling technique that is common in the Puerto Rican stateside diaspora, rendered here with pen on paper.

Of course, in the library itself Belpré was also an inspiration. One of her devotees, Hildamar Escalante, went on to translate Walt Whitman's poetry into Spanish and dedicated a volume to Belpré with the following inscription: "A mi maestra bibliotecaria que despertó en mi el amor por los libros" (To my library teacher, who awakened my love of books) (Belpré Papers, "Discurso" 1978: 1). Under Belpré's care, the children's reading room of the public library became a wondrous and inviting place where children's natural restlessness and curiosity could be transformed into active reading and all that this reading implies. Of the summer months she writes: "It is the time to rejoice with a group of children who had followed a butterfly into the children's room, only to lose her through an open window, but settled down to admire the illustrations in a butterfly book" (Belpré Papers, "Library Work with Bilingual Children" 1968: 8). And "joy," plain and simple, is the term Belpré likes to use when she describes this activity in the children's room, evident in the following passage:

> This paper should be filled with statistics, but no statistic can show the joy of a child who runs around the room to tell his friends: "She speaks Spanish. She can help you with your books." Nor the joy of a young Puerto Rican mother waiting for her son, who discovered a copy of Jimenez['], *Platero y Yo*. Hugging the book, she exclaimed: "How I enjoyed this book in Puerto Rico. I love it as much as I love '*El Quixote*.'" Picture the pathos and glee of the Cuban girl who stumbled into a copy of Andersen's Fairy Tales. "This," she said, "was the last book I read when I left Cuba in a boat to come here." No form of figures can describe the satisfaction of a boy who tells you he has re-read all the stories you had told so far. What statistics can explain the rapport of a group of boys from Colombia, Santo Domingo and Cuba, who brought a friend to hear more stories about Juan Bobo. Or, the little girl who ran into her mother's arms and said "She told us stories from Puerto Rico." (Belpré Papers)

Belpré adds that the story books the children heard read out loud would become springboards for them to retell other versions of the story they had learned at home. Under Belpré's supervision, the children's reading room must have been a loud place, signifying as much a transgression of that near sacred silence maintained in most public libraries as an affirmation of the love of verbal communication and highly stylized modes of orature common in Harlem's Boricua, African American, and other working-class communities. Children running, laughing, and talking, a mother hugging a book she thought perhaps she would never see again after moving to the United States—all of this "joy" seemed to have been the prime, living aesthetic that Belpré curated in her corner of the library.

In 1940, while attending a librarianship conference in Cincinnati, Belpré met her future husband, Clarence Cameron White, a composer, conductor, musicologist, and concert violinist, whose work required constant traveling. They fell in love and married in 1943, and soon after, Belpré decided to take a leave of absence to travel with her husband. This leave ended up lasting nearly two decades.

However, Belpré's work in children's librarianship was not completely suspended during her hiatus from the NYPL. She mentions in her archival papers that she would always come back to Harlem for the Christmas festivities at the Aguilar branch, though otherwise she was constantly on the road. While traveling, she did presentations and lectures across the country, and kept in touch with her colleagues through visits, correspondence, and conference meetings. Belpré recalls that she also told stories across the United States by invitation at community centers, public parks, and other recreation facilities, ranging to places as far from Harlem as Bakersfield, California, where she did a reading for a group of agricultural workers. In her words, "storytelling kept alive my library experience, wherever we went. And I had time to write!" (Belpré Papers, "Bilingual Story Telling" n.d.: 10).

Belpré's Published Fiction: 1932–1961

Indeed, Belpré's marriage did give her time to write, and it is during this period of traveling with her husband that Belpré finally seems to have focused on her writing rather than her librarianship.

In my research on Belpré I was shocked to find that there is not a single article in academic circulation that analyzes *any* of her published or unpublished books and stories. Yet, as the previous chapters have illustrated, this critical silence is part of a pattern of neglect in Puerto Rican and American studies concerning Boricua narrative during the first half of the twentieth century. Like Luisa Capetillo and Arturo Schomburg, Pura Belpré is often cited as a curious or important activist, and an occasional essay will appear celebrating her contributions to the Puerto Rican community, but no one has taken a serious look at her writing as a literary corpus.

It is impossible in the space of a single essay to do justice to every text Belpré authored. My reading of her literary corpus as a whole revolves around Belpré's creative uses of orature and written folklore as pedagogical source material for children of color. The initial key to Belpré's narrative strategies as a children's author is her first story book, *Perez and Martina,* which she published in 1932. Within this apparently simple story is a packed allegory of colonial Puerto Rican race and gender relations. An analysis of her second publication, a major collection of children's stories entitled *The Tiger and the Rabbit and Other Tales* (1946), also reveals that in Belpré's fiction even the most "universal" themes of childhood are rendered in allegories relevant to Puerto Rican and Boricua social history. Furthermore, as my close textual analyses suggest, sexual subtexts underlie most of Belpré's writing between 1932 and 1961, and these subtexts function as encoded messages for girls and young women about sexuality, courtship, marriage, and the social mores that dictate their conventional forms. As I discuss at length in the next section, her later publications (1962–1978) depart from this allegorical-pedagogical narrative strategy in crucial ways, and reflect Belpré's development as a researcher and civil rights–era advocate in New York City's public library system.

Belpré's earliest texts improvise on orature's explicitly pedagogical functions in Puerto Rican culture. Indeed, storytelling and other forms of discourse between women in Puerto Rican and Boricua households are often "meant to be overheard" by young women and girls, ostensibly to teach them lessons about their prescribed roles in an oblique but impressive fashion (Ortiz Cofer 1990: 14). Oral traditions in subaltern contexts can also provide a sort of alternative educational institution. The performativity and memorization of tales ensure that a community's culturally specific storehouse of wisdom survives in highly stylized speech acts that help orient children, whether they are formally literate or not, to conceptualize their own roles in life as adults and/or parents.

According to the frontispiece of the text, *Perez and Martina* was a story Belpré heard from her grandmother when she was a child.[3] *Perez and Martina* contains some of the stylistic tendencies found throughout Belpré's literary corpus: bilingual passages, more dialogue between characters than omniscient narration, and a quick pace. Like many of her stories, *Perez and Martina* is also an animal fable, which suggests her familiarity with an African diasporan oral tradition, or even more generally, an African basis for certain aspects of Puerto Rican orature. Most important, beyond these general narrative tendencies, *Perez and Martina* also employs more subtle literary allusions to the politics of race and language. These narrative maneuvers, which are typical of Belpré's work with orature and folklore as a whole, prompt allegorical readings of insular Puerto Rican social history. In this instance, the story's allegory can be read as an implicit critique of social stratification rooted in colonial history, especially the hierarchies pertaining to women.

As an animal fable, *Perez and Martina* is motivated by a core allegory that concerns marriage, or, more precisely, how a single but apparently self-sufficient Puerto Rican woman in colonial times might choose a husband. Martina, the "cockroach" protagonist of the story, is "Spanish." She is "a pretty cockroach with black eyes and soft brown skin" (oddly rendered pink in the illustrations), the narrator tells us at the outset of the story, a cockroach who is "very refined and exceedingly proud of her descent."[4] Martina is a good housekeeper. She sweeps her patio every day, keeps her pots "bright and shining," and according to the book's illustrations (based on the puppets and scenery Belpré used for the original performances of this story in the public library), she has a handsome if simple and well-accoutred home.

Where did Martina gain the resources to own such a lovely house? She is not a widow, nor does she have a father or other relative around who supervises her home and courtship, nor is she an entrepreneur in licit or illicit commerce, situations that would provide some historical footing for her relatively high social status as a single woman during Puerto Rico's Spanish colonial era. Instead, as in virtually all fairy tales, history is highly encoded in *Perez and Martina*. Martina's privilege is a function of her imaginary social standing; her light brown skin, Spanish descent, and good housekeeping skills establish her privilege and vice versa. Rather than performing as a mere tautology, this automatic, mutual constitution of Martina's good fortune, southern European good looks, and "proper" womanly habits could be read as a tacit endorsement of Spanish colonial socioeconomic stratification, in which Spanish descent or (dis)simulation and color-caste standing were forms of cultural capital for women.

Yet this endorsement is critically undercut as the story progresses. The crux of the allegorical reading I want to propose for *Perez and Martina* relies on a reading of caste, class, and racially symbolic capital for women in colonial Puerto Rican context, a form of symbolic signification that Belpré's story implicitly critiques. The story's plot moves into motion when Martina finds a *peseta*—a Spanish coin—while sweeping her patio. This coin becomes Martina's mode of access to marriage, not as a dowry per se, but as a means for her to acquire a feminine tool of racialized empowerment—face powder:

> [S]he again thought what to buy with her money. "It cannot be a dress," said she, "for I had a dress made to order not long ago. Perhaps a box of candy, but candy never lasts me long. What shall I buy with it? Oh, I know, I must get a box of powder."
>
> So she bought a box of powder, and that day she powdered her little face as she had not done for a long time. Then she put on her best dress, took a little fan and sat on her chair again. "I wonder," said she as she sat there, "if Perez the Mouse will come to visit me today."

Does mentioning that Martina had not worn powder "for a long time" imply that she is older, perhaps even on the brink of becoming a stereotypical *jamona* (old maid)? Or is it that her previous situation included a profession, such as prostitution, that would regularly require such makeup? Or perhaps, as a younger woman, Martina had access to such courtly luxuries, intimating she had once belonged to a somewhat wealthy family that, for the purposes of this story, no longer exists for her? Or that, despite her lovely home, she has no source of income and, like Jean Rhys's characters in *Wide Sargasso Sea* (1966), Martina is a "white cockroach" (a derisive term for the leftover, disempowered European colonists in the Caribbean after the abolition of slavery), desperate to marry, with nothing left to shore up her social standing but a single, serviceable dress, an old house (bought with money gained through slavery), and her European(-ish) looks? One could also examine what kinds of things Martina does *not* buy with the peseta: eyeliner (to enhance her dark eyes), lip dye (to make her mouth more shapely), curlers (to straighten or wave her hair), lotion (to make her skin softer), perfume (to make her smell sweet), costume jewelry (to adorn her body), a new scarf or ribbon (to embellish her hair). Martina also regards candy as an ephemeral, purely private pleasure, hardly worth the investment of a rarely won coin. Despite all the options, face powder is her obvious and immediate first choice.

What the story thus tells us is, first, that whitening one's face with powder is a sign of beauty (clearly, the powder will lighten her "soft brown skin," which was already "pretty," the narrator tells us at the beginning, *au naturel*); second, that this particular trait and/or feminine stylization—a lighter face—makes her more marriageable, since sitting on her porch wearing the new powder and almost-new dress signifies an open invitation for suitors in the story; third, that, barring a new dress, the face powder is the sine qua non for attracting appropriate suitors, subtly suggesting that the appearance of moderate wealth (a new, professionally tailored dress) is paramount over the appearance of light skin (face powder); and, finally, that even though she is going through the motions of entertaining various marriage proposals, she already has an eye on Perez the Mouse. On the surface, choosing the face powder seems like a somewhat neutral act in the story; the narrator does not interject with any positive or negative assessment of this purchase. However, as the story progresses we find that Martina and Perez are headed for disaster and, in a pivotal way, the coin and then the powder it buys set this disaster in motion.

Martina chooses Perez the Mouse because of his refinement, his own form of colonial symbolic capital:

> Now Perez was a gallant little mouse who lived in the same town as Martina. There was no one else who could bow just as Perez could. No one else danced and talked as he did, and many a one wondered if Perez had not come from royal descent.

Perez's recommendations as a suitor are his apparent courtly mannerisms, which impress those in Martina's town as nearly synonymous with "royal descent." His skill with language is especially important. The bulk of the story details various suitors' proposals to Martina—Señor Cat's, Señor Cricket's (Coquí's), Señor Rooster's, Señor Frog's, Señor Duck's—which are rejected not because of any express concern with the merit of the offers themselves, but because of each suitor's way of talking. All the suitors are well dressed, polite, attentive, and quite enamored of the cockroach (most cry when their offers are rejected). But Martina does not like the way any of them speak: Señor Cat's "miaow" frightens her, Señor Cock's "qui-quiri-qui" is too noisy for her, Señor Duck's "quack quack" is a bore for her, Señor Cricket's "coquí, coquí" is too sad for her, and Señor Frog's "Borom, Borom" is not pleasant to her ear and, besides, she complains, frogs talk too much. In the end, only Perez the Mouse's "chui, chui" will do. Perez describes his manner of speaking as "the language of [his] forefathers," to which Martina responds, "Oh, how lovely! It sounds just like music," accepting his marriage proposal on the spot.

Thus, according to the story's logic, Perez is the most appropriate suitor, Martina is "exceedingly proud" of her Spanish descent, Perez is ostensibly the most authentic Spaniard among her suitors, and what distinguishes him from the rest is primarily his way of talking. Perhaps more to the point, his way of talking—a sociolinguistic form, again, of symbolic capital in colonial context—becomes a convenient excuse for Martina to reject the others. Given the proper argument, "chui, chui," after all, is not more musical, aesthetically speaking, than the other animal sounds. Martina makes a completely subjective judgment call on the poetics of language, and the reader already knows that she is partial to what would more easily pass in colonial Puerto Rico as Spanish, that is, as culturally "refined." Therefore, of all the suitors, and as absurd as he is, Perez best complements her class and caste aspirations.

The argument might be made that this is merely a typical children's story, in which animals and the sounds they utter are incorporated humorously and formulaically into the text in a kind of pedagogical mode; younger children learn to distinguish sounds, name voices in a story, attach meaning to characters, and so forth, with such stories. All of this is of course true. But the text does not end with Martina's marriage. This suggests that the pedagogical function of the story does not conclude with the linguistic competition. And, importantly, the story does not end happily; instead, Perez falls into a cauldron of food Martina is preparing for a special Christmas supper, he is cooked to death, and Martina mourns him unhappily ever after in a song.

During my first reading of this text I felt that the story's conclusion was rather morbid. Why not have a cheerful ending? There seemed to me to be some disjunction in the text, because my sensibilities as a reader were thrown off course when Perez dies. The story is cute, entertaining, and culturally familiar—therefore pleasant—until the final few pages, when we hear of Perez's gruesome death by boiling; hardly, I thought at first reading, an appropriate story for young children.

But the key to the story's conclusion is the subtle colonial allegory we can trace in the text. The coin and the face powder it buys set something specific into motion, something that the narrative ecology organically transforms from a comedic into a tragi-satiric mode. What else could be accomplished by having Perez the Mouse die in this fashion, to have the narrative's tone shift so drastically, unless an allegory is at work? In a kind of moral reading, the allegory could suggest that Martina is being punished for having rejected the other suitors for unfair, elitist, pseudo-aesthetic reasons arguably common among the colonial elite (or those who aspired to or frequented the social circles of these elites), reasons she tries to represent as private and cultural, but that are at root racially and economically motivated in both the public and private spheres. Another reading is that the narrative offers a kind of punitive satisfaction in seeing the mouse who put on such airs burned to death precisely in the extraordinarily delicious dish his airs alone made possible. Notice how Perez moves into Martina's house after they marry, meaning that whatever home he had or could afford to have would be substandard to hers—they do not move away to Spain or to his family's estate, but remain in Martina's home—therefore Perez's only capital (his affectations) appears to be purely symbolic.

An allegorical reading of the sexual subtext probably makes the most sense, since the story is fundamentally about a tragicomic marriage. Indeed, remarks related to cooking provide a whole category of sexually doubled meanings in Puerto Rican vernacular. More specifically, Martina may have been too "hot" for the dilettante mouse, so her very skill in "the kitchen" (sex) is so vigorous that it kills him. This interpretation would intimate a life-threatening impotence among pretentious and/or elite Spaniards. Notice, for example, that the rest of the suitors in the illustrations (based, again, on the original puppets) have no shoes. Except for Señor Frog, who wears a pair of (non–gender-specific) slippers, the suitors go completely barefoot, while Perez the Mouse wears a pair of very effeminate high-heeled pumps. Consider too that the suitor whose way of talking frightened Martina, Señor Cat, was a strong and imposing blue-black cat with large paws,[5] and that he and Señor Cock (the slippage of language is self-evident here) are also by far the largest suitors to scale in the illustrations. Señor Duck is large too, but he almost immediately breaks into tears; he is somewhat sentimental, more pathetic than the others, and therefore less imposing. And of all the suitors, Perez the Mouse is the only one small enough to converse with the cockroach protagonist eye to eye. Importantly, averting the tragedy would require the young reader or listener to imagine Martina choosing the Duck, Cock, Cat, Coquí, or Frog as the more appropriate suitor, which converts the apparently morbid conclusion into a pedagogical lesson; in other words, put on airs and powder like Martina, set your eyes on the town's dandy, let yourself be seduced by the "chui chui" and all it implies, and you shall end up with a dead (heterosexually impotent) husband.

These interpretations of carnivalesque allegory in *Perez and Martina* capture a kind of reading specific to the cultural imaginary of Puerto Rico, an imaginary whose class and racial layering was pertinent to the working-class migrants of the 1920s and 1930s. Encoded in the tale is a culturally specific set of meanings alongside and in between the more general considerations that animal fables automatically bring into their frames of reference. The immediate context and performance of *Perez and Martina*'s telling could produce manifold meanings for manifold listeners as well. And considering its popularity—as the cornerstone performance at the Aguilar branch Epiphany celebrations (events that brought Harlem's Boricua community to the library every holiday season for decades), as Belpré's first book published in Spanish (and Braille), as her first bilingual recording—*Perez and Martina* is a pivotal work of early-to-mid-twentieth-century Nuyorican literary history.

Belpré credits a wide variety of sources for her folktales, and in her archival papers she frequently comments on the multiple ethnic roots of Puerto Rican culture.[6] In Belpré's assessment, insular Puerto Rican culture is an extraordinarily global hybrid, since it reflects both centuries of reinvention in the New World and millennia of improvisation on "Asiatic" (her general term for the indigenous—Taíno—influences), European, Mediterranean, and African diasporan aesthetic traditions (Belpré Papers, "I Wished to Be Like Johnny Appleseed" 1977: 1). Furthermore, she suggests that the Spanish influences on this folklore retain elements of a (perhaps exaggerated) multiplicity of other traditions as well. The imbrication of global traditions in Spanish folklore is, she writes, "not surprising considering that Spain at one time or another was occupied by Arabs, Romans, Jews, Iberians, Celts, Phoenicians, Greeks, Carthaginians and others" (Belpré Papers, "The Folklore of the Puerto Rican Child" n.d.: 3). Thus, while carefully noting the specific cultural and historical contexts of Puerto Rican legends in her essays and research, Belpré also attributes these legends to a worldwide cache of folklore, primarily via premodern Spain. Given its ancient and globally syncretic history, Belpré claims that folklore "is one of the purest forms of literature," bringing together through local variations an archetypal set of figures, plots, and dilemmas that are pedagogically geared to a younger audience (Belpré Papers, "Writing for Bilingual Children" n.d.: 4).

Most of Belpré's stories are adaptations of Puerto Rican legends that she heard as a child and/or researched as an adult. Occasionally, her stories are direct translations of Spanish-language originals. Evident in her two major collections of folktales, *The Tiger and the Rabbit and Other Tales* and *Once in Puerto Rico* (1973), are allegorical functions akin to those in *Perez and Martina*. *Once in Puerto Rico* is an important collection of tales that are explicitly concerned with Puerto Rico's colonial history, and this text seems a likely result of Belpré's later political trajectories when she worked with the South Bronx Library Project in the 1960s. We will return to this text below.

The Tiger and the Rabbit and Other Tales is Belpré's first collection of animal fables. In these tales, originally published in 1946 and twice reissued (1965 and 1977), we find stock folkloric characters, plots, and stylistic devices, some from African orature, others from Spanish folktales, and still others that seem borrowed from paradigmatic, written folklore. Belpré merges these traditions. As her introduction to the edition suggests, she was attracted to the art of storytelling long before her experiences working in New York City's libraries:

> Growing up on the island of Puerto Rico in an atmosphere of natural story-tellers was fun: a father whose occupation took him all over the island; a grandmother whose stories always ended with a nonsense rhyme or song, setting feet to jump, skip or dance; elder sisters who still remembered tales told by a mother; and finally, a stepmother whose literary taste was universal. (1946: 5)

Belpré's childhood experiences include African diasporan orature. This influence is obvious in the collection's title story, "The Tiger and the Rabbit," which is a trickster tale of a cunning rabbit whose wits alone suffice to bring him safely out of impossible dilemmas. Likewise, "The Wolf, the Fox, and the Jug of Honey" involves a trickster fox, and Perez the Mouse's incarnation in this collection is as a formidably witty and wily creature as well. There are apparently African phrases (what Belpré terms "nonsense") in these stories as well, particularly the songs and incantations, such as "Casi Lampu'a Lentemué" and "ay toro—toronjil" (in "Nangato") which, as the citation above implies, Belpré probably initially heard from her grandmother. Fantastic tales about witches, such as "The Jurga," and a number of Juan Bobo (Simple John) stories suggest a Spanish folk influence reconstructed in colonial Caribbean context, while tales about clever girls who marry kings or clever princesses who marry commoners reflect the more "universal" lineages in world literature she discusses in her essays.

My reading of *The Tiger and the Rabbit and Other Tales* focuses on what I see as Belpré's revisions of archetypal stories, revisions that are specific to the unrelenting colonial experience in Puerto Rico and, by extension, to an experience in which slavery, poverty, and the threat of sexual violence would contribute to shaping improvisations on these stories in women's orature.

Perhaps the best example of this allegorical signification is "The Earrings," which deals with a set of characters that might be found in any number of children's tales: a mean old man, a naïve young woman, and her mother. The plot is basic. After the mother warns her daughter to stay close to home, the daughter disregards the warning, gets captured by the ill-intentioned old man, is put into a life-threatening situation, and is later rescued having learned the primary lesson—obedience.

Yet the peculiarities of this story implicitly allude to the colonial Caribbean. The mother, who is the only adult in her humble household, works on a pineapple plantation. This reference to a plantation could suggest Puerto Rico's late-nineteenth-century economy, in which fieldwork was one of the few available employments for rural women; it could likewise suggest the era of slavery, during which a single mother might live in small quarters with her children who, as a consequence of their mother's enslavement, might be left unsupervised between dawn and dusk during the planting and harvesting seasons. Indeed, since it is an oral tale, both of these historical experiences for subaltern women probably inform Belpré's twentieth-century version, which in turn would logically resonate with similar fears of loss or abduction of children in the bustle of the city's streets among mothers in the Nuyorican community. The earrings of this tale suggest the mother's and daughter's subaltern status as well, since historically, jewelry of this sort for girls is not particularly common outside low-income communities of color in the Caribbean and the continental United States.

Like *Perez and Martina,* "The Earrings" has a sexual subtext, which also reveals maternal fears that are clearly residual concerns from the era of plantation economies in Puerto Rico. The young protagonist of this story, Julia, is warned by her mother about bathing in a certain river. This river is taboo in the community, "for people said the river was haunted and that there was a time when children had been carried away and never brought back" (27). Leaving her children unsupervised near water, of course, would worry any working mother. But there is a further inscription here, the threat of children being sold "down river," and thus separated forever from their mothers, was a reality during slavery, and rivers in African diasporan literature are definitive tropes marking anxieties of death/salvation and irremediable familial separation (see Danticat 1998; Kincaid 1996).

Julia is, however, tempted by the river: "Its waters were so clean that she could clearly see the little pebbles and the silvery fish which swam in it" (28). The river lures Julia, and "suddenly" she is "seized with a desire to plunge in," intimating an adolescent craving for sensual pleasure along with the typically adolescent tendency to test the limits of parental authority (28). Julia removes all her clothes and, finally, her earrings, leaving them on a rock on the river's edge. But when she is through playing in the water, dresses, and starts her journey home, she realizes she forgot her earrings. Thus, not only has Julia misbehaved by disobeying her mother's explicit orders, but her indulgence in physical pleasure has made her negligent about her only valuable material possession as well. A sexual connotation is implied by the lost earrings, which symbolize virginity; like her earrings, Julia's chastity is one of the few socially valuable attributes a young woman of her social class could control or at least guard, which she puts at risk once she takes "the plunge" and experiments with forbidden pleasures.

When Julia returns to the riverside for her earrings, the threat of abduction is realized and the threat of rape is imminent. An old man is waiting for her, holding her earrings in his hand. He asks Julia,

> "Are these your earrings?"
> "Sí Señor" said Julia. "I left them here just a short while ago after my bath. Won't you give them to me? I must return home before my mother comes back from the pineapple fields."
> "Here," said the old man, stretching the hand in which rested the beautiful pair of earrings. As Julia reached for them, the old man seized her and put her into a sack. He slung the sack on his back, drew a long lance from behind the rock and started on his way home. (28)

Julia's vulnerability is compounded by her naïveté; she either trusts the old man or her dread of returning home to her mother without her earrings trumps her fear of him. Once she reaches out to his hand, the old man's ruse is a success. Importantly, hidden behind the rock is a "long lance" that the old man is hiding from view, hinting at ulterior, sexual motives.

Indeed, the "long lance" becomes the old man's tool for exploiting Julia. He carries her from town to town in the sack and makes money entertaining onlookers who believe that the sack magically sings. To make sure that Julia sings on cue, he recites the same threat in his song:

> "Canta, saquito, canta
> Si no cantas, te espeto la lanza"
>
> "Sing, little sack, sing,
> Or with my lance
> I'll thee pierce." (29)[7]

To which Julia is forced to respond in song:

> "Por los arcillitos, madre,
> Que en la peña yo dejé,
> Por los arcillitos, madre,
> A ti nunca volveré."
>
> "Because of the earrings, mother,
> Which in the stone I left,
> Because of those earrings, mother,
> To you I'll never return." (29)

There is something fetal in the image of Julia rolled up in the sack, a kind of grotesquely inverted representation of her mother's womb and, by extension, the love and protection of her mother's home. Pedagogically, Julia's abduction is a lesson for young girls about obedience, and the punishment she receives seems to fit the anxiety her transgressions (metaphorically) produce; not only is Julia at risk of death (relevant to the residual maternal anxieties of slavery) by the lance's penetration (with a violent, phallic connotation), but this risk also forces Julia to obey the malevolent old man in public, forcing her into his "sack" forever. Therefore there might be a further significance in the text relating to unsanctioned relationships with men, since Julia now literally belongs to the man who caught her bathing in the river her mother forbade her to use and is now hopelessly trapped in a radically unequal relationship that this disobedience has instigated.

Ultimately, this story has a happy ending. Julia's friend—another young woman—recognizes her voice during one of the old man's public performances, sneaks up on him while he sleeps, rescues Julia from the sack, and puts a bunch of stones in her stead. The next morning, when the old man begins his song in public, the sack is silent. As promised, he lances the sack, only to spurt mud on the onlookers. In retaliation, the mayor orders his men to run the old man out of town, and Julia returns home to her mother permanently cured of the desire to bathe in the forbidden river. That she is saved by another young woman is pedagogically significant, because it implies that young women must be alert to their friends' distress and, whenever possible, be vigilant and helpful when their friends fall prey to this kind of (sexual) abuse or potentially dangerous adolescent desire.

Other stories in *The Tiger and the Rabbit and Other Tales* can be read in a similar fashion. "The Cat, the Mountain Goat and the Fox" teaches a lesson in how to deal with a lazy neighbor, and warns young girls about how vanity—represented by a cat who refuses to leave her house for fear of ruining her fur—can make a woman behave in unhealthy and ridiculous ways. The Juan Bobo stories in the collection, in which a young, penniless simpleton manages to get himself out of seemingly impossible predicaments with his twisted wits, have a particular pedagogical significance for boys, while other stories seem intended to inform girls and young women about marriage. Non–gender-specific stories, like "The Jurga," have moralistic overtones, indicting practices of abuse and exploitation in the context of slavery and colonialism. *The Tiger and the Rabbit and Other Tales* addresses a wide range of implied audiences, and includes silly word game stories for younger children.

Belpré's second collection of children's stories, *Once in Puerto Rico* (1973), was published nearly thirty years after the first edition of *The Tiger and the Rabbit and Other Tales*. *Once in Puerto Rico* reflects Belpré's lifelong interests and hands-on experience as a Caribbean folklorist, and includes tales that she arduously researched. These tales are either direct translations into English from primary sources in Spanish or Belpré's own variations on common themes and plots in Puerto Rican folklore. Given its generic milieu, *Once in Puerto Rico* is also much more consciously concerned with cultural history; unlike the stories in *The Tiger and the Rabbit and Other Tales*, which seem to have been chosen because they were Belpré's personal favorites, the stories in *Once in Puerto Rico* are more deliberate selections of Spanish colonial-era myths and legends. Consequently, her second collection dovetails quite conspicuously with nationalist versions of cultural formation in Puerto Rico, lingering on fictions of *mestizaje* (miscegenation) and aboriginal culture that are meant to be understood as historical fact.

The 1960s and 1970s: Belpré's Work in the Civil Rights Era

Published as late as it is in Belpré's life—after she had lived in the States for over half a century—we might not be surprised to find that *Once in Puerto Rico* dwells on the Islands' culture and social history in a romantic (or, at the very least, nostalgic) fashion. Considering too the political context of Belpré's final decades in the NYPL system, we might expect that her writing, along with the programs and projects she advocated, were influenced by her work in the milieu of the civil rights movement.

Chapter 4 explores in further detail Nuyorican narrative's ethical and aesthetic relationship with the civil rights movement. For our purposes here, it is crucial to note that Belpré's return to the NYPL occurred in the early 1960s, when it appears that Belpré as a respected elder was beckoned by a younger, politically motivated generation mobilizing for structural changes in public institutions. Her work in the final phase of her career is epitomized by her involvement with the South Bronx Library Project (SBLP), which began in June 1967 and was funded largely by a grant from the federal Library Services and Constructions Act (Title 1). The SBLP, which provided administration and monies for library services in the South Bronx community, developed a number of special projects. Belpré mentions a few of these projects in her archival papers, which include details on how she and others in the SBLP compiled information for bilingual programs in the public school system, formed an award-winning traveling puppet show (which visited schools, day care centers, hospitals, parks, and orphanages), and published annotated bibliographical pamphlets, such as *Libros en Español: An Annotated List of Children's Books in Spanish* (South Bronx Library Project 1977) and *Puerto Rico in Children's Books.*[8] From her writing on this experience as well as her publication record during these two decades, we can see that Belpré's professional life was more prodigious than it had ever been. She was rehired first as a "Spanish Children's Specialist," then in 1968 as a per diem paid consultant for the SBLP (after her forced retirement from the NYPL at age sixty-five). Belpré's literary corpus burgeoned with a number of new texts and reprints in the 1960s and 1970s. Her work during this period was no doubt inspired to some extent by the growing cultural nationalist sentiment among the younger generation in the Nuyorican community, which formed an avid audience for her work recuperating oral traditions.

Fabricating a kind of quasi-historical narrative out of the Islands' legends and myths is an innovative device for exploring Puerto Rico's Spanish colonial history; this strategy is engaging, entertaining, and educational, and might certainly appeal to a broad readership in the stateside community. Furthermore, Belpré's sustained interest in orature made her one of the precious few autodidactic Boricua scholars of the period who could responsibly meet the challenge of this kind of narrative enterprise. Without qualification, *Once in Puerto Rico* should be considered an important Boricua text. However, this text reflects a certain confluence of narrative desires that merit critique.

The opening illustrations of *Once in Puerto Rico* foreground a line of dancing Taínos, providing a visual hint of the tales to follow. In this text, understanding modern Puerto Rican history means returning to the pre-Columbian era, when one of the peoples popularly considered ancestors of the contemporary Puerto Rican population reigned in complete autochthonous control of the main island, which they reputedly called *Boriquén* or *Borinquen*. The introduction avers that Puerto Rico's post-Columbian history is the syncretic legacy of three distinct racial groups: Asian (aboriginal Aruak), European, and African. The tales themselves, in the words of the author, offer "a key with which to unlock the door of time" and return—in medias res—to foundational moments of Puerto Rican history (12).

While a number of stories in this collection focus on proper ethical behavior, courtship, and marriage, and are thus reminiscent of Belpré's earlier literary texts, *Once in Puerto Rico* employs an allegorical pedagogy that is clearly infused with nationalist ideologies of social formation in Puerto Rico. Consequently, mythic versions of cultural fusion are depicted in folktales that effectively erase the history of racial and cultural conflicts, inequalities, and, in the case of the Islands' indigenous peoples, genocide. This complicity between an apparently "innocent" literary genre and nationalist fantasies is a symptom common to national canons throughout the Americas.[9] As a set of "truth effects" (Foucault 1972–77) propagated by national discourses of mestizaje, this kind of folkloric invention glosses over the violent (sometimes in lethal proportion) history of colonization and slavery in Puerto Rico for the purposes of representing a unique national character voluntarily—even passionately—forged in a context of conspicuous racial equality.

The best illustration of this narrative strategy is the story "Yuisa and Pedro Mexias" (45–50).[10] According to popular legend in Puerto Rico,

Yuisa, a Taína chieftain or *cacica,* and Pedro Mexias, a Spanish-born "mulatto" immigrant, are the figurative ancestral parents of the modern Puerto Rican population. This legend has spawned literary variations on how the two meet, fall in love, and marry amid the armed struggle between the Taínos and the Spanish invaders sometime in the early sixteenth century. Belpré's version is a translation of María Cadilla Martínez's "Yuisa y Pedro Mexias," which she found in an anthology of folklore entitled *Rememorando el pasado histórico* (Cadilla n.d.).

Belpré's English-language version of the folktale begins with the initial contact between Spaniards and Taínos. Accordingly, the Spaniards encounter seventeen *caciques* on Borinquen when they first arrive, and find the main island's territory divvied up between these leaders in seventeen *yuayeques* (parcels). Yuisa is the *cacica* of a yuayeque called Jaimanio (today known as Loiza Aldea), while Pedro Mexias is a young Andalusian of African descent who grew up in the household of Hispaniola's viceroy and became his personal valet. Mexias receives the viceroy's permission to leave Hispaniola in order to join the colonists in Borinquen when gold is discovered there. After he arrives, Mexias and Yuisa somehow meet and fall in love, but the Taíno *bohiques* (spiritual leaders) demand that Yuisa give up her title and lands upon marrying Mexias. The couple start a household on the banks of the Canóbana River, which is shortly invaded by an army of Taíno and Carib warriors. Together, Mexias and Yuisa die defending the Spanish settlement during this battle, but not before they manage to kill the Carib chief. The final battle of sovereignty occurs soon afterwards on the island of Vieques, the Spaniards prevail, and Yuisa and Pedro Mexias become the martyrs of the Spanish colonial cause and, by extension, the foundational couple of the incipient Puerto Rican nation.

There are a number of strange, ahistorical, and possibly unique aspects of this story as a myth of national formation in the Americas.[11] The first and most obvious of these is the fact that no Spaniards seem to be involved as key characters. Unlike, for example, the myth of Malintzin Tenepal (also known as Doña Marina and, derogatorily, as La Malinche) and Hernán Cortés in Mexican legend, or the myth of John Smith and Pocahontas in United Statesian legend, Yuisa and Pedro Mexias—a conquered cacica and an indentured or enslaved man of African descent—are both subaltern subjects in colonial context. Likewise, it is odd—even illogical—that as national ancestors the couple never have children. But these two aspects of the story, together, ironically suggest some core contradictions of *mestizaje* (or more specifically, in this case, of Afro-mestizaje) discourse. By keeping the Spanish characters conspicuously out of the war's significance, the story narrates the island's formational violence as a struggle between subalterns, thereby obfuscating the actual historical record, and also suggesting that Puerto Rico's communities of color were central actors and, therefore, the victors, in the battles of colonial conquest. Likewise, by hailing an African diasporan-indigenous couple who never reproduce as Puerto Rico's iconic, ancestral parents, the story implies that, while seminal in the national imagination, this foundational fusion, in the form of a highly packed allegorical marriage, is sterile. Crucially, slavery is never mentioned. Analyzed as such, the legend at once celebrates the "multiculturalism" of the Islands' social history and figuratively eliminates all possibility in the narrative of any historically engendered multicultural or multiracial progeny in the present.

Other folktales in *Once in Puerto Rico*, such as "Iviahoca," elaborate on similar legends. A few of the tales also seem to blend elements of African oral traditions with Spanish colonial Taíno legends. Overall, the text basically offers an English-language reader a peek into insular Puerto Rican folkloric inventions. Again, given its date of publication—1973—we can assume that Belpré, whose writing on Puerto Rico's perennial "status question" suggests that she supported independence (Belpré Papers, "Statehood—Commonwealth" n.d.), was targeting a Nuyorican reading public, offering this community its first anthology in English of stories that could fill the gaps of their understanding about the Islands' cultural nationalist imaginary. This text also fulfills the vision of bilingual education Belpré advocated for Puerto Rican children in New York, by affirming "that we are not a group without a past, and that in the past was dignity and spiritual strength to struggle ahead" (Belpré Papers, "Cultural Thoughts and Facts about the Puerto Rican Children in a Bilingual Bi-Cultural Set Up" n.d.: 1).

Belpré's Literary Contributions: Hints for Further Research

There are a number of other monographs Belpré published in the 1960s and 1970s: *Juan Bobo and the Queen's Necklace* (1962), a reprint of a story originally published in *The Tiger and the Rabbit and Other Tales*; *Oté: A Puerto Rican Folk Tale* (1969a); *Santiago* (1969b), a delightful story about a little boy who overcomes prejudice in school with the help of a stray chicken; *Dance of the Animals* (1972), another reprint of a story originally published in *The Tiger and the Rabbit and Other Tales*; and *The Rainbow-Colored Horse* (1978). The bulk of Belpré's most important work was published when she was in her sixth and seventh decades. Her productivity as a writer and successes as an advocate for the South Bronx Library Project during the final twenty years of her life affirm the fact that elders in our community constitute an invaluable and vital presence in even the most contemporary narrative and political struggles.

Early on June 31, 1982, the morning after she was honored for her life's work by the NYPL's Coordinating Council, Belpré's brother Pedro stopped by her apartment for a visit and found that she had passed on (Hernández-Delgado 1992: 435–36). During her eighty-year lifetime, most of which she had spent working and living in the United States, Belpré made a huge contribution to the Boricua community, the New York Public Library system, and New York City's children of all backgrounds.

Belpré's pedagogical projects in both literature and public institutions constitute an important precursor to civil rights–era Boricua literature. However, the next generation of Boricua authors defined themselves more assertively as part of an integral, U.S.-based community of color, and their aesthetic and ethical priorities evince a more self-conscious effort to reinvent traditional literary genres and colonial discourses. Akin to earlier Boricua narrative experimentation, social justice is still an intrinsic and ideal desire in this period's literary enterprises. Language itself is put under question in this corpus, along with colonialism, cultural nationalism, internalized racism, sexism, and other broad concepts that help mediate and organize power in everyday life. Similar to Luisa Capetillo's and Arturo Schomburg's supranational influences and identifications, the civil rights generation's thematic concerns also dovetail with the radicalism of its historical milieu. Chapter 4 thus explores how Boricua authors of the 1960s and 1970s reinvigorate the narrative tensions and tendencies that emerged in the first half-century of Boricua literature.

4

The Boricua Novel

Civil Rights and "New School" Nuyorican Narratives

> Our cry is a very simple and logical one. Puerto Ricans came to this country hoping to get a decent job and to provide for their families; but it didn't take long to find out that the American dream that was publicized so nicely on our island turned out to be the Amerikkkan nightmare.
>
> —David Pérez, Young Lords Party

The ethical and aesthetic motives of the earliest extant Boricua narratives—Arturo Schomburg's African diasporan research, Luisa Capetillo's anarcho-feminist fiction, William Carlos Williams's historical deconstructive poetics, Pura Belpré's allegorical pedagogy—set the epistemic foundations for an entire century of Boricua literature. The first three chapters' discussions also suggest a template for considering what we might term the "Old School" Boricua cultural intellectual tradition, which dates roughly from the turn of the century to the early 1960s. In this tradition, a set of writers and a corpus of writing emerge that are characterized by progressive and even radical social, historical, and philosophical critique. Moreover, this kind of critique informs both the narrative and institutional interventions of the first generations of Boricua writers. Even William Carlos Williams, the most widely recognized and celebrated author in this group, felt he had a public trust in his profession as a medical doctor and, accordingly, he cared for patients from low-income communities whether or not they could afford his services. Williams, like Belpré, was also a proponent of educational reform. One of his latest publications, a polemical book on American education, *The Embodiment of Knowledge* (1974), attests to the kind of progressive politics he advocated in his public intellectual life. Thus, explicitly centered in an analysis of Boricua literary history, the narrative writers of the first half of this study form an insurgent cultural intellectual tradition based in radical aesthetic enterprises that openly challenge a number of core problems endemic to twentieth-century American social history.

As a period that inaugurates a "New School" of cultural intellectual politics, the late 1960s and early 1970s might be aptly termed the Nuyorican Renaissance. Like the Old School tradition, this generation's literature is characteristically concerned with social justice, but the New School's narrative politics revolve around more conventional genres, especially the novel, and more contemporary discourses of anticolonial resistance and civil rights. The writers of this generation are poets, playwrights, journalists, essayists, and novelists, and include Juan González, Miguel Piñero, Pablo "Yoruba" Guzmán, Sandra María Esteves, Piri Thomas, Tato Laviera, Iris Morales, Miguel Algarín, Pedro Pietri, and Nicholasa Mohr, all of whom were born and/or raised in the New York City area during the 1940s and 1950s. Although these writers represent a vast range of lifestyles and varied political perspectives, the primary underlying concern among them as a group is the construction, through literature, of Boricua cultural citizenship as an organic—and organically resistant—North American formation. Each of these artists explores dimensions of thought and action specific to life in the Boricua community around midcentury. Historically, both the transition from the pre–World War II era to the civil rights movement and the biggest wave to date of Puerto Rican migration to the States shape these writers' context.

Arguably, the most extensive articulation of this new Boricua literary sensibility may be found in the novel, and two of the first Boricua texts of this era, Piri Thomas's autobiographical novel *Down These Mean Streets* (1967) and Nicholasa Mohr's novel *Nilda* (1973), are the most emblematic works of this generation's narrative experimentation.[1] As civil rights–era fictions, both novels explore how the Boricua community responded to the tremendous historical shifts that occurred during the postwar period in the continental United States. From the late 1940s to the 1960s, the stateside Puerto Rican population grew from about seventy thousand to almost one and a half million people strong, over half of whom took up residence in the New York City area (Picó 1988: 266, table 14.2). This demographic surge strengthened the sense of community that had been nurtured within the New York *colonias* during the first half of the century. The mainland influx also set the stage for a significant Boricua presence in the period's grassroots political mobilization of people of color in the United States.[2]

The appropriation of the novel during the era of the civil rights movement enabled writers of color in general to articulate a collectivized and collectivizing historical sensibility (see Jaimes 1992; Jones and Neal 1968). Taking thematic cues from anticolonial writers in Africa and the Caribbean, such as Amilcar Cabral, Frantz Fanon, Aimé Césaire, Pedro Albizu Campos, and Albert Memmi, these writers developed a literary perspective that offered creative and critical reevaluations of cultural history (see Fanon 1961; Césaire 1955; Memmi 1957). Cultural nationalist perspectives are particularly acute in American civil rights–era fiction, as writers elaborated how their communities' histories were integrally bound to a violent past, beginning many centuries ago with the European invasion of the continent, continuing on through the eras of slavery and North American expansion, and culminating in the widespread poverty and political disenfranchisement of people of color in the present. Unconvinced by the hegemonically endorsed versions of history in circulation at the time, these writers tapped their own cultural resources—their own idioms, family histories, and narrative devices—for ways of signifying that could subvert what they understood as "Amerikkkan" narratives that maligned, erased, or otherwise misrepresented their communal histories. Overall, the literature (and orature) of the civil rights generation testifies to a resurgence and rearticulation of a centuries-old struggle over signification in the United States that resurfaces in the 1960s and early 1970s with a vigor unparalleled in U.S. literary history.

This rearticulation was prompted as much by anticolonial movements and writing as it was by the more immediate discursive and political struggles that erupted with the close of World War II, the rise of U.S. global imperialism, and the onset of the Cold War, as the Truman administration staked the United States' moral high ground on the postwar world stage. That is, while the "communist threat" became the ideological shield of U.S. intervention in Greece, Turkey, Iran, Guatemala, and Cuba during the 1950s (acts inspired less by ideals of "free expression" and "democracy" than desires to secure foreign market domination and curb the nationalization of corporate and natural resources), critics of the waxing U.S. military-industrial complex could—and often did—cite the oppression of Blacks and other minority populations in the United States as proof that the U.S. rhetoric of equality and "democratic freedom" was a sham. In other words, as long as African Americans and other people of color were denied basic human and civil rights as U.S. citizens, the United States could not justify its bids to rescue the rest of the world from the "red menace." According to this perspective, politicians such as Harry Truman (and later presidents Eisenhower, Kennedy, and Johnson) did nothing more than gloss over the country's racism with rhetoric and empty federal legislation.[3] In response, civil rights leaders and groups spawned by the movement were involved in direct political action, demanding that what the United States celebrated as its democratic values be equally applied to all citizens, regardless of race and gender. Hence the domestic flip side of the Cold War was played out in the struggle for human rights, which proved to be a war of sorts as well, fought both discursively and literally on the streets.[4]

Boricua civil rights–era novels form part of this larger enunciation of dissent (Marable 1991; Morris 1984; Warrior 1995). Galvanized by movement activities and philosophies, these writers turned to fiction as one of the few media readily available to them as producers of knowledge, since mainstream television, newspapers, radio, and film devoted little or no substantive coverage to the movement's events and perspectives. Not surprisingly, this appropriation entails a reformulation of discourse in the novel that critically reshapes or ignores many conventions associated with the genre. Furthermore, these writers wrote for a wide, popular audience; in both a literal and figurative sense, their novels constitute a paperback challenge to the fantastic fictions of American democracy and racial equality.

Among Boricua writers, the work of Piri Thomas and Nicholasa Mohr together represents the significance of this literary appropriation for both men and women of color. Their first published works, Mohr's *Nilda* and Thomas's *Down These Mean Streets,* best illustrate the innovations entailed in the Boricua civil rights–era novel, particularly the narrative strategies involving child protagonists' reflections on, and journeys through, a world that is hostile to their very being. These novels narrate less the "coming of age" often associated with the *bildungsroman* than particular ways of coming to consciousness, a process by which the subject must critically evaluate his or her sociohistorical context and, accordingly, create alternative strategies for both literal and metaphysical survival.[5] The protagonists in *Nilda* and *Down These Mean Streets* are subjects in process who must negotiate their antagonized place in U.S. society, a negotiation that foregrounds a dynamic and threatening rubric of colonialism, racism, sexism, and their effects.

The particularity of this rubric itself undermines the ideological substance allied with the Euro-American novel's development, since it portrays social context not as a given, static set of conditions, but rather as a contradictory and flexible situation in which characters not only can but must create new models of social agency in order to situate themselves more comfortably and integrally in the existing social order. This narrative strategy may represent an improvisation on what Mikhail Bakhtin analyzes in the European tradition as the novel of "becoming," which revolves around a protagonist who is not "ready-made" but rather "emerges" in concert with the progress of history. Bakhtin designates this type of fiction a subgenre of the "novel of emergence," which, he writes,

> is the most significant [type of novel]. In it man's individual emergence is inseparably linked to historical emergence. Man's emergence is accomplished in real historical time, with all of its necessity, its fullness, its future, and its profoundly chronotopic nature. [In other types of novels] man's emergence proceeded against the immobile background of the world, ready-made and basically quite stable. If changes did take place in this world, they were peripheral, in no way affecting its foundations. Man emerged, developed, and changed within one epoch. The world, existing and stable in this existence, required that man adapt to it, that he recognize and submit to the existing laws of life. Man emerged, but the world itself did not. (Bakhtin 1986: 23)

Rather than crafting the protagonist's submission to the status quo in this manner, Bakhtin argues, certain novels represent the way s/he "emerges along with the world and . . . reflects the historical emergence of the world itself." Although Bakhtin is perhaps more interested in describing this new "typology" as an outline of the trans-epochal novel, his discussion suggests a new approximation to social change and social critique in fiction. Among other things, this notion of emergence may also provide a useful concept for analyzing a certain "commitment" to the articulation of not only class but also cultural, colonial, diasporan, gendered, and racial consciousness via a new species of social realism specific to U.S. communities of color during the aftermath of World War II and the rise of the civil rights movement.[6]

This commitment is elaborated in both *Nilda* and *Down These Mean Streets* in the narration of the adolescent protagonists' journeys of self-discovery. For the Boricua novel, the emergent historical context includes New York City during and in the wake of World War II, the colonial maldevelopment of Puerto Rico (Operation Bootstrap), and the civil rights movement. The protagonists' most immediate lives are explored through realist renditions of situations they experience, avoid, or attempt to transform at home, at school, at work, in public agencies, and on the "mean streets" of Spanish Harlem. Visible around and underneath these situations is a palimpsest of larger antagonistic forces, including racism, colonialism, poverty, sexism, and other problems that arise as Puerto Rican youths attempt to make sense of themselves in a society and in institutions that actively refuse to accommodate them, that at moments even attempt to annihilate them. Adapting the realist technique of including "idiomatic" speech, both texts employ the languages of the Boricua community, through not only the use of Espanglish, but also other ways of speaking and signifying, ranging from Anglicized renditions of Spanish phrases to word games (such as the "dozens" in Thomas's text) and tropes of "paradise lost" in family remembrances of Puerto Rico. However, unlike works in the Euro-American realist tradition, these texts use so-called idiomatic speech as the core language, including all first-person direct or indirect discourse and third-person narration. Both texts thus disregard the standardization of English in the novel, opting instead to create narrators and characters who speak and signify completely in Boricua and other urban vernaculars.

Mean Streets and Hombre *Hermeneutics: Piri Thomas*

The hostilities that young Boricuas face in their U.S. social context are fundamental concerns for Piri Thomas, and his writing unapologetically explores the rage, confusion, and violence that these hostilities can cause for young men in urban settings. My discussion of *Down These Mean Streets* analyzes its protagonist's apparent "identity crisis" as a hermeneutical crisis that forces the narrator to establish his authority as an integral speaking subject in the autobiographical novel. The narrator's search for an authentic understanding of himself in the world progresses in a series of escapes or attempts to run away from his immediate context and, in the process, from his dilemma as a character interpellated by apparently contradictory yet commonsense racial and ethnic identities.

Down These Mean Streets opens with the protagonist, Piri, running away from home. Indeed, what "home" ideally implies for Piri—belonging, unconditional love, safety, and security—is presented at the outset in absentia, both literally, when Piri runs away, and figuratively, when he returns only to find that no one noticed he had left. Piri's initial escape and isolation prefigure his perpetual flight from confusing and contradictory familial and social contexts in the novel. As a darker person in the Boricua color spectrum, he feels as if he never quite fits, not in his family, nor in his "gang," nor among his African American friends. The novel implies that in order to make sense (of himself), Piri must legitimate both his Puerto Rican and African American identities, that he must somehow find a way to conceptualize himself as both simultaneously by trying to adapt the prevailing constructs of racial, national, and cultural citizenship to his reality as culturally marked Puerto Rican, economically marked poor, racially marked Black, and nationally marked colonial in the United States.

Yet as the novel develops it is clear that these identity constructs are too rigidly fixed, that the people and institutions around him will force him to make a choice between understanding himself as Black and understanding himself as Puerto Rican, no matter how hard he tries to make these two social identities meet. Thus Piri's insistence on coming to terms with himself in terms that refuse to accommodate him represents an allegorical journey that charts both what being Boricua means in the racial context of the United States and how difficult articulating this meaning is in U.S.-based terminology. Ultimately in the novel, as I discuss further below, this journey hits a dead end, when Piri capitulates his will and word to a divine and conspicuously white father figure whose omniscience is absolute and unfathomable, thus permanently deferring the text's hermeneutical crisis. His failure to revise successfully the common criteria and languages of racial and cultural belonging in the United States parallels how the Puerto Rican colonial diaspora has faced, confronted, and transgressed (though never transcended) the definitive boundaries between ethnic, racial, and national constituencies and consciousness (also discussed in chapter 2). Ultimately, Piri's hermeneutical crisis indicates how inadequate these social identities and languages can be, that in fact Boricua cultural, racial, national, and ethnic "identifications" (Clifford 1994) cannot always be entirely subsumed by the terms "Black," "Puerto Rican," or even hyphenized "American."

Internalized and externalized racisms are important thematic concerns throughout *Down These Mean Streets*. In the first chapter of the novel it becomes evident that, with reason, Piri feels ostracized by his family because, unlike his brothers and sister (who look more European, like Piri's mother), Piri is the only child who has his father's African features. He feels that his father treats him unfairly precisely because he reminds him of his own Blackness, and indeed Piri, the eldest child, is a convenient target for his father's frustrations and anger. In the opening scene, Piri's brother José starts a chain of events that results in a broken jar of coffee and, as usual it seems, Piri receives all the blame and corporal punishment. Piri's first words in the novel illustrate how his personal struggle is inextricably meshed with a struggle of articulation:

> I could feel my mouth making the motions of wanting to say something in my defense. Of how it wasn't my fault that José had almost knocked the toaster off the table, and how I had tried to save it from falling, and in trying had finished knocking it to the floor along with a large jar of black coffee. But I just couldn't get the words out. Poppa just stood there, eyes swollen and hurting from too much work, looking at a river of black coffee. He didn't give me a chance. Even before the first burning slap of his belt awakened tears of pain, I was still trying to get words out that would make everything all right again. The second whap of the belt brought words of pain to my lips, and my blind running retreat was a mixture of tears and "I hate you." (1967: 3–4)

As this scene intimates, coming to terms with himself means coming to terms with his father, who becomes the embodiment of all the painful contradictions he must untangle in his search for self-understanding. The frustrated desire to explain himself, to say something in his own defense, to find the words that can make things "all right," signals how the novel will provide (by proxy) a way to "get the words"—or Piri's (side of the) story—"out." Running away from his father, who stands in for the menacing quandary of Piri's vexed relationship with authority and, ultimately, with his own narrative voice, prefigures the series of conflicts and escapes that form the cyclical struggle shaping the rest of the novel. Until he can make peace with his father and what he signifies in the novel, Piri cannot stand still (as a signifier) in his own text.

Piri's initial escape is a Harlem rooftop at night. Although the streets are "mean" like his father, they become an alternative home. In fact, in many ways the street life represents a surrogate father for Piri during his adolescence. Learning to be a native son of Harlem "is a sort of science," he soon explains, which is "all part of becoming *hombre*" (an adult male) (15–17). As a teenager Piri finds companions also orphaned to the streets, and as his gang these other youngsters become a surrogate family as well. Harlem is depicted as a harsh but fair father, whose only rule is that boys become men by "having heart" or *corazón,* a catchphrase denoting the courage and strength to fight for your space and reputation. Whether proving he has heart in Spanish Harlem, in an Italian neighborhood, or on Long Island, Piri manages to prove his manhood by fighting it out with his aggressors. That is, he is able to establish himself on the street by being an hombre as the street codes define it, defending himself against racism in "foreign" neighborhoods and engaging in an equally violent struggle to win respect in his own community. On the generic level of this struggle, Piri confirms Lukács's claim that, of all literary genres, "[t]he novel is the art-form of virile maturity" and, consequently, "the most hazardous genre" (1971: 71–73). Piri responds to these struggles and hazards by "deterritorializing" and "reterritorializing" the English language novel—played out in the text as turf wars—which enables him to take and remake the "foreign" turf/text his to control through sheer force of will (Deleuze and Guattari 1986: 18–23).

But while Piri's elaboration of and adherence to the street's ethical code do force open a space in the text to represent his character's rather violent and often illicit behavior as a young man, this process does not enable him to integrate his narrative voice completely and thus establish a stable hermeneutical center in the novel; as much as he can fend off the aggressors on the street (and in the process become an aggressor himself), another, apparently insuperable friction postpones the narrator's own constitution as an integral speaking subject. That is, even though Piri has established his turf in the neighborhood, he still has to come to terms with himself as the author (of his own identity and text). For although he can prove his authority (his socially constituted power) to others, he is yet unsure of what his author-ity (his constitutive power as a speaking subject in the text) means. Articulated in *Down These Mean Streets* as a question of who he is and "where he's at"—or the question of his existential legitimacy and an explication of the speaking subject's self-authorization—the internal/external narrative voice or "I" of the text craves more solid ground. Again, language itself seems to be at fault in all of this, since it renders his pressing questions unanswerable or eternally deferred. Piri's explanation of this dilemma is that he feels "hung up between two sticks" or polarized affinities—Blackness and Puerto Ricanness—as a character in his own life story, which leaves him dangling precariously between wor(l)ds (127).

This process of achieving authentic self-understanding—of the "I" making peace with its (con)text, if you will—guides the course of Piri's narrative journey, of his varied attempts to escape the streets of Harlem, his family, and all they signify in the hope of finding clues to un-dangling his existence. Even within his street family, Piri feels compelled to choose between being "stone Porty-Rican" and being a Black man, and trying to make this choice engenders a whole series of irreconcilable dilemmas (130). He cannot choose to adopt a quasi-white Puerto Rican identity, because he recognizes how his father's internalized racism has strained their relationship. On the other hand, he is reluctant to assume a U.S.-centric Black identity, for this would deny his unique cultural legacy as a member of the African diaspora by way of Puerto Rico and Spanish Harlem. Moreover, he knows that categorically disidentifying with whiteness means rejecting those he loves—his mother especially, but also his siblings. Later in the novel, while he prepares to search for a more definitive answer to his racial/cultural quandary, Piri ponders this affective tug-of-war:

> I look like Poppa, I thought, we really favor each other. I wondered if it was too mean to hate your brothers a little for looking white like Momma. I felt my hair—thick, black, and wiry. Mentally I compared my hair with my brothers' hair. My face screwed up at the memory of the jillion tons of stickum hair oils splashed down in a vain attempt to make it like theirs. I felt my nose. "Shit, it ain't so flat," I said aloud. But mentally I measured it against my brothers', whose noses were sharp, straight, and placed neat-like in the middle of their paddy fair faces.
>
> Why did this have to happen to me? Why couldn't I be born like them? I asked myself. I felt sort of chicken-shit thinking like that. I felt shame creep into me. It wasn't right to be ashamed of what one was. It was like hating Momma for the color she was and Poppa for the color he wasn't. (129)

Piri's gang activities at first apparently offer a way to avoid this painful quandary by lending unconditional love via a type of familial membership that, at least superficially, is uncomplicated by racial or cultural division. What unites the gang is the drinking, the pot they smoke together, the sexual encounters they plan (and sometimes execute) together, and the "turf wars" they fight out in the streets. The mood-altering drugs they share deepen their sense of comradery as "a young army going to war" (images Piri borrows from World War II–era films) and intensify the drama of rumbles that end when one gang routs the other or their common enemy—the police—arrives:

> You feel so good that when the cops make it up them five flights, they ain't gonna find nothing but a sad Puerto Rican record playing a sad bolero called "Adiós, motherfuckers."
>
> Yeah. But the best is the walk back to the block, with the talk about the heart shown in the rumble, the questions put down and the answers given. The look of pride and the warmth of hurts received and given. And each cat makes it to his pad to cop a nod and have his dreams sweetened by his show of corazón. (65)

Piri relates these inclusive feelings while "stoned," suggesting that his biochemical experience on drugs induces the feeling of belonging (and vice versa). The youths' ultimate victory against their common enemy ends as music—a "sad Puerto Rican record playing a sad bolero"—confronts, confuses, and effectively stops the "paddies" in their tracks, symbolizing the strange (if suggestive) possibility that Nuyorican aesthetic forms may help thwart the lethal threat to children and young adults posed by the NYPD. The gang's unity is then expressed in tidy lists of "questions," "answers," and "hurts" that are easily tallied as physically "received" or "given" in the rumble, thereby eluding any of the more involved questions that his hermeneutical "hang-up" entails. This episode indicates that being "stoned"—and "a stone Porty-Rican"—are mutual but surreal grounds for securing the narrator's authority, safety, and self-understanding.

The illusory nature of gang solidarity is likewise represented in a scene that again provokes the question of authenticity, in this instance involving sexuality. In this episode, Piri's thoughts emerge while he and his comrades are "getting stoned" with three transvestites who give alcohol, drugs, and some cash to the young men in exchange for being allowed to "service" them sexually (59–68). Here Piri is "hung up" between two polarized affinities. On the one "stick" is the conviction of his heterosexual identity; while one of the transvestites gives him a "blow job," Piri "chants" in his head, "I like broads, I like muchachas, I like girls" (66). On the other "stick," the scene makes him feel "both good and bad," both "strong and drained," contradictory sensations that seem only reconcilable within the surreality induced by being "high" (67). Ultimately, although Piri seems to enjoy the encounter while it is happening—"I dug the lie before me" are his words—he later explains his homoerotic pleasure as merely another episode in a life defined by getting by:

> I hadn't liked the scene, but if a guy gotta live, he gotta do it from the bottom of his heart; he has to want it, to feel it. It's no easy shake to hold off the pressure with one hand while you hold up your sagging pants with the other. But the game's made as you go along, and you got to pick up what you have or dive out the top-floor window. (67)

Piri claims he was reluctant to go the transvestites' apartment, but agreed to go with his partners only because the fear of seeming to be a coward in front of his "boys" outweighed his fear of homosexual desire. He argues to himself that he neither "wanted" nor completely "felt" the experience, but rather participated as a method to validate his manhood among his friends, suggesting that not only the gang but also the paternal codes to which Piri subscribes on the street can be defined within a certain logic that is both homoerotic and homophobic. Since this logic is psychologically troubling and chemically induced, Piri's narrative voice is left hanging again once he sobers up.

Leaving the gang aside, the narrative then shifts to another escape, as Piri attempts to find and keep a regular job. The logic here moves from the paternalism of the streets to that of the capitalist workforce, which is equally contradictory in his experiences. Piri's first job is as a shoe-shine boy. The scene among shoe-shiners is also a "turf war," and the role he acts out with his customers is a "Sí, señor, sir" game that requires him to play yet another prescribed and unauthentic part (76). This segment of the novel illustrates the illusory logic of both capitalism and the Protestant work ethic among urban youths with scant resources, as it dawns on Piri that at the rate he is being paid he would be "987 years old" before he makes his first million (77).

This critique of capitalist ethics for Black and Boricua youths becomes more specifically a problem of racism in the next section of the novel, entitled "How to Be a Negro without Really Trying," which forges the connections between the "turf wars," racism in the U.S.

workforce, and the unanswered questions of Piri's identity (101–11). In this episode, he and a friend go together to apply for advertised entry-level jobs in insurance sales. Once he sees Piri, the prospective employer tells him that all the positions have already been filled, but his friend (a light-skinned Boricua), who goes into the office immediately after Piri, is hired on the spot. Racism is the main ingredient in Piri's realization that being identified by others as Black effectively bars him from employment in even the lowest-paying, entry-level jobs available to others who share his class and cultural background. Thus the problem of the way the world identifies him as a "Negro" without his consent erupts all over again, and Piri is left dangling once more as the author of his own identity in the novel.

After numerous other failed attempts to "go legit" as a worker, Piri resolves to make sense of his dilemma by visiting the Deep South with his African American friend Brew. Brew is the text's representation of prototypical U.S. Black male consciousness, with which Piri must dialogue in order to begin the process of untangling his hermeneutic "hang-up." According to Brew, Piri must recognize and valorize his Blackness in order to make sense of family, society, the job market, and the very essence of who he is. But on the eve of their departure, as Piri sits listening to Brew's argument that phenotype is the key to his only authentic social identity, Brew's girlfriend, Alayce, argues that cultural difference trumps racial affiliation:

> Alayce burst out. "He's a Porto Rican and that's whar he is. We's Negroes and that's whar we're at." . . .
>
> "Hold on, baby," Brew said. "Sure he's Porty Rican, but his skin makes him a member of the black man's race an' hit don't make no difference he can talk that Porty Rican talk. His skin is dark an' that makes him jus' anudder rock right along wif the res' of us, an' tha' goes for all the rest of them foreign talkin' black men all ovah' the world. When you're born a shoe, yuh stays a shoe." . . .
>
> "But honey," Alayce insisted, "Porto Ricans act different from us. They got different ways of dancin' an' cookin', like a different culture or something."
>
> "What's culture gotta do with the color of your skin?" Brew asked sarcastically.
>
> "I dunno, but Ah've met a whole lot of dark Porto Ricans, an' I ain't met a one yet who wants to be a Negro. An I don't blame 'em. I mean, like anything's better'n being a li'l ole darkie." (171)

This dialogue encapsulates Piri's dilemma. On the one hand, Brew claims that African descent is paramount over any and all cultural and historical differences. For Brew, the color of Piri's skin in New York makes him a U.S. Black, and all "foreign-talkin' black men," regardless of cultural difference, should understand themselves as such. On the other hand, Alayce thinks that cultural difference does matter, that Boricuas "got different ways" than African Americans, and therefore Piri more centrally belongs to this other community. And as Alayce duly adds, she thinks that part of the resistance among "dark Porto Ricans" to calling themselves "Negro" is the reluctance to become part of this constituency or, as Alayce reads it, to become another "li'l ole darkie," suggesting a rejection based on shame of association. Though this brief dialogue clearly outlines Piri's dilemma in the second half of the novel, it does not resolve it: Piri craves a stable identity, and Black is an option, but his conflict has to do with his particular experience of Blackness as a Boricua in New York, which Brew's definition of Black identity, based in his experience of migration from the Deep South to the Northeast, cannot completely encompass or unravel.

Piri is, nevertheless, intrigued by Brew's diagnosis of his "hang-up"—that he is "but one mudderfuckin' part of all this hurtin' shit"—a reflection that prepares the text's final direct confrontation with U.S. Blackness as Piri's potential identity (199). This leads to Brew and Piri's decision to travel south so that Piri can confront Brew's pain in full blown proportion. The two sign up for the merchant marine to make the trip. The first stop is in Virginia, where they encounter Gerald, a very light-skinned African American who has opted to be "white" and feels he has more in common with people of "Spanish extraction" as a result. Gerald's rationalization of this device for passing occurs during a long monologue, in which he explains his position to Brew and Piri:

> I would like you to know that if, because of genetic interbreeding, I cannot truly identify with white or black, I have the right to identify with whatever race or nationality approximates my emotional feeling and physical characteristics. If I feel comfortable being of Spanish extraction, then that's what I'll be. You might very well feel the same way, were you in my place. (190)

Gerald is an academic from the North, and much of what he has to say about his biracial identity seems ridiculous and opportunistic; he can adopt a Black identity at his convenience, but his racial identity of choice is "white" as a person "of Spanish extraction." Gerald's project in going south parallels Piri's in certain ways: Gerald journeys to learn the "Negro" perspective for a book he is writing, while Piri is likewise trying to acquire his own interpretive lenses as a "Negro." As Piri puts it: "Gerald had problems something like mine. Except that he was a Negro trying to make Puerto Rican and I was a Puerto Rican trying to make Negro."

When Gerald leaves the bar, Piri is left confused, pondering what this dialogue means in the context of his voyage of self-discovery. But again there are no ready answers and the narrative thus moves toward another escape from the metacritical interpretation required for Piri to solve the riddle of his identity. As with his gang partners, alcohol and sex become the diversions, and sexist behavior and modes of thought become his (meta)physical escape from pursuing the very questions that instigated his trip south. Indeed, Piri is no feminist, and his interaction with U.S. Black male consciousness in the novel never involves the obvious imbrication of gender with race, culture, and nation. What distracts Piri from his discussion with Gerald at the end of this chapter is a "broad" who is "coming on" to him at a bar, and the oddly reassuring and clearly problematic thought that "pussy's the same in every color" (191).[7]

At this point in the narrative, it is evident that Piri's trip south has created more questions than answers, and that he is bound toward his old methods of coping. After he and Brew hire a pair of prostitutes, Brew disappears for good, and with him goes the African American male consciousness he represents in the novel. Piri now must brave it alone, and although he recognizes that in fact sex is not a race-neutral diversion when he is almost barred from entry into a "whites-only" brothel, the issue is dropped along with his quest for self-understanding. He stays enlisted in the merchant marine and travels all over the hemisphere. When he finally returns to New York, the only conclusion he seems to have reached is that whiteness is the equivalent of evil.

The second half of the novel begins with Piri's return to where he began, to his phrase "I hate you" diverted from his father and what he signifies toward white supremacy, as he explains that he "came back to New York with a big hate for anything white" (209). That his hermeneutical crisis has not been solved is suggested by the title of the subsequent segment, "Hung Down," alluding to the fact that his "hang-up" has transformed into an all-encompassing malaise (214). Back in Harlem, Piri's desire to escape escalates, to the point where he becomes *embalao,* or addicted to heroin. The drug is clearly a new way for Piri to try to evade the dilemma he had hoped to resolve by finding his Black "essence" in the South. In his words, "mainline is the best time," because "when that good-o smack was making it with you, nothing in the whole mundo world made no difference, nothing—neither paddies nor Poppa and strange other people" (220). Although he ultimately survives his addiction and detoxes, Piri's life becomes again a series of evasions. He tries to escape from poverty by becoming a professional thief, but gets arrested. Then once he is incarcerated, he tries to avoid thinking about his predicament by concentrating on his girlfriend, Trina, back home. He also dabbles in a Black Muslim religion while in jail, yet none of these alternatives pans out. He decides he never wants to be in prison again, therefore crime is no longer an option. Trina eventually marries someone else while he is doing time, so she is no longer an option. And try as he might to fall in with the Muslim brothers, their religion never really suffices for him either. Again, Piri's desire to find a conceptual space in which to find peace and piece for his narrative voice is thwarted.

When Piri is finally let out on parole, he returns to his aunt's apartment in Harlem to start over again. He vows to stay off drugs and out of trouble with the law, which leaves him with few familiar activities. He never figures out how to articulate himself through the available racial and cultural terminology, which suggests that there are no simple answers, that being culturally and historically shaped by Africa, Puerto Rico, and Harlem simultaneously is simply that and, for all its apparent contradictions, that is "where he's at," perhaps suggesting a new diasporan hermeneutics in the making somewhere outside the text with the reader's critical response to this unresolved crisis. But in the novel's closing moments, Piri's final escape seems to be Christianity, as he projects a compassionate father figure onto the Christian god and thus feels part of a new family in his aunt's church congregation. The promise he makes to his new "father" in exchange for religion and help is telling:

> If God is right, so what if He's white? I thought, God, I wanna get out of this hole. Help me out. I promise if You help me climb out, I ain't gonna push the cover back on that cesspool. Let me out and I'll push my arm back down there and help some other guy get a break. (346)

The novel closes with Piri finding religion and translating his fervor into a commitment to helping others out of the "cesspool" of rage, drugs, crime, violence, and pain he has suffered and survived. In effect, the novel forecloses the quest to constitute an omniscient, self-authorizing narrative voice in deference to the primal Word of divinity itself. This closure might also suggest that the protagonist has exacted symbolic revenge on his father by rejecting him for an archetypal father figure who is as unquestionably white as his actual father wanted to be but never really could be.

Although this final escape from the world into the "family of God" could be read as yet another diversion, the commitment Piri makes to helping others begins a much more detailed process of self-discovery explored in the two sequels to *Down These Mean Streets*. *Savior, Savior Hold My Hand* (1972) depicts how Piri's coming to consciousness as a Christian engenders even more dilemmas. His work with a community church helps him recognize the hypocrisy of religious missionaries in the inner cities of the United States, and he ultimately rejects the church for a career as an activist and writer. In *Seven Long Times* (1974) Piri returns to his prison years and narrates the process he underwent as an inmate who successfully de-institutionalized his mind by educating himself during his incarceration. The question of his racial identity rendered moot by the end of *Down These Mean Streets*, Thomas's subsequent novels focus on the more concrete problems Black and Boricua young men face in New York's urban ghettos, barrios, and prisons.

The unresolved hermeneutical crisis I am reading in *Down These Mean Streets* gives way to an important set of thematics in Thomas's later works, thematics that focus on the importance of direct intervention in the lives of urban youths rather than identity per se. Both *Savior, Savior Hold My Hand* and *Seven Long Times* illustrate that progressive community services, committed activism, and nonracist education can be effective in creating positive social change for young men who encounter a confusing, hostile, and violent societal context similar to Piri's. In its fictionalized call to action, Thomas's vision in the trilogy as a whole echoes the sentiments and politics of the Young Lords Party activist Pablo "Yoruba" Guzmán:

> [I]n New York, we found that on a grass-roots level a high degree of racism existed between Puerto Ricans and Blacks, and between light-skinned and dark-skinned Puerto Ricans. We had to deal with this racism because it blocked any kind of growth for our people, any understanding

> of the things Black people had gone through. So rather than watching Rap Brown on TV, rather than learning from that and saying, "Well, that should affect me too," Puerto Ricans said, "Well, yeah, those Blacks got a hard time, you know, but we ain't going through the same thing." This was especially true for light-skinned Puerto Ricans. Puerto Ricans like myself, who are darker-skinned, who look like Afro-Americans, couldn't do that, 'cause to do that would be to escape into a kind of fantasy. Because before people called me a spic, they called me a nigger. So that was, like, one reason as to why we felt the Young Lords Party should exist.
>
> At first many of us felt why have a Young Lords Party when there existed a Black Panther Party, and wouldn't it be to our advantage to try to consolidate our efforts into getting Third World people into something that already existed? It became apparent to us that that would be impractical, because we wouldn't be recognizing the national question. We felt we each had to organize where we were at—so that Chicanos were gonna have to organize Chicanos, Blacks were gonna have to organize Blacks, Puerto Ricans Puerto Ricans, etc., until we came to that level where we could deal with one umbrella organization that could speak for everybody. But until we eliminate the racism that separates everybody, that will not be possible. (Young Lords Party 1971: 74–75)

Guzmán's narrative explains that educating the community about internalized racism and its noxious effects on people of color was a priority for the Boricua civil rights generation's most important grassroots organization, the Young Lords Party. Inspired by the Young Lords Organization in Chicago, and modeled on the Black Panther Party, the New York Young Lords' grass-roots projects and programs were directly involved with children and young adults in their communities, focusing on both practical and symbolic interventions. Guzmán's proposal, like the implicit message of Thomas's narrative trilogy, is that cultural differences between African diasporan communities should not foreclose a meaningful political engagement within and between them; in fact, internalized racism may be one of the things communities of color have in common across the board. Furthermore, as Guzmán avers, the "national question"—Puerto Rico's colonial status—alerted Boricua civil rights activists to what they considered important differences between communities of color in the United States, and led to their assessment that attending to these differences should help rather than hinder political collaboration between Blacks, Boricuas, and other internally colonized groups.

Storytelling and Boricua Womanist Hermeneutics: Nicholasa Mohr's Nilda

Iris Morales, another founding member of the Young Lords Party, echoes the motivations of the next civil rights–era author under discussion in this chapter, Nicholasa Mohr. Morales's narration of her coming to consciousness as a political activist not only employs storytelling devices similar to Mohr's, but reiterates many of the themes that Mohr explores in her fiction—the daily stress of confronting racism and sexism in public institutions, the complications of confronting sexism at home, and the resistance to indoctrination that young girls in the Boricua community perform in both of these contexts:

> You resign yourself to poverty—my mother did this. Your face is rubbed in shit so much that you begin to accept that shit as a reality. You've never seen anything else. Like the only thing we knew was that block. You never went out of that block. I didn't know there was a Museum of Modern Art. I didn't know that there were people who were living much, much better. I didn't know about racism. I mean we were just on that block—and that block was our home, it was all we knew.
>
> The images of that poverty. . . . My stomach rumbling. My mother beating me when I knew it was because of my father—you know, they just had an argument where he almost hit her. The welfare investigator cursing out my mother because what she wants is spring clothing for her children and he's telling her how she just can't have it—when I read in the magazines that people—you know, other people—had spring clothes. Why couldn't we have clothes for Easter? And he's telling her, like, in a sense, "Fuck you." And I remember images of my saying, "When I grow up I'm gonna kill every welfare investigator I see, every one of them—you know, strangle them." (Young Lords Party 1971: 29)

Morales's testimonial further explains that her involvement in the Young Lords Party helped her critically reconsider the context of her childhood, a context that she hoped not only to critique but to change for the next generation of young women in the Boricua community. Nicholasa Mohr's protagonist, Nilda, experiences a critical coming to consciousness akin to Morales's, under similar circumstances to those Morales describes above, and narrated in a similar fashion. Like the work of Luisa Capetillo and Pura Belpré, Mohr's fiction elaborates the scenes of everyday life for women and children in her community, and not unlike Morales's almost novelistic narration of her memories of childhood, Mohr's *Nilda* is a carefully crafted testimonial to the indignities of life in a Boricua barrio, one that employs narrative tactics that capture, critique, and ultimately help her protagonist—and by extension, her readers—prevail over the racism, sexism, and material poverty that she experiences as a child in New York City.

Like Thomas's *Down These Mean Streets*, Nicholasa Mohr's *Nilda* is the story of a child growing up around midcentury in East Harlem. But while both texts respond to the same generation of children, Nilda's story evolves within a different mode of writing gender and power. Characteristically less concerned with the search for socially and textually constituted authority, Mohr's woman-centered prose is more concerned with orchestrating a hermeneutic co-participation with the reader. The child protagonist's sometimes sketchy—yet always acutely felt—understanding of the hostile forces bearing down on her daily life prompts the sympathetic reader to interpret Nilda's story with more thorough critical acumen than the child protagonist herself is mature enough to assume. This is a subtle technique that matches the sophistication of Belpré's skill merging critical pedagogy with storytelling.

This strategy begins with the selection of a young female protagonist. Unlike Piri, Nilda never grows up, thus the simplicity and clarity of the prose stay constant throughout the text. Furthermore, representing Nilda's thoughts as an indirect narrative voice positions her character as a subject in process simultaneously with the progress of the novel; in this way Nilda's, the novel's, and the reader's understanding of the world emerge together. Likewise, by having Nilda articulate the dilemmas she faces in direct and reactive ways, as a child would, Mohr emphasizes the more raw emotional dimensions of childhood. Meanwhile related historical, cultural, and political issues are inscribed around the child's voice, couched in spaces and moments that are juxtaposed with Nilda's limited understanding. This broader context, which the protagonist may not completely or explicitly comprehend, is consistently presented in pieces that the reader, intimately involved in Nilda's personal story, must consolidate for herself. Thus, the site of understanding the larger significance of Nilda's story resides outside the text with its readers.

Throughout the novel, Mohr crafts Nilda's life as similar to most children's lives: wanting to have friends, dealing with parents, going to school, asking questions about the world, and pondering one's place in it. However, at each turn in Nilda's childhood she is faced with oppressive structures of power that continually interrupt her world and impose themselves in obnoxious and threatening ways. The first hint of these impositions comes at the opening of the text, on a hot summer day in Nilda's neighborhood, El Barrio, or Spanish Harlem. The children are enjoying a reprieve from the sizzling heat by playing in an open fire hydrant. The scene is described as a shared pleasure for the whole neighborhood that abruptly ends when the police arrive, spewing abusive and racist remarks at the folk standing by. The fun immediately stops, the relief is gone, and Nilda walks home with a lingering sense of resentment toward the policemen who so rudely and crassly intervened. Her strategy is to think of being somewhere else, to use her imagination to project herself into an imaginary diorama that can divert her thoughts and thus "erase" her resentment:

> She walked home, trying to step only on the areas where the pavement was still wet. Nilda started thinking of camp and what it might be like with all kinds of trees and grass and maybe a lake. Like Central Park, she thought, or something like that. She tried to guess what might be ahead for her, maybe something better. These thoughts helped erase the image of the two white policemen who loomed larger and more powerful than all the other people in her life. (Mohr 1973: 7)

Here, despite its troubling catalyst, a simple daydream opens the tableau of Nilda's innocence. The scene she creates in her mind reaches beyond the immediate intrusion to another, imagined realm where policemen and all they signify are absent from the picture. The power structure represented by the armed white authority figures is the first of a series of imposing presences that signal the reader to beware for Nilda as she comes to terms with a hostile world and her place in it.

Nilda's ability to reimagine the scenes of immediate conflict in her own hopeful way provides the guiding metaphor for the novel. Like Piri, Nilda is always looking for an escape, but in lieu of drugs, sex, and religion, her routes "out" are made possible by her creative powers and active imagination. Her art is to draw new scenes in "a world of magic," not only with lines and colors, but also with the words in her head and the images she can paint with words. Although her desire to escape is always spurred by her feeling that she is trapped, misunderstood, and abused, she takes what little control of the situation she can by aesthetically decomposing and recomposing the world around her. Mohr explores this creative impulse and process with a description of Nilda's "box of things":

> As she often did when she was upset, she took her "box of things" out from under the bed. . . . She sat looking at her cardboard box affectionately. Carefully she began to stack her cardboard cutouts. Her stepfather would give her the light grey cardboard that was in his shirts whenever they came back from the Chinese laundry. She cut these into different shapes, making people dolls, animals, cars, buildings, or whatever she fancied. Then she would draw on them, filling in the form and color of whatever she wanted. She had no more cardboard but she had some white, lined paper that Victor had given her. Drawing a line and then another, she had a sense of happiness. Slowly working, she began to divide the space, adding color and making different size forms. Her picture began to take shape and she lost herself in a world of magic achieved with some forms, lines and color.
>
> She finished her picture feeling that she had completed a voyage all by herself, far away but in a place she knew quite well. (50)

As an analog for the process of writing, Mohr alludes to the aesthetic necessity to construct an alternative space, by whatever means available, in fiction. Using what few materials to which she has access, such as the cardboard shirt inserts from the laundry and pieces of loose-leaf paper, Nilda re-creates the world around her in her own fashion, refiguring common objects in the cityscape ("people dolls, animals, cars, buildings, or whatever she fancied") into unique, imaginative, and positive possibilities. Although Nilda's favorite thing is to cut, paste, and color, her art becomes a vehicle for storytelling too. Mirroring the novel's palimpsestic representation of social and historical contexts, Nilda, inspired by her crafts, narrates and thus curates the pieces she creates.

The next episode in the novel details Nilda's first trip to summer camp. Although the summer camp appears to offer refuge from what the policemen signify in her life, it is soon evident that the program is designed and implemented as a charity by yet another imposing and menacing institution, the Catholic Church. Thus in place of the idyllic scene she imagines, the reader finds Nilda in something more like a concentration camp designed to modify children's behavior and indoctrinate them into the Catholic religion.

This episode starts with the common childhood trauma of leaving home for the first time, when Nilda becomes somewhat nervous and scared as she boards the train leaving Grand Central Station. But when she and the other children arrive at the camp in upstate New York, the reader soon discovers that Nilda's anxieties about leaving home for the first time in her life are warranted. Nilda at once observes that other campers already settled in "don't look so happy" (10). Her reading of the setting itself is reminiscent of a gothic novel meshed with urban degradation; Nilda notes that the weather is "gloomy, adding to the bleakness of the place," while there is a "thin layer of oily film covering the water," and the camp's housing quarters remind her of an "abandoned factory." The opening scene at the summer camp also reveals that the nuns and priests have an ulterior agenda, and that their arguably fascist designs will quash the children's natural curiosity and their desire to play. Accordingly, the first order of business is to get the children to line up and "march" in order to the buildings. They then receive the command of "silence" along with the injunction to defer to the priest's authority. The third order is that all children not yet through the rite of First Communion be separated out and prepared for the ritual; after all, the priest warns, "[w]e want no Judas or Jew!" (11).

Allusions to war-era charity work are also made throughout this segment of the novel. The children are provided with army surplus blankets and supplies, the housing barracks are lined with cots in neat rows for the children, and the showers and commodes have no doors. An allusion to fascist concentration camps is perhaps less evident but nevertheless suggested. The children's forced feeding of laxatives before bedtime, the priest's anti-Semitic comments, and the cruel order that they line up for showers in freezing cold water altogether evoke the coercion, humiliation, xenophobia, and toxicity of Nazi concentration camps.

On the second day at camp, the racism endemic to the Catholic Church comes into clearer focus for the reader. When Nilda observes that "[a]ll the nuns, priests, and brothers were very white and had blue or light brown eyes," that "[o]nly among the children were there dark faces" and wonders "if Puerto Ricans were ever allowed to be nuns, fathers, or brothers," Mohr subtly implicates the church's institutional racism as a source of the emotional pain and physical indignities Nilda and the other children experience at this camp (16). Nilda partially recognizes the racial stratification implicit in Catholic charity work through the adult faces and features she sees around her. However, she leaves off thinking about the whiteness around her and begins to internalize the blame for her misery. In good Catholic form, she worries that she is being punished by a vengeful god for something wrong she has done to him, then prays that night in her cot for a "miracle," which comes the next day in the form of the decision to shut down the camp because of plumbing problems (17–19).

Although Mohr implies that Nilda sincerely believes the plumbing problems were somehow an act of divine intervention, the careful reader notices that other episodes in the text suggest that Nilda is much more ambivalent about religious dogma. That is, Mohr narrates her mother's rather fanatical Catholic influence unpersuasively in the novel, while her stepfather's politicized atheism makes a lot more sense to the young child as she attempts to figure out her spiritual orientations. For example, on her first day at camp, Nilda "thought of her stepfather's constant blasphemy and his many arguments with her mother, as he attacked the Catholic Church" and wishes that he could rescue her from the grips of the nuns and priests (11). When Nilda returns home from the miserable Catholic camp, her religious doubts are again evident during a heated argument between her parents. While her mother insists that Nilda go to Sunday mass at the local Catholic church (her brothers are relieved of this duty simply because they are boys), her stepfather argues that Nilda should not be forced to emulate her mother's religious fervor. "Bunch of shit," her stepfather argues, "filling her head with that phony stuff. Fairy tales in order to oppress the masses. Teaching them that to be good is not to fight back, is to take crap" (20–21). When Nilda tries to intervene and to explain her mother's conviction to her stepfather—that "[f]aith is very powerful" and "God will provide"—he counters with an anglicized, popular Spanish curse: "I shit on the priest's bird, is what I do." Nilda then ponders the "possibilities of truth set before her" and tries to adapt to her mother's religious sensibility by doing as her mother asks, but ultimately Mohr suggests that Nilda is not passive enough to be swayed into believing in the church's absolute authority. Although the text never explicitly states Nilda's rejection of Catholicism (perhaps in order not to offend the sensibilities of the novel's prospective readers), her sympathy with her stepfather's position is alluded to in the way she chomps on the sacramental Host (a sin in the eyes of church authorities), her disappointment after taking Communion because she fails to feel the "magic transformation" she was told it would inspire, and her attendance at a neighborhood storefront Protestant service for no better reason than as an excuse to hang out with her friends and to eat some of the food they share at the end of the service (24, 102ff).

If Nilda's rejection of Catholicism is subtly portrayed in these episodes and arguments, her resistant entanglements with other forms of institutional racism and sexism are far more explicit in the novel. Among these, public education constitutes yet another scene of oppression and illuminates the whole process of indoctrination to which Boricuas were subjected in New York City's public school system in the 1940s and 1950s.

The representation of Nilda's school days begins with Miss Langhorn (dubbed "Miss Foghorn" by her students), an aging and decrepit Anglo-American teacher, who starts the class by reciting a litany of reasons for locking the classroom supply closet, all of which insinuate her unsubstantiated belief that students of color are prone to theft (51). Miss Langhorn is portrayed as yet another type of police officer and, in fact, an ideological drill sergeant. Part of "Foghorn's" policing duties is to ward off any attempt to speak Spanish, which is punished by insults and physical abuse. As Nilda explains,

> Anybody caught speaking or even saying one word of Spanish had to put out both arms and clench his hands into fists. "None of that," she would say, "if you are ever going to be good Americans. You will never amount to anything worthwhile unless you learn English. You'll stay just like your parents. Is that what you people want? Eh?" (52)

Recalcitrant students are taunted by Miss Langhorn as she smacks their knuckles with a ruler; presumably they must respond by affirming that Spanish is un-American in order to stop the beating, while the teacher/policewoman also tries to teach them to be ashamed of their own parents as the epitome of all that not being a "good American" implies. Infractions of school rule and active resistance to this sort of xenophobic Anglo-nationalist indoctrination are grounds for corporal punishment, and those who will not submit to punishment are put in the back of the class on a stool with a "dunce" hat, a stool to which Nilda has been sent no less than three times in the current term. But Nilda's ultimate resistance to Miss Langhorn, the English-only rule, the class discipline, and their denigrating objectives is reflected in her ability to tune it all out by daydreaming. The classroom episode ends as Nilda gets lost in the stories and images in her mind. The teacher's voice then drifts "far, far away," as the text drowns out the teacher's discourse and captures the range of Nilda's thoughts instead (54).

In addition to describing the public school system, the novel details

Nilda's resistant tactics in her interactions with the social services establishment institutionalized during the New Deal. Again, Nilda's response is to displace the humiliation and anger she experiences in a government office by drifting off into her own thoughts and narrating an alternative ending to the episode. And like Iris Morales, who desired vengeance against the welfare investigators of her childhood, Nilda covertly imagines the scene of her tormentor's demise.

This scene begins as Nilda and her mother visit the "Home Relief" office to request assistance when her stepfather is hospitalized and, therefore, temporarily cannot work to support the family. Again the figure of the menacing, lower-middle-class Anglo-American woman poses as an antagonist who represents the imposition of white supremacist ideology. Here the "policewoman" is a social worker named Miss Heinz, whom Nilda nicknames the "cellophane lady" in her internal dialogue because of her hermetically sealed appearance and the transparency of her skin. Miss Heinz will not help Nilda's mother fill out the necessary paperwork without first humiliating her and insinuating that Nilda is physically dirty and ill-groomed. Nilda tries to talk back, but her mother insists she be quiet. Miss Heinz then forces Nilda to accept the "gift" of a nail file (an object she overtly suggests Nilda has never seen before), while her mother forces her to say "thank you." Once again, however, Nilda fights back with a story she tells to herself on the way to the bus stop:

> Still holding the nail file, Nilda thought about Miss Heinz. Oh how I hate her. She's horrible, she said to herself. I would like to stick her with this stupid nail file, that's what. When no one was looking I would sneak up behind her and stick her with the nail file. Then she would begin to die. No blood would come out because she hasn't any. But just like that . . . poof! She would begin to empty out into a large mess of cellophane. Everybody in that big office would be looking for her. "Oh, where is Miss Heinz?" they would all say. They would be searching for her all over. Poor Miss Heinz. Oh, poor Miss Heinz. First her eyebrows disappeared. Did you know that? She had no eyebrows. And now she's all gone. Disappeared just like that! Poor thing. My, what a pity.
>
> The bus pulled up. As Nilda climbed inside she felt the nail file slipping between her fingers and heard a faint clink when it hit the pavement. (71)

Nilda thus turns a denigrating experience into the material of a story that can make Miss Heinz and all she signifies literally—and literarily—disappear from her thoughts. The daydreamed story is elaborated as if it were a rough draft of a short story, including narrator, indirect discourse, and the voices of the other characters looking for the missing "murder victim." Nilda's dreamscape enables her to dismiss the intentionally oppressive effects of the social services establishment, the imposition of which is represented in the nail file that she lets slip to the ground. Nilda's rage, provoked by a humiliating episode in which she is forced (for her family's sake) to be silent, echoes the source, substance, and intensity of Morales's, Piri's, and even the potential reader's responses to similar situations.

While Mohr presents the bulk of Nilda's experiences in the intimate confines of childhood, the larger historical context is finally made manifest in the story with the outbreak of World War II. This war marks a turning point, not only for the United States on the global scene, but for Puerto Ricans on the Islands and in the diaspora, who are both U.S. citizens and U.S. colonial subjects. Mohr represents in the novel the dilemma that arises for the Boricua community during this period as the pressure to assimilate, to feel fully "American," and to participate in the war effort in whatever way possible—by buying bonds, organizing community drives, and, for the young men, either being drafted or enlisting in the U.S. armed services. For the men as colonial subjects, of course, enlistment signified the total submission to the metropole's cause. In the novel, Mohr offers a glimpse into how this dilemma reads for Nilda's older brothers, Victor and Jimmy.

Victor is her mother's favorite—he is the child who always blindly obeys and can be counted on to help around the house—while Jimmy (like Piri in Thomas's first text) stakes his manhood on the street codes and tries to escape the oppressive situation by selling drugs and living life on the edge. Thus when Victor announces that he is going to enlist after his high school graduation, Jimmy is enraged, and accuses his brother of being a "sucketa." Victor counters that he feels a patriotic duty to fight for his country as "an American," but Jimmy disagrees:

> "Man, you wasn't even born here; you was born in Puerto Rico. What country? What country you talking about?"
>
> "Puerto Rico is part of the United States. And anyway, what if I was born there! I've been here since I was six years old and I am an American," Victor answered.
>
> "Oh, yeah?" Jimmy said, getting angry. "You're a spick. You can call yourself an American, all right. But they are gonna call you a spick!"

> "If that's the way you want to think about things, Jimmy, then I really feel sorry for you. You got no feelings for your own country. In this country, if you work hard you can be somebody, get an education and accomplish something!"
>
> "First of all I was brought here, man. I didn't ask to come! And in the second place, I don't believe in that sucker stuff, Victor. You wanna believe that, O.K.! Go ahead. It is more blessed to take, baby, than to receive leftovers. That's my motto. I don't want for them to give me no shit. I take and I get." (132–33)

That "sucker stuff" (i.e., the U.S. capitalist work ethic) is part of the colonial indoctrination process Nilda has been resisting throughout the novel, while the option of "take and get" resembles Piri's street philosophy in *Down These Mean Streets*. Although Jimmy's life is sparsely depicted in the novel, it is clear that his "way out" has been crime and a problematic sexual relationship with a white woman—neither of which seems to provide a workable alternative to any of the dilemmas Mohr portrays him facing. The brothers' argument reflects the two options young Puerto Rican men faced at the outbreak of World War II, that is, to support the "democratic mission" of the rising U.S. military-industrial apparatus or to invent some other belief system. Neither brother wins the argument in this episode, ostensibly because neither has really come up with a convincing position.

By the end of the novel, however, Mohr suggests that Nilda has begun the process of coming to terms with her predicament, of resisting the more threatening forces of racism and assimilation while still managing to make sense of herself and the world around her in productive ways via her art. As such, Nilda's emergence in the novel is a success. During her second stay at a summer camp (this time a "paid" camp and not a Catholic charity ordeal), Nilda discovers a secret clearing that represents for her the beauty she imagines of Puerto Rico from the stories her mother has told her. The clearing is not only an escape from some of the other girls at the camp who taunt Nilda about being Puerto Rican, but also that magical space all her own that she imagines finding during the novel's opening scene.

The clearing provides a diorama not unlike the vivid imaginary spaces Nilda creates in her drawings, daydreams, and cut out pastiches, and it is especially akin to what she describes earlier in the novel as a special "far away" place she nevertheless "knew quite well" (50).

Importantly, the clearing is not merely an escape, but something reconcilable with her home in El Barrio:

> Breathless, she stared at the flowers, almost unbelieving for a moment, thinking that she might be in a movie theater waiting for the hard, flat, blank screen to appear, putting an end to a manufactured fantasy which had engrossed and possessed her so completely. Nilda walked over to the flowers and touched them. Inhaling the sweet fragrance, she felt slightly dizzy, almost reeling. She sat down on the dark earth and felt the sun on her face, slipping down her body and over the shrubs covered with roses. The bright sash of warm sunlight enveloped her and the flowers; she was part of them; they were part of her.
>
> She took off her socks and sneakers, and dug her feet into the earth like the roots of shrubs. Shutting her eyes, Nilda sat there for a long time, eyes closed, feeling a sense of pure happiness; no one had given her anything or spoken a word to her. The happiness was inside, a new feeling, and although it was intense, Nilda accepted it as part of a life that now belonged to her. (154–55)

Like Piri's drug-induced escapes, Nilda's experience in the clearing is extra-worldly—it is something that is both a sensual pleasure and a mind-altering experience. But rather than being a self-destructive coping device, Nilda's "high" is a feeling produced from "pure happiness," a sense of peace and tranquility induced by an uninterrupted landscape rather than the religious fervor, patriotic zeal, and angry rebellion offered in the examples set by her family members.

Furthermore, the "secret garden" becomes something Nilda actively shares with her two friends, both of whom are also cruelly ostracized by the condescending girls at the camp. She invites these friends to come with her to her special place, and as they approach, Nilda begins a story. Their time together in the garden is spent with storytelling, making plans to visit when they return home, and talking, activities that suggest that her "secret garden" is not an isolating, fantasy-like escape, but rather a shared imaginary space that helps her to build a sense of community with others and to share a common pleasure in the exchange of words and ideas. Ultimately, the "secret garden" in this text may be read as a metaphor for the act of fiction itself.

The novel concludes in a Harlem apartment with an allusion back to the "secret garden." Here it is clear that Nilda—now orphaned and living with her extended family—will continue to share her special place with her cousins as both a refuge from her daily life and a site of imaginative transformation within her daily life. Here Mohr explains the motives of the artist as a young woman. Most important, the pieces Nilda creates are vehicles for the stories she can tell of what they mean:

> "Let me show you." Opening her closet door, she pulled out a drawing pad. "Now, these drawings are ones I made when I was a little kid; they are of a camp I went to once." Holding up the pad excitedly, she pointed to a drawing on a page. "Here is the cabin where we all slept; there were eight of us. And that's the inside here; that's my bed, and," Nilda turned the page, "here is a special trail in the woods. You see how it winds . . . well, that trail leads to a secret garden." (292)

In the text's final paragraph, the path leading to the garden suggests that Nilda has already found the tools she can use for demystifying an oppressive social order in the United States and successfully reconceptualizing herself as an integral and sovereign subject in the world. "Turning the page" with Nilda in this final moment also underscores how the reader has been part of the text's meaning—its winding paths and dead ends—bearing witness to her "secret garden," her art, all that this art has already signified in the novel, along with all that it may signify beyond the novel's closure as well.

While the institutions and relations of power Nilda experiences and challenges at an early age seem superficially disconnected from any larger historical circumstances, these circumstances are still inscribed palimpsestically in the text as the manifestation of what occurred in New York's Boricua neighborhoods during the 1940s and 1950s (including social problems that, in many respects, continue to this day). Rampant unemployment, the hostile police force, highly problematic educational and social services systems, in sum, the entire context of most Boricuas' family history is tangentially explored in the novel. Extrapolating further, we can contextualize Nilda's adolescence as the community survived through the era of the New Deal, culminating in World War II, which finally emerges in the text as a turning point for Nilda's family and which, in many ways, was also a turning point for the Boricua community at large.

Novels of Emergence and Social Emergencies

Although Mohr's protagonist, Nilda, and Thomas's protagonist, Piri, are different genders, their common starting point is in a society hostile to their very being. Both texts explore how emblematic characters cope with multiple and overlapping structures of oppression and devise strategies and tactics they hope will help them to transcend this oppression or, at the very least, to resist the noxious institutions that hail them for indoctrination as children and young adults. Both narratives are elaborated with episodes that illustrate the dynamic interplay between the young protagonists' immediate scene or dilemma and the imaginary or literal escapes they contrive in the effort to create a less compromising conceptual space for themselves. This realm is often a deferred dream of liberation, something to be realized at another time, in another place, or via another set of possibilities. Nilda learns to make her dream manifest in the act of creation, in the pictures she draws and the stories she tells to herself, her young friends, and her cousins. Like the textual logic of Luisa Capetillo's final writings, Mohr's work may imply that Boricua womanist praxis is most comfortably at home in fiction and other creative subversions. For Piri, on the other hand, the deferral is never ending, but Thomas's autobiographical trilogy suggests that the process of coming to consciousness for him in the novel logically concluded with an endorsement of extratextual interventions. Similar to Arturo Schomburg's project, Thomas's explication of the predicament of being marked Puerto Rican as well as Black in the United States implies a particular identity that must be ideologically deconstructed simultaneously as it is politically constructed, intimating a set of group identifications and active collaboration as yet in process for African diasporan communities in the States.

The civil rights generation's narratives constitute a specific type of "resistance literature" (Harlow 1987), one that—like the work of the Old School writers before them—subverts the very language and literary forms of the colonial metropole from within the proverbial "belly of the beast." Overall, *Down These Mean Streets* and *Nilda* begin to trace the contours of the diaspora's coming to consciousness as a distinct community of color, addressing its own conflicts and remedies in its own idiomatically rendered and generically improvised narratives during the postwar period. Yet the initial articulation of a new Boricua sensibility represents more the desire to elaborate on the contradictions confronted by the colonial diaspora than to reconcile them with simple, static evocations of identity. In other words, although both Thomas and Mohr sketch Boricua youths' desire to be "at home" in the United States, neither of them portrays the diaspora finding a ready-made and uncompromised physical and conceptual space in which they can settle in perfect safety and comfort. As novels of emergence, these texts reject the conventional "coming-of-age" novel's tacit endorsement of the status quo by presenting protagonists whose journeys of self-discovery are also indictments of U.S. colonialism and the racist-sexist society in which U.S. subaltern youths face the daily struggle to survive physically, emotionally, spiritually, aesthetically, and philosophically. And, unlike the works examined in the next chapter, these ethically motivated aesthetic inventions are also interventions that respond to the experiences of the Boricua community at large, literary interventions that challenge, in intimate detail, the unconscionable conditions that continue to surround many children's and young adults' lives in New York City.

5

"I Like to Be in America" [*sic*]

Three Women's Texts

The U.S. publishing industry learned to profit from civil rights–era texts that could be advertised as "ghetto" testimonials, which helped create a new and lucrative pulp fiction niche during the mid- to late 1960s and 1970s. Most of the less notable Boricua narratives in this category are unimaginative reiterations of the popular "gang-banger" novel. These texts include Manuel Manrique's *Island in Harlem* (1966), Nicky Cruz's *Run, Baby, Run* (1968), Humberto Cintrón's *Frankie Cristo* (1972), and Edwin Torres's *Carlito's Way* (1975).

Meanwhile, the 1980s and 1990s have witnessed a resurgence of published texts by Boricua writers. Along with some authors of the civil rights generation who are publishing new work and reissuing some of their older titles, an entirely new spectrum of voices has come to print, including the novelists Ed Vega, Soledad Santiago, Oswald Rivera, Carmen de Monteflores, Judith Ortiz Cofer, Abraham Rodríguez, Edward Rivera, and Esmeralda Santiago, as well as a host of short story writers, poets, and playwrights. The proliferation of these authors' work has been due in part to an interest in "ethnic" American fiction on a popular scale that was catalyzed by the civil rights movement. As new utterances of "minority" sensibilities, these texts offered wide audiences access to the American "Other" in paperback form, creating the possibility of armchair cultural voyeurism, high school and college ethnic studies courses, as well as a full generation (even, perhaps now, two generations) of critically engaged readers from within the communities depicted in these fictions.

This new interest in what might be termed the "minority condition" created not only a market for selling these texts in bookstores but also institutional apparatuses for nurturing the growth of these literatures, including the establishment of journals, ethnic studies centers, writers' fellowships, bibliographic databases, and even new publishing houses.

Although Boricua writers have not proven to be as much of a commercial and institutional success as other ethnic market niche writers, a few presses—most notably Arte Público Press at the University of Houston and Bilingual Press/Edición Bilingüe at the University of Arizona—have provided somewhat stable (if limited) resources for both emerging and established Boricua authors.

Yet as much as the most recent texts and their criticism have enjoyed some measure of institutional accommodation, the content of the most currently popularized literature seems to be renegotiating the overt ideological challenges offered by earlier generations. It is as if this literature's narrative politics have migrated toward the conservative epistemological center in tandem with its academic and industrial institutionalization, despite the effort on the part of more progressive educators to establish Boricua studies as a "legitimate" but definitively contestatory academic discipline. Some of the texts enjoying the widest audiences are outright reactionary and self-aggrandizing, while others are wildly satirical or otherwise spectacular renditions of the Puerto Rican cultural legacy in the diaspora as exotically and/or psychotically episodic. Meanwhile the most important literature of protest from the late 1960s and early 1970s has disappeared from the shelves, as classic texts such as Pedro Pietri's *Puerto Rican Obituary* (1973) and Piri Thomas's *Savior, Savior Hold My Hand* (1972) have gone out of print. And given these new institutional and industrial dynamics, along with the critical tendency to read "minority" literature as allegory for the community at large, contemporary literary criticism is facing the challenge of sorting out questions of aesthetic and ethical motivation in a unique post-movement context.

Latina (in the politicized sense of the term) feminist critique has prompted my analysis of this context.[1] Generally, the predicament of writing culture, gender, and power for the Boricua and Chicana critic is described as a hermeneutical reconnaissance mission, by which culturally specific modes of seeing, knowing, being, feeling, and understanding are transformed from orature to scripture, then aggressively and unapologetically thrust into the public sphere (Moraga et al. 1983; Gomez et al. 1983; Anzaldúa 1990). Latina critics tend to claim that these transformations are motivated by a subversive desire to rehumanize Latinas, that is, to "put flesh" back on the reviled object of study in academia. Among these critics, the very act of Latina print articulation connotes not so much an individualist will to power as a counterhegemonic will to a collective and collectivizing *empowerment,* creating a reinvigorated textual and extratextual sense of communal agency. In Chicana literary studies, this kind of articulation has been theorized as an expression of the subalternization and displacement of Mexicans caused by U.S. territorial expansion (Sánchez and Pita 1992), particularly among the earliest extant women authors (Castañeda 1990, 1993; Lomas 1993, 1994; Sánchez 1993).

It is difficult to disagree with this notion of Latina studies as academic guerrilla warfare, especially when deployed in analyzing social movement literature, and most especially when analyzing social movement and nineteenth-century literature authored by women of color. Yet today in the United States the burgeoning market for "Hispanic" women's writing complicates the issues for literary historians. The small post-movement aperture that opened for Chicana and Boricua women writers in the late 1970s and 1980s has led to a cottage industry in the 1990s, one that even Latin American elites posturing as "Latinas" are rushing to exploit. Given this growing market and the industry's profit motives, certain priorities that respond to industry readings of market potential determine which titles get published and promoted. In the worst of cases, a sort of incestuous loop of consumer orchestration prevails, one created and maintained by corporate conglomerates that have increasingly monopolized control over supply, promotion, and, consequently, demand for such books.

Compare, for example, the "Hispanic," "Southwest," or "Latino Studies" (as they are usually labeled) sections of major chain bookstores in large or medium-sized U.S. cities, and in every store you will find the same titles, from the same catalog lists, ordered from the same distributors. Independent bookstores, which catered to a small but consistent clientele that included critics like myself only a decade ago, cannot successfully compete with these corporate giants. Even university bookstores, once largely owned and operated by student cooperatives and staffed by experts who prided themselves on their intimate knowledge of university and alternative presses, have sold or sublet their spaces to the likes of Barnes and Noble. The titles stocked in these chain stores are dictated by market analysts in corporate headquarters who purchase bulk from distributors, who purchase bulk from major publishers, who spend bulk on advertising and author contracts and then force-feed the products of their investments to the major book reviews. This is how a variety of arguably hackneyed "Latina" books find their way to the market stalls, while the genuinely innovative and provocative work of Chicana and Boricua prose writers like Helena Maria Viramontes, Nicholasa Mohr, and Emma Pérez is relatively difficult to find.

Gone are the days when Latina writers were clearly outside the realm of commodification, when their significance, by virtue of this literature's historical moment and modes of production, automatically sidestepped and outmaneuvered the distortion of mainstream marketing. Without begrudging the success of those ubiquitous and celebrated writers who have "made it" financially (or at least symbolically), we have to recognize the fact that the book market's late-capitalist logic—its simulacra of diversity, of aesthetic autonomy, and of international, gender, racial, or ethnic sensitivity—has essentially changed the playing field for contemporary American women writers of color. Furthermore, as public universities are cutting budgets in library staff and acquisitions, the last safe place for recuperating and archiving Chicana and Boricua women's literature is under threat, while cyberspace has yet to prove itself a sustainable venue for progressive or radical literary experimentation in our communities.

We might accept all this as an unfortunate side effect of the publishing industry's vested interest in marketing culture, and leave it be as such, but as cultural critics and literary historians we know there is more at stake, that literary self-representation is institutional self-preservation as well. Furthermore, these representational politics are played out in the context of worsening material conditions and other prospects for survival among Boricua women, as well as Chicanas, Mexicanas, and their children in the United States. These Latinas have hit rock bottom on the socioeconomic scales, sharing the very highest poverty rates of any group in the United States with American Indian and some Asian American women and children. Although current public debates about cutbacks in social services and the affirmative action backlash persist in misreading these issues as a Black versus white socioeconomic impasse, the truth is that in the states that have launched the most virulent legislative attacks on low-income women and people of color—California and Texas—the largest nonwhite group under fire is lower-income Latinas *and* their children (Moran 1996). The city and state of New York may be avoiding the legislative grandstanding occurring in California and Texas, but cutbacks in education and social services there disproportionately affect Boricua women, Dominicanas, low-income migrant Mexicanas, and their children in similar ways.

Although these Latinas live and work in the First World, their quality of life index matches those in the Third World. African Americans are also living in Third World conditions in the United States, for sometimes distinct but usually overlapping historical reasons. Meanwhile white women collectively in the United States enjoy the highest quality of life index in the world today (United Nations Development Programme 1993).

This, the gruesome underbelly of U.S. representational politics in the era of late capitalism, the hidden or obscured realities belied by the popularity of noncontestatory "Latina" and other "minority" writings that are read as communal allegory in the public sphere, provokes a specific hermeneutical crisis for the Latina public intellectual. For me at least, acknowledging that I speak in near solitude as a Boricua English professor in the States, this crisis renders the reconnaissance model of literary historical critique inadequate to the entire task of analyzing Latina narrative. I think this notion of intellectual guerrilla warfare in large public universities may still be effective, but it requires a constant—even dizzying—tactical flexibility and no small patience and skill navigating the surreal antinomies of academia. And lately, dwelling consciously in the academic underbelly, with fewer and often seriously wounded comrades, I feel not so much the need to insist on filling in the gaps of understanding between the margin and the center, but instead the pressure to theorize a certain discursive "unreality," to borrow Vine Deloria's (1969) concept, of actual Latina existence in print and elsewhere, along with a certain intransigent brutality at work in this rendering unreal.

That is, positing the layers of Latina oppression, the usual Richter scale or exponential effects of multiple, simultaneous disempowerment, is not enough; the sort of humanist premise that merely articulating our experiences, or moving from silence to speech, can begin to undo this disempowerment and dehumanization often fails, because we speak and speak and speak and, though we may get louder and more analytically astute, or call for backup, people around us do not care, refuse to listen, or, in public protest, simply have us incarcerated, most especially when we make perfect sense. I have witnessed this not only in academia, but at the grassroots political level as well. It is difficult to analyze this phenomenon as post-humanist, since the struggle for human status has never been completely successful for our communities, one of our post-Columbian legacies perhaps, being our tendency toward subhuman interpellation by the multiple, often transnational powers that be. Quite literally, it is unreal.

Thus, for the Latina critic, I see a set of mutually contradictory impossibilities rather than possibilities deriving from print articulation. For the moment, we might identify three of these in relation to publicly scripted Latina criticism: the impossibility of writing Latina feminism, the impossibility of not writing Latina feminism, and the impossibility of not writing, since writing itself, for feminist critics of color, proposes our only insurance against nihilism, our own bottomless pit of hope.[2]

Since the Feminism that prevails in academia today has managed to create a conceptually hegemonic claim to Truth on women, normed to an Anglo-American women's experience and collaborative agenda so clearly distinct from our own, Latina feminism is a contradiction in terms, a practical oxymoron. Speaking from this contradictory space renders the Latina feminist quite painfully global, local, and, ultimately, *loca en la boca,* transforming experience into an *escritura* both capable and incapable of "competing with food" in our mouths (Deleuze and Guattari 1986). Latina feminism (minus the institutional authority that the capital *F* implies) cannot help but be geopolitical (Saldívar-Hull 1991). It cannot help but be preoccupied (Zamudio-Taylor 1993). And considering, for example, Amalia Mesa-Baines's artwork or Susana Almanza's and Sylvia Herrera's environmental justice work, progressive Latina interventions cannot help but reterritorialize both physical and metaphysical fields in ways that cannot be analyzed exclusively as a discursive practice.

Loca-lizing theory is often construed as a hysterical project, since speaking to and from a collective, radicalized, and unapologetically Latina-centric *lengua y sitio* (tongue and location) (Pérez 1991) means upsetting the Feminist establishment, only, in the end, to be dismissed, forgotten, or plagiarized. This act is often self-referential, since the identity politics we are forced to play are often inescapably autobiographical (Chabram 1990). It is also often highly metaphorical and densely theoretical (Sandoval 1991) and sometimes simultaneously romantic, materialist, and meta-metaphysical (Anzaldúa 1987). Certain strains are passionately empirical (López 1994; Colón and Fabián 1995). Others are timely structural Marxist critiques of things like development, patriarchy, and colonialism (Acosta-Belén and Bose 1990). Yet there is a certain suspicion, intolerance, and, ugliest of all, indifference toward the repetition, multivalence, and virtuosity of this critical corpus, and toward the very problems that are motivating this realm of scholarship at its most urgent edges.

As it was for Sycorax, our first rebel icon, I would argue, for post-Columbian Caribeña feminist theory, the possibility of constitutive articulation as uncompromised historical agency is always already dead for American Indian and other subaltern feminists in the United States (Silko 1991). Or, as in the Chicana tradition, as Norma Alarcón avers, *la mestiza* (à La Malinche) cannot help but betray herself and her people as she speaks in the master's tongue, her monstrous doubling having everything to do with the historical (dis)articulation of women in Mexican nationalist discourse (Alarcón 1989). *Traducción es ya siempre traición*—translation is always already betrayal—for our intentionality (in English *or* Spanish) cannot *be*. But this is not because we blaspheme the (sexist) "Cause," but because we are betrayed by the communicative promise of language itself; that is, when we speak no one seems to know how to *listen*. We are thus not merely subsumed by existing discourse, but quite literally consumed by what I would like to propose is its *xanthagunephagic* (brown-woman-eating) logic. This creates a sort of communicative brutality I have discussed elsewhere, a discursive cannibalism that renders subaltern feminist articulation (almost) impossible in contemporary academic discourse (Sánchez González 1993–94).

This cannibalism, in concert with the publishing industry, has helped to center quite problematic versions of a mainland Puerto Rican feminist sensibility in books both popularly and academically advertized as Latina literature. Again, while I do not begrudge these writers' accomplishments as professional authors, the centering of their uncritical expressions of upward class mobility as representative texts for the community at large demands critical attention as a networked connection to xanthagunephagic technologies. In terms of Boricua literary history more specifically, as the previous chapters should indicate, this literary trend in the 1990s marks a clean break with the progressive and radical narrative politics characteristic of the Boricua feminist literary enterprise throughout the twentieth century.

In striking contrast with earlier writing by Boricua women—such as the work of Luisa Capetillo, Pura Belpré, Nicholasa Mohr, and others—these mainstreamed Latina feminist texts narrate personal experiences of the feminine condition to the near total exclusion of a collective predicament that entails growing problems with racism, poverty, reproductive rights, education, and colonial maldevelopment. As a metaphor, Puerto Rico and its diaspora collapse in these texts into a tropical dystopia from which women must seek refuge or permanent exile. This dystopic vision relies on stereotypical representations of island culture as definitively *machista* in implicit contrast with mainstream U.S. culture. In many ways, this work might be defined as a literature of mutual betrayal, not just between women of color and women of cash (if you will), or between women and men, but between the "Islands" and "America" as acts of signification. For the most part, a certain simplistic trope in these texts—the "Islands" (Puerto Rico)—represents outgrown, retrograde communal and family values, while in the final instance "America" (that is, any area of the mainland United States unpopulated by Boricuas) is celebrated as the utopia of the mature female protagonist's liberatory exile.

The imagined landscape of this liberation involves the projection of individual socioeconomic self-sufficiency, self-imposed or class-motivated exile from the Boricua community, and the rather uncanny ability to pack one's cultural baggage at will. When labeled and therefore authorized as Latina feminist texts, this solipsistic version of empowerment, however accurate it might be for particular women writers with particular experiences, performs in the public sphere as an outright denial of the structural inequalities—the severely restricted access to material, ideational, and institutional power—that the overwhelmingly working-class majority of Boricua women endure collectively as a colonial diasporan community (Benmayor, Torruellas, and Juarbe 1992; Cooney and Colón 1996). In the absence of other voices who would contradict them in actual demographic proportion, these mainstreamed women's texts harmonize with the culture of poverty theory's anthem—*I leik tu vee een A-may-ree-ka*—only this time in flawless English.[3]

Carmen de Monteflores's *Cantando bajito/Singing Softly* (1989), Judith Ortiz Cofer's *The Line of the Sun* (1989), and Esmeralda Santiago's *When I Was Puerto Rican* (1993) represent the widest span of these concerns, presenting the trials and tribulations of upper- , middle- , and lower-class female protagonists respectively. None of these texts portrays the gendered subject's transition to an uncomplicated "American" social location as painless; in fact, all three texts portray this process as a traumatic endeavor to leave behind personal and familial legacies that simultaneously represent home and estrangement, belonging and ostracism, love and brutality. But this trauma is portrayed in a certain romantic register that ultimately proposes alienation as both a symptom *and* cure for the protagonists' disaffection with their cultural legacies. Each of these three texts thus attempts to come to terms with a feminine Puerto Rican diasporan legacy by rejecting it, in the final instance, as obsolete. The issue of coming to consciousness as sexual beings underscores the three texts, as the protagonists identify the source of Puerto Rican women's oppression in intimate relationships whose broader historical contexts are either absent or so highly encoded that the average reader will not ascertain them. To foil her exceptional intelligence and, consequently, her natural adaptability or predisposition to mainstream American values, each protagonist is also surrounded in her childhood by martyred, ignorant, lascivious, alcoholic, backward, or otherwise unidimensional adult Puerto Rican and Bori-cua characters who cannot see beyond, and therefore transcend, their dysfunctional culture. In this, predictably perhaps, the protagonists' respective class identifications further complicate matters.

Monteflores's novel traces the process of this alienation by a multiple "*streams* of consciousness" narrative that explores why the protagonist, Meli, simultaneously resists and insists on returning—both literally and figuratively—to Puerto Rico and the pathology it signifies for her. The novel thus charts the narrator's flight to the main island, a flight that transforms into a historical journey traversing three generations of psychologically tortured women in Meli's family. These women's emotional trials bleed from one character into the next, forming clusters of at times indistinguishable female voices. Monteflores depicts the collective intergenerational plight/flight with sudden temporal and narrative shifts. Passages in Puerto Rican vernacular Spanish are immediately spliced with standard English translations. Time in the present is suspended and time in the past is measured by a certain transgenerational longing among the family's women, who wait interminably for their husbands and fathers to come home.

Throughout the text, this longing and waiting surface as Meli's emotionally charged recollection of a certain definitive feminine alienation in her family's history. The suspension of both time and place lent by the flight helps situate the isolated subject in a kind of sociohistorical limbo. When the plane actually lands at the very end of the novel, Meli emerges out of San Juan's Muñoz Marín airport into an otherworldly place populated by the "ghosts" and "ugliness" of her past (197). What Meli ostensibly hopes to—but cannot—recuperate is suggested on the author's dedication page, which introduces the novel as "a piece of the land we had lost." Thus the novel proposes itself as a figurative recuperation of a lost personal inheritance, a *terruño* denied an elite female protagonist. Paralleling her lost inheritance, and as if in poetic retaliation, the island itself in the text becomes a mere figment of Meli's haunted imagination.

Monteflores ultimately explains that the land Meli lost is her literal patrimony; she is the granddaughter of a wealthy Spanish merchant who lived with her grandmother as her common-law husband. Reclaiming this patrimony—ironically recuperated via women—constitutes a type of masculine authority, of ownership ultimately, and with it a sort of textual sense of female primogeniture. In this fictional recuperation of her inheritance, the text never directly confronts the Spanish plantation economy's disintegration and the rise of mercantilism in Puerto Rican history in the realist fashion of Mohr's or Thomas's fiction, nor does Monteflores's feminist agenda erupt in the polemical passion of Luisa Capetillo's prose. Instead, Meli's disinheritance as a granddaughter of a wealthy Spaniard defines her transhistorical quest and poses as the primordial cause of each dysfunctional relationship in her mother's, aunts', and grandmother's lives.

The machismo that perpetually triggers this dysfunction begins with the story of Meli's grandmother, Pilar, whose common-law husband does not love or care for her properly. Apparently overwhelmed with adolescent desire, Pilar, a young peasant woman who (unlike her mother and sister) can pass for white in their rural town, abandons her family to live with a Spanish colonist named Juan. Pilar elopes with Juan despite the consequences; she knows that her parents will disapprove of her legally unsanctioned marriage, that she will be ostracized by Juan's family (for although she is light-skinned, she is still not of their caste), and that living with him means her own family will never be allowed in their house (poor Black folk being unwelcome guests in Spanish homes). But apparently Pilar is undaunted by this guaranteed isolation from any extended family. Rather, Juan's long business trips abroad represent Pilar's immediate source of suffering after their marriage. The narrator describes Pilar as a victim of her love and desire for Juan; even though the relationship is emotionally unsatisfying, she craves his companionship and their lovemaking. Monteflores avers that Pilar cannot name (and therefore escape) the real source of her torment, and instead waits patiently for Juan to return while blaming herself for her distress:

> Pilar slipped into her nightgown. The one Juan liked most. She wore it when she missed him.
>
> He always brought her presents. She didn't want presents. Her dresser and wardrobe closet were full of them. She wanted him.
>
> But she couldn't say anything. She was so happy to see him she forgot she had been sad. When he was home she forgot nearly everything else.
>
> It must be her fault too that the children couldn't talk to him. She wanted him all to herself when he was there.
>
> She had been selfish, she thought as she turned off the kerosene lamp and slipped under the mosquito netting (Monteflores 1989: 43–44).

Pilar's scattered thoughts, like those of a dimestore romance heroine, pivot around her desire for Juan, a character who embodies virtually nothing more than her misguided affections. Her sensual pleasure is defined by her projection of her partner's pleasure, evident in the way she wears Juan's favorite piece of lingerie in order to assuage her longing for him. Moreover, the reason "she can't say anything" in her defense when he does occasionally return is her dependency on him, not merely as a provider (she lives well enough even during his absences), but as her lover and as the father of her children. And while Juan and Pilar apparently share a mutual sexual attraction, the text seems to suggest that Juan's affection is not nearly as consistent or intensely felt as Pilar's, and that in fact he may have a fiancée on another island. But rather than making her needs an issue, Pilar internalizes the blame for her own emotional suffering. Her children's alienation from their father "must be her fault too," she says, attributing all responsibility for the family's problems to her own "selfishness."

The economic and social stratification bearing on women's lives in fin-de-siècle Puerto Rico is absent in the text. Instead of depicting Juan and Pilar as emblematic characters of this complicated sociohistorical milieu, Monteflores again squarely attributes the couple's problems to misguided love and lust. Pilar, wanting her husband more than she feels she needs his wealth, is a victim of her own desires, including her desire for his more permanent residence in their home, which is never satisfied. Before Juan fulfills his promise to legally marry Pilar and settle down with her and their children, he dies during one of his trips, leaving Pilar and her children without legal entitlement to his lands and fortune. Pilar's daughter Luisa consequently resents both her parents for her precarious socioeconomic position, which erupts in her aspiration to reject her mother's role as a victim and to assume her father's role as a landowner:

> [Pilar:] "[E]h que tengo miedo que vayah a parar como tanta gente pobre por ahí. Yo sé que te vah a casar y Dioh quiera que te salga bueno el hombre. Como Juan. Pero si no. . . ." *It's just that I'm afraid you're going to end up like so many poor people around. I know you're going to get married and I hope he turns out to be a good man. Like Juan. But if not. . . .*
>
> "Yo no me voy a casar." *I'm not going to get married*, Luisa muttered stubbornly, still looking down at her plate.
>
> "Eso lo diceh ahora, pero dehpuéh . . . ya tú vah a ver, cuando empiecen a andar loh muchachoh detráh de tí." *That's what you say now, but later . . . you'll see when boys start to chase after you.*
>
> Luisa shook her head while still looking down.
>
> "Yo no quiero que mi marido me deje sola mientrah él va de viajeh. Yo quiero una finca." *I don't want my husband to leave me by myself while he goes on trips. I want a farm.* (69–70)

Pilar expects that Luisa will find a man whom she loves with the intensity of her own misguided devotion to Juan, who courted her in the way she describes her daughter's suitors soon will. But it is precisely this unerring devotion that Luisa feels is at the root of her mother's victimization, and Luisa does not want to fall into the same trap, to be left waiting, hurting, and dependent like her mother "mientrah él va de viajeh." In Luisa's mind, owning land poses a better alternative, and the text avers that she will devote herself to farming as soon as she inherits the title to her father's property. But Luisa's ambition is dashed when the narrator reveals that Juan's family destroyed his letter promising to wed Pilar on his return. In order to pass the inheritance on to another male relative, Juan's family also destroyed his final testament, which left the house and surrounding land to Pilar and her children.

Later in the novel, when Pilar's daughters convene as adults to discuss contesting their grandfather's will in court, the text implies that Juan should have legitimated Pilar as his wife and her children as his heirs, posing wealth and property again as a final solution to the daughters' many problems. However, by this time the family has become entrenched in the professional middle class and, fearing the public scrutiny of a legal battle, Pilar's daughters prefer to keep their illegitimacy a family secret (173–75). The many changes that occur in Puerto

Rico's legal system and colonial status during the turn of the century are never broached as the family's context, nor the subsequent historical and economic shifts that would have contextualized the second and third generation's transition from landless, "illegitimate" *criollos* (Island-born Spaniards) to Puerto Rico's professional classes. All of these broader issues are completely omitted from the novel. In their stead, a lingering resentment pivots around Pilar and Juan's romantic liaison, especially Juan's irresponsibility as a husband and father. Importantly, Pilar's Black family ties utterly disappear, though a stereotypical Black *curandera* (healer or witch) figure, "Seña Alba," hovers inexplicably, protectively, and sometimes drunkenly around Pilar for her entire life.

Although Luisa vows to avoid marriage because of its inescapably damaging effects on women in her family, she somehow ends up becoming another version of Pilar, only lacking Pilar's naïveté. Overall, Luisa is represented as a casebook study of clinical depression. Traumatized at the age of twelve when she witnesses a girl's rape (163–64), unhappily married to an emotionally abusive husband, and incapable of relating to her own daughter, Luisa is a chronically depressed character who has more or less lost her grip on reality. Luisa's daughter Meli becomes the resentful witness to her mother's suffering, perpetuating the cycle of misery that Luisa once planned to break as a younger woman. Almost word for word Meli reiterates Luisa's rage against her father:

> "¡Yo no voy a ser como mami! ¡Sentada ahí ehperando que tú vengah! ¡Yo nunca voy a ser como ella!" *I'm not going to be like mami! Sitting there waiting for you to come! I'm never going to be like her!* (160–61)

Again the cause of this anger is the uncaring husband/father, whose unidimensional characterization is basically a repository for blame and resentment. But the difference here is that Meli actually confronts her father, and by the end of the text the reader is alerted to the fact that she has successfully escaped the intergenerational cycle of psychological abuse by going on her own interminable "viajeh."

That is, we learn at the end of the novel that Meli has left Puerto Rico and is narrating her family story on a flight. The teenage Meli went to art school in the United States in what seems to have been a well-financed, self-imposed exile. Unlike Nicholasa Mohr's and Luisa Capetillo's fiction, here art is not that imaginative terrain where the artist comes to grips with her situation and creatively conceptualizes collective change. Rather, for Meli, art as a discipline of study becomes a vehicle of escape that is unhindered by such mundane concerns as money or the oppression of working-class women and their children. The life Meli saves is thus literally her own.

Meli's motive for returning to Puerto Rico is to visit her grandmother's deathbed, but when the plane touches ground she intuits that Pilar has already passed on. When she debarks, Puerto Rico is portrayed as the "ruins" of her past:

> When I arrived at the airport I realized how long I had been gone. I felt like a tourist in my own past: arriving by plane, in the morning dampness which clings to the skin. The cement defeated by rain. Becoming mold. Becoming ruins to be looked at.
>
> In my body I knew already she had died. (132)

Pilar's death signals the end of the narrator's access to the main informant of her family history, and Meli buries Puerto Rico's significance as a living legacy with her grandmother. She now describes herself as a character like the North American tourists who visit the Islands as strangers, while Puerto Rico is narrated as nothing more than "dampness," "mold," "ruins," and "defeat." Monteflores closes the novel with Meli's sense of being "outside of time," somewhere "[s]uspended between sky and sea, between past and future," "[b]etween worlds" (197). This is her home, which can only be comfortably made away from Puerto Rican signification. Yet this home is equally devoid of Boricua signification as well. No doubt Meli flies first-class. And what, after all, is the cultural space of a first-class cabin en route to San Juan from the States? Thus apparently alienated on all cultural fronts, but comfortably sitting in the front row of the plane, the disinherited (yet wealthy) *criolla* exile visits the Islands as a tourist, and takes home with her a metaphorical "piece of land" as a virtual souvenir representing the failed romance and decline of Puerto Rico's Spanish colonial past.

While *Cantando bajito/Singing Softly* perhaps offers itself up for a Puerto Rican feminist critique of Spanish colonialism, such a critique would require the teasing out of allegorical subtexts that the novel arguably does not intimate. At best, the feminine issues that surface in the novel may suggest the relative unimportance of colonialism in wealthier Puerto Rican women's lives today, the particular forms of sexism at work in the formation of Puerto Rico's upper-middle classes and wealthier women's collusion with this sexism during the Spanish colonial era. Ironically perhaps, bogged down by its racist subtexts and solipsistic Euro-*criolla* logic, the novel also mirrors key discursive elements of Puerto Rico's myths of national formation. However, the unspoken center of the novel is the United States; as Meli's tacitly articulated home away from the Islands and their realms of signification, the United States represents the uncomplicated site of her liberatory exile.

Judith Ortiz Cofer's novel *The Line of the Sun* also interrogates the ghosts of a Puerto Rican past in order to make sense of the emigrant female protagonist's relative comfort and security in the present. However, Ortiz Cofer's narrative is less a story of disinheritance than one of what we might call *re/creation,* or recreational re-creation. While her collection of essays, *Silent Dancing* (1990), offers what could be read as a feminist theorization of storytelling and family history, Ortiz Cofer's novel presents the past as something that can be revisited and revised simply for pleasure. *The Line of the Sun* therefore reads as a re/creational narrative of the author's family history, the composition of which provides the author with what she explains at the end of the novel as a commodity she can "trade" in North America for what she "want[s] out of life" (1989: 283).

The Line of the Sun is a composite of two narratives. The first half of the text is the story of the near mythical hero Guzmán, a sort of trickster figure whose misadventures as a young man in Puerto Rico are narrated in a series of picaresque episodes. Guzmán is the family "troublemaker," the wayward child whose life begins with an agonized pregnancy that, in rather tidy poetic form, foreshadows his perpetual friction with the world around him. This character is a narrative device for presenting an ersatz sketch of small town life in Puerto Rico during the 1940s, and his misadventures enable the author to present and test the social mores of his sociocultural milieu. As a trickster, Guzmán is foiled by the unidimensional characters around him: his sister Ramona, who is forced to stay home and take care of the house and younger children; his brother, who enlists in the U.S. armed services and is killed in the Korean War; his father, who is a bookish recluse; his mother, whose only role is as his constantly worried protector/antagonist; and his best friend, the troubled son of an abusive overseer in the town's sugar refinery. All the surrounding characters provide the mundane setting against which Guzmán's wild exploits seem colorful, romantic, and exciting.

These exploits portray Guzmán as an inexplicably wild character who spurs the desires of a set of odd townswomen who can apparently match his passion but not his manly freedom to express it. The first and most important of these women is the curandera Rosa. Like Monteflores's depiction of Seña Alba, the curandera figure in Ortiz Cofer's text is stereotypically and moralistically defined by her excesses and turpitude; Rosa, also known as La Cabra or "She-goat" in the novel, is a whore. Initially, Guzmán's mother sends him to Rosa to be "cured" of his wanton ways, but Rosa apparently seduces him instead. She then becomes Guzmán's "true love," the focus of his life's dreams, with whom he decides to live as a young adult. Rosa accepts him into her idyllic home (replete with a moat) in a secluded valley on the edge of town. But the local "authorities"—namely, the bourgeois matrons of the Catholic Rosary Society—run Rosa out of town by threatening to tell her daughter (whom Rosa has sent away to a convent school) that her mother is a prostitute. Thus Rosa disappears, and with her the potential fairy tale ending of Guzmán's life.

The rest of the first half of the text introduces the other women in Guzmán's career as a young lover, all of whom see in him the masculine complement to their own independent spirit. But at the novel's midpoint, as Guzmán's story seems just about to elaborate his departure for the United States, the narration shifts to his sister Ramona's story, and the "I" of the text emerges with a new narrator, Ramona's daughter Marisol. Abruptly, the story becomes what seems at first to be a digression into the woman's world that Guzmán never fully enters. However, the narrative soon evolves into yet another plot when Ramona marries Guzmán's best friend and they begin a family whose home is Paterson, New Jersey.

If the first half of *The Line of the Sun* is a fairy tale rendition of Marisol's Island heritage, the remainder of the novel exposes the protagonist's disenchantment with this heritage. Marisol's sexual coming to consciousness drives the remaining text, and like the women in Monteflores's novel both she and her mother clock their lives by waiting for the absent patriarch to return home from his many long trips abroad. This sudden midpoint plot shift seems a bit forced in the novel, as if two texts—a series of trickster tales and a *bildungsroman*—are being artificially spliced together. As the bildungsroman begins, Ramona's story is likewise pushed to the margin to make room for the narrator's autobiographical concerns. Here we learn that Marisol's father is a member of the U.S. armed forces, employment that gives his family financial security but sends him out of their lives for months at a time. But unlike the wives and daughters in *Cantando bajito*, Ramona does not seem to mind her husband's extended absences from home as much as Marisol does. Marisol's longing for her father's presence is exacerbated by the shame she feels for her mother's "dark beauty" and lively *jíbara* (hillbilly) ways in public, which are narrated in sharp contrast with her father's introversion and white North American cultural affinities.

Marisol eventually explains that the stories woven into the first half of the novel are her own imaginative re/creations of her mother's, father's, and uncle's childhoods. The plot finally merges the two narratives when Guzmán arrives to stay with his sister's family in New Jersey. At first thrilled to have the trickster character of her imagination at hand, Marisol slowly realizes that her uncle is less than the heroic character onto which she had projected the magic and mystique of Puerto Rico. Once in Paterson, Guzmán is shortly stabbed in a mysterious disagreement, and his convalescence enables Marisol to ask him about his life, to have him narrate for her what she had already constructed as a series of fairy tales. But hearing Guzmán tell his own story makes Marisol feel sorry for herself:

> Talking with my uncle, listening to stories about his life on the Island, and hearing Ramona's constant rhapsodizing about that tropical paradise—all conspired to make me feel deprived. I should have grown up there. I should have been able to play in emerald-green pastures, to eat sweet bananas right off the trees, to learn about life from the women who were strong and wise. (222)

Soon disappointed with the actual Guzmán, she feels "deprived" of the romantic and nostalgic possibilities he once represented for her, which in turn creates a sort of diasporically marked ambivalence in the narrative; on the one hand, Marisol somewhat realizes that the Puerto Rico she created in her imagination was mythic, and that her ideas about Puerto Rico were romanticized musings, but on the other hand, she *still* resents the presence of the other Puerto Ricans in her neighborhood, the deflated characters of everyday life, if you will, whom she considers noisy, violent, superstitious, and parodic in their customs.

In other words, Marisol cannot reconcile herself within any positive conceptualization of the diaspora, and thus relentlessly clings to an illusory myth of Puerto Rico as an enchanted island. Living in "El Building," an apartment complex that portrays the collective experience of Paterson's lower-income Boricua population, Marisol explains that she resents the way people around her perform an unauthentic "parody" of Puerto Rican culture. On her way to the market, Marisol explains,

> I put on my coat and left the apartment. The smells of beans boiling in a dozen kitchens assailed my nostrils. Rice and beans, the unimaginative staple food of all these people who re-created every day the same routines they had followed in their mamá's [*sic*] houses so long ago. Except that here in Paterson, in the cold rooms stories above the frozen ground, the smells and sounds of a lost way of life could only be a parody. (223)

Considering herself forced to make a choice between "parody" and romantic re/creations, Marisol opts for the latter.

Consequently Marisol's character is alienated, not only from the families around her in El Building and the white North American children at the private school she attends, but also from the romantic trappings of Puerto Rico she has carefully crafted and guarded in her imagination. There are certain events that she can use as material for spectacularizing her own life—the fire in El Building, for example, or the trips to her grandmother's house in Puerto Rico—but ultimately Marisol is left to re/create for herself an imaginary and colorful little island only tangentially related to her family's actual history. Preferring the fantasy of her books to interaction with her peers, at a young age Marisol retreats from the world emerging around her and finds refuge in rewriting her Puerto Rican heritage in exotic and tantalizing ways.

The impact of this alienation and the force of this imaginary refuge are soon evident in the text when Marisol's memories of El Building are buried in its ashes and Guzmán, now a crippled and deflated character, returns to Puerto Rico:

> This broken man taking one step at a time into the belly of the airplane had little to do with the wild boy I had created in my imagination, but I loved him too. He was a good man and brave, even if finally not the hero of my myth. In a way I was glad that he would no longer be around to confuse me. He and El Building would be gone but not forgotten. (282)

Thus Marisol is freed from Guzmán's "confusing" influence and the demystification of Puerto Rico he represents as well as the intrusive presence of the other Boricuas in El Building. Importantly, although she loves her uncle, "in a way" he disappoints her, and she is "glad" he leaves.

Guzmán's departure sets the stage for Marisol's ultimate exile from her community in the States as well. When her father returns from his next military tour, he buys a house in an apparently segregated section of the city's suburbs while her mother is on a visit to Puerto Rico. Marisol helps her father decorate their new home in what she considers "the best middle-class American taste." In this, Marisol enjoys her role as her father's surrogate partner, sharing and decorating their new home with him, but when Ramona returns she intrudes on Marisol's new suburban fantasy:

> With the help of a Sears catalogue, we had color-coordinated everything: curtains, sheets, throw rugs, and cushions matched in the best middle-class American taste. Though it was a pleasure for me to set up this house in the soothing hues that appealed to my father and me, I had a feeling that Ramona would feel like a stranger in it. . . .
>
> So it was with mixed feelings that I dusted and polished everything and opened windows . . . the day Mother came home. Rafael pulled up in the driveway in the rented car, and when she stepped out, I could see that she was darker, her cinnamon skin several shades deeper. . . . She wore sandals and carried a shopping bag. To our neighbors . . . she must have looked like a new immigrant. Though she was lovelier than ever, it hurt me to see how easily Ramona had given herself back to the Island. (283–84)

When Ramona returns to live in their new house as the proverbial (tropical) bird in a gilded cage, the narrative suggests that Ramona and her dark tan have become threats to Marisol's "pleasure." The narrative also avers that, as long as Ramona is not present, Marisol feels that she and her father might successfully aspire to the suburban white middle-class ideal, which would ostensibly compel her father to stay home more often. Why else would her mother's dark beauty "hurt" Marisol, if not because she is ashamed of what might be construed as her mother's racial difference, and because she is worried about losing her father's attention and affection?

Ultimately, the silence, isolation, and cultural homogeneity of the suburbs are a relief for Marisol, who takes up residence in an attic room where she can finally read and be at peace with herself and her imagination. Marisol's alienation thus ultimately fulfills the formula of American success and assimilation. The novel's conclusion also provides an explication of the role of her fiction, which is to make history enchanting, romantic, beautiful, and unreal. This irreality is foregrounded in the epilogue, in which Marisol picks up the story of Guzmán back in Puerto Rico, imagining him married to Rosa "La Cabra's" daughter in a tight, fairy tale ending. But she admits that "Guzmán's story did not end happily at the altar as all good fairy tales and love stories should," so she contrived a "lie" that would lend the story a happy ending (290–91).

Overall, while the colonial history concomitant with the period covered in Ortiz Cofer's novel is occasionally (albeit faintly) discernible in the text—the enlistment of Puerto Rican men during the Korean War, the Cuban "Missile Crisis," and the advent of television are a few examples—the significance of this history is preempted by a portrait of the artist as a young woman, whose emergence as a storyteller in the second half of the text is more or less the dissection of the third-person narrator guiding the first half. Although the narrative techniques here are sometimes interesting and the stories are often entertaining, the novel tends toward the solipsistic and indulges a problematic (internalized) racism-sexism in the exoticized and racialized depiction of cultural difference among emigrant Puerto Rican women (Ramona) and the Boricua community at large (El Building).

However, as I shall elaborate below, Ortiz Cofer's self-conscious discussion of her romanticizing impulses in the novel's epilogue is perhaps a subtle hint to the reader that the text's meanings are mythical in direct proportion to the realities they mask. That is, Marisol's seemingly simple assimilation—her willful estrangement from her community, her economic upward mobility, her teenage transition from conflicted "Other" to uncomplicated "Woman" (minus sociohistoric adjectives)—might also be construed as a fairy tale. Perhaps Ortiz Cofer, true to her own prescriptions, purposely suppresses the more complicated endings that might also be pertinent to stories contrived from her family history. But all her published monographs return, in a similar fashion, to the same autobiographical material and diasporan angst, leaving the impression that the re/creational story of Marisol's life and her problematic perspective of her Puerto Rican heritage will remain the author's recurring thematic material (Ortiz Cofer 1990, 1993, 1995, 1998).

The final novel in this vein is Esmeralda Santiago's *When I Was Puerto Rican*. This text—aggressively marketed as a memoir—reads, I would argue, more like a realist novel. Like Monteflores's and Ortiz Cofer's work, Santiago's major themes revolve around intergenerational female bonds, the meandering patriarch, and the young female protagonist's alienation and sexual coming to consciousness. However, Santiago's text overtly depicts the confluences of poverty, colonial maldevelopment, and gendered oppression—particularly the feminization of poverty in Puerto Rico—as mutually determining forces for both Boricua and Puerto Rican women. In a way, this narrative reads as an antithesis of the *bildungs*-romantic urges evident in both *Cantando bajito* and *The Line of the Sun,* especially in the ways the individualistic Puerto Rican female subjects in Monteflores's and Ortiz Cofer's texts are comfortably and conclusively situated in the existing social order. Within the integral body of the novel, Santiago's protagonist, Negi, on the other hand, never quite finds this comfortable fit. However, like Ortiz Cofer's subtle subversion at the end of *The Line of the Sun*, Santiago's epilogue effectively upends the novel's implicit critique of colonial racism-sexism in its closing pages.[4]

While Santiago's novel may compromise the blatant rejection of Puerto Rican and Boricua signification so clearly evident in Monteflores's and Ortiz Cofer's narrative strategies, her writing is also more innovative. *When I Was Puerto Rican* plays with Puerto Rican orature—music, lyrics, and *refranes* as well as a culturally specific articulation of humor in engaging and provocative ways. Although some moments of the text are perhaps giddy, none are exactly flippant in tone, nor is the novel utterly reductive of the complex history surrounding the protagonist's childhood.

When I Was Puerto Rican narrates the success story of a working-class child nicknamed Negi who, through luck, hard work, and determination, "makes it" in the United States. Like Monteflores's novel, a good part of Santiago's representation of Puerto Rico revolves around the perpetually absent father, whose adulterous liaisons cause her mother no end of frustration and emotional agony. Yet unlike the all-suffering martyr Pilar, Negi's mother refuses to tolerate her husband's "viajes," and retaliates by taking her children from their home on a number of her own trips to live with other families in the capital. Negi's parents, however, keep renegotiating their relationship. This constant moving away and returning home makes Negi skeptical of romance, and, like Luisa and Meli in *Cantando bajito,* she decides never to be a victim, like her mother, of marriage:

> It seemed to me . . . that remaining *jamona* [spinster] could not possibly hurt this much. That a woman alone, even if ugly, could not suffer as much as my beautiful mother did. I hated Papi. . . . I would just as soon remain *jamona* than shed that many tears over a man. (Santiago 1993: 104)

The empathetic relationship between Negi and her mother builds as her mother's suffering increases, but the juxtaposition of this episode with the next segment, entitled "Mami Goes to Work," intimates that the final cure for her mother's pain is self-sufficiency. Unlike the story of Meli's mother and grandmother, Negi and her mother literally cannot afford to wait around for the patriarchal figure to return home. Thus Negi's hope of breaking the intergenerational feminine cycle of longing is realized early in the text, when her mother enters the workforce and then shortly after decides to leave her husband behind in order to start a new life for herself and her children in New York.

As soon as Negi's mother strikes out on her own, becoming the first woman in her rural town to secure a factory job, it becomes clear that her newly won economic freedom will set the stage for the final break with her partner. Although her job causes a sensation among the neighborhood gossips, Negi's mother persists in her employment, despite the fact that tending to her family's needs before and after a full day's work is a tremendous labor. The money she earns helps the family afford more basic necessities, but her husband resents her success. In Negi's words,

> Papi seemed to have the same opinion about Mami's job as the neighbors. He looked at her with a puzzled expression, and several times I heard her defend herself: "If it weren't for the money I bring in, we'd still be living like savages." He'd withdraw to his hammers and nails, to the mysterious books in his dresser, to the newspapers and magazines he brought home rolled up in his wooden box. (123)

At this point in the narrative, Negi's father arrives less frequently, ostensibly intimidated by his wife's wages and threatened by the independence these wages imply. As the oldest daughter, Negi must therefore help out as surrogate parent while her mother is at work. Even though she is somewhat resentful of the chore, her sympathy lies with her mother's effort to make life more comfortable.

Released from the pressures of a generally miserable marriage, and free to do more of what she pleases with her income, Negi's mother begins to travel regularly to New York on visits to relatives there and to seek treatment for her youngest child's ailing foot. While Negi's mother flies back and forth to New York preparing for what will be the final move, Negi is left to her own devices while making sense of the apparently unhappy condition of heterosexual desire on the Islands. The most accessible hints for understanding this complicated phenomenon come at first from the songs she hears on the radio, which complement the scene in her home:

> I will not forgive you again.
> I've closed my heart.
> It is useless to cry.
> It is useless to call.
> I will never forgive you.

> The jukebox blared the lover's troubles. His voice cracked a little when he sang that his heart was closed. But no matter how final he meant it to sound, eventually he would forgive his woman, and they would go on living, loving, and fighting. Just like Mami and Papi. (155)

Indeed, popular music is a handy alternative text for Negi's understanding of the world, since the family has moved into a room behind a bar in Santurce. Her parents do "go on living, loving, and fighting," but after each reconciliation her mother is left at home in cramped quarters, taking what odd jobs she can to get by while her common-law husband reverts to his carousing. Negi contrasts her parents' behavior with the radio *novelas* (soap operas) to which she regularly listens, which star men and women who live tortured but ultimately fulfilling lives according to the usual formulas. Inspired by these romantic tales, Negi creates her own renditions of such stories to help herself forget the bitter and more frequent fights between her parents.

As Negi's understanding of love and its effects emerges in the novel, so does the history of U.S. colonization. With more definite strokes than Ortiz Cofer, Santiago depicts the effects of colonialism in Puerto Rico, including the political corruption among the Islands' elite, which forms the context of her protagonist's childhood. The first signal of this historical backdrop is suggested with Negi's mother's factory job. Attracting U.S. corporations to Puerto Rico was the main planning priority for the industrialization project Operation Bootstrap which began in the 1940s, and the bra factory where Negi's mother works alludes to this project.[5] Likewise the English classes Negi suffers at school, forced by the U.S. mandate of bilingual education in Puerto Rico, illustrates the colonial imposition of English in the classroom. The various homes her family inhabits around the Islands also allude to the migration of rural families in search of scarce employment, while the rise of the tourist industry, the infrastructural development for facilitating industrial growth (such as bringing roads and electricity to the rural regions where factories would be built), and the free school breakfasts (*Americano* style—powdered milk and eggs, and sausages that taste like "cardboard"—which are of course suspended once the insular elections are over) all portray how U.S. colonialism evolved in Puerto Rico during the 1950s and 1960s (63–83).

The novel's elaboration of colonialism in Puerto Rico shifts to the metropole when Negi's mother makes the final decision to leave her husband for good by moving with her children to New York City. Once there, her mother finds another job in yet another bra factory, reflecting the continuation of the working-class colonial predicament as it was played out in the States: the continued exploitation of female labor, the same or worse living conditions, and the hostile way that English as a second language is taught in New York's public schools. At the same time, Negi's talents as a storyteller emerge with her determination to learn English well enough to get to the top of her class. Resentful of the "dumbbell" classes to which she is assigned because of her native Spanish, she hits the books with a fervor similar to that of Ortiz Cofer's protagonist. But unlike Marisol's private pleasure writing and reading fairy tales, Negi assumes the role of a bard whose stories keep her and her family entertained, transforming their cold and crowded Brooklyn apartment into the scene of magical adventures:

> The room looked larger when we were all together like this, leaning toward the warmth. The walls seemed higher and steeper, the ceilings further away, the sounds of the city, its constant roar, disappeared. . . . Brooklyn became just a memory as I led them to distant lands where palaces shimmered against desert sand and paupers became princes with the whush of a magic wand.
>
> Every night that first winter we gathered in the kitchen around the oven door, and I embellished fairy tales in which the main characters were named after my sisters and brothers, who, no matter how big the odds, always triumphed and always went on to live happily ever after. (235–36)

Their apartment is thus transformed, appearing much larger than before, while Negi tells her siblings and other relatives stories that help them imagine themselves as heroes and heroines someplace far away from their struggle to survive in Brooklyn and the oven around which they convene for warmth. The magic "whush" is Negi's skill as a storyteller, which is enhanced by the books she voraciously reads in the effort to master English.

Akin to Nilda's "secret garden," Negi's stories help to alleviate the despair that daily threatens to surface for her family in the United States. In contrast to the happy ending of Negi's fairy tales, however, her mother's life in New York turns out to be a continuation of the exploitation and emotional suffering she underwent in Puerto Rico: she works long hours, falls in love, and becomes pregnant, only to lose her new partner to cancer (243–44). Life has not really improved much for her mother in New York City, and Negi explains how fearful she is that "whatever Mami had been looking for when she brought us to Brooklyn was not there, just as it wasn't in Puerto Rico" (247). Thus, unlike Ortiz Cofer's fairy tale prescription for forgetting the past, Santiago's protagonist confronts and represents the unhappy endings in dual national contexts that for many women, unfortunately, closely reflect the colonial diasporan experience.

The hope in the text is thus projected onto Negi, whose tenacity (and audacity) in public school lands her enrollment in New York City's prestigious High School for the Performing Arts despite what she narrates as a flawed performance in her audition. The novel ends with the teenage Negi dreaming of an illustrious career that will make her somehow famous, with hints to the reader that she is exaggerating her potential. The integral body of the text concludes with this dream as yet unfulfilled; Negi has, through luck and hard work, found herself in a privileged position from which she may transform many more lives with her art, but we never hear of how or whether such transformations will happen. In subtle ways, the closure of her narrative suggests that the protagonist, like Nicholasa Mohr's Nilda, may be able to reshape the world around her by revising it with her creative talents, not only for herself but for others as well. But like Ortiz Cofer's and Monteflores's texts, Santiago's book abruptly shifts in its ultimate moment—here, in the epilogue—with the protagonist's Harvard scholarship. The epilogue is a quick tally of Negi's subsequent personal successes, once more suggesting that the life this protagonist saves is exclusively her own. The novel's closure also gives hints to the title; ostensibly, Negi "was Puerto Rican" as a semiliterate child living in a dank Brooklyn apartment, but once she escapes this poverty and earns an Ivy League degree, she becomes something else. And if no longer Puerto Rican or Boricua, what is she in the present tense?

Cantando bajito, The Line of the Sun, and *When I Was Puerto Rican* each exploit the author's Puerto Rican heritage as dystopic historical dreamwork, while simultaneously and aggressively embracing assimilationist tenets of the "American dream," whereby the colonial female protagonist will be able to undo her alienation in and exile to the metropole by claiming authorial intentionality over herself and her highly personalized life story via the written word. The Feminist trappings in this corpus are compelling; it is, however, the absence of an ethical imperative expressed by the pronominal split between the "I" and the "we" that has aggravated—even angered—so many Boricua feminists.[6] Why? Because representing Puerto Rican women as fragile, wounded children tormented by their Puerto Rican fathers' and grandfathers' abandonment or their mothers' and grandmothers' dysfunctional relationships with these men, or as ambitious fairy tale and romance writers, or as disingenuously assimilating youths, all of whom find contentment in their all but automatic stateside socioeconomic freedom, tends to satisfy a certain hegemonic thirst (and market demand) for the subaltern woman's acceptance—even celebration—of colonial paternalism.

Crucially, however, as much as they fail as Boricua feminist allegories, these texts do suggest a new category of textual and sexual politics worth analyzing. When we read them precisely *as failed allegories,* we see how these texts undermine their own authority in ways that mainstream public and feminist audiences in the United States may not perceive. That is, none of these novels' protagonists ever really confronts the possibilities and complications of the present; rather, they are literally transfixed in the clouds, consciously mythologizing, or quite obviously tacking on happy endings, as Monteflores, Ortiz Cofer, and Santiago respectively make evident in the closing moments of their novels. Consequently, although these texts posit the female Boricua or Puerto Rican subject as a willfully assimilating exile who yearns for and simultaneously rejects a nostalgic past, they also emphasize the Kafkaesque underpinnings of their American success stories when each character's ruggedly individualistic intentionality is rendered fantastic, albeit subtly, at the very last moment in each text.

Perhaps these self-subversions can be read as Sycoraxean traces—the reviled (m)Other invoking herself out of death and, ambiguously, as all spirits do, hexing the text. Or perhaps this desire to find a Sycoraxean subversion is willful thinking. From a Boricua feminist perspective, *Cantando bajito, The Line of the Sun,* and *When I Was Puerto Rican* are very *esneaky* texts, too *esneaky* perhaps. They also articulate far too many internally racist-sexist attitudes to speak progressively and productively as allegories for the community at large. This genre of

Boricua women's literature offers a quasi-autobiographical rendition of a tiny minority of women within the colonial diaspora for whom economic upward mobility has been possible. But in the public sphere these texts also represent the conscription of Boricua narrative into the ranks of North America's literary mainstream as utterances that speak from the margin only to validate its center. In the absence of other voices, we might be perfectly entitled to argue that this kind of narrative politics is, at worst, not even feminist, or at best, insufficient; that while the uppity white female "I" of the assimilation novel might like to be in America without qualification, the brown and down female "we" outside has many valid reasons *not* to.

So where can we go from here? Or more to the point, if we are looking for more poetically and politically engaged forms of Boricua self-representation, what is left to read?

Beyond literature proper, there are all sorts of contemporary forms of Boricua signification that speak from margin to center, and from margin to margin, in aesthetically and ethically sophisticated ways. These forms of signification are often referred to as *social texts* in contemporary cultural studies scholarship. Like literature, these texts can be read and interpreted, but unlike literature, social texts are not exclusively written materials, but also include things like street art, word games, break dancing, tattoos, poetry slams, and other visual, physical, and verbal self-stylizations that people create in their everyday lives.

Cultural studies scholars have begun to approach these lived aesthetics as performance arts that constitute a serious arena of socio-symbolic engagement. In Puerto Rican studies, for example, the performance, marketing, reception, and folklorization of salsa, plena, bomba, and hip-hop have become important topics in an emerging discussion of popular music, insular cultural formation, diasporan history, and urban resistance (Aparicio 1998; Glasser 1995; Flores 2000; Quintero Rivera 1998). Moving toward what I propose as an epi-*fenomenal* approach to Boricua cultural studies, chapter 6 reclaims salsa as an insurgent form of transnational aesthetic collaboration among and between Boricuas and other violently dispersed communities of color. In a deliberately supra-literary finale to an outline of twentieth-century Boricua literary history, the next chapter suggests the limitations of analyzing only published and archival documents as artifacts of Boricua cultural production, and ultimately proposes salsa as the Boricua social text par excellence at the turn of the twenty-first century.

6

¡Ya Deja Eso!

Toward an Epi-fenomenal *Approach to Boricua Cultural Studies*

Más allá de los textos que demarca la preceptiva,
más acá de los textos que se confían a la tradición,
se asientan los subgéneros, los postgéneros,
los géneros híbridos y fronterizos, los géneros mestizos.
A pesar de la marginalidad, a pesar del asiento en la periferia,
ellos reclaman, también, una sugerencia de lectura,
una llave de acceso.

—Luis Rafael Sánchez

Los Puertorriqueños are always looking for a place to sleep.

—Martín Espada

Luis Rafael Sanchez's *La guaracha del Macho Camacho* (1976) narrates a day in the life of Puerto Rico. The novel's opening line—"Si se vuelven ahora, recatadas la vuelta y la mirada, la verán"—propels the text into motion with the reader literally "re/turning" to watch "her" (13).[1] "She" is a young, underemployed and nameless woman "sitting," sweating, and waiting for "el Viejo" (the Old Man), a corrupt politician who pays her for sexual "favors." The narrative turns and turns upon itself and the woman, as the phrase "vuelta y vuelta" repeats in nearly every paragraph, bringing the reader into the commotion of the text, just as the novel will continue to glide through different moments of daily life with narrative glimpses, the only momentum between them being a prose that turns and turns around itself, unwinding and rewinding the scene. To read *La guaracha* is to dance with it, turning and returning with each paragraph.

In the opening pages the woman comes alive, yet not with dialogue, a history, or any of the other usual contextualizing devices in fiction. Instead, she begins to dance. More than anything else, it is her sexuality that she performs, not as a direct encounter with el Viejo but as a means "to while away" (espantar) the wait. Bored with the situation, she gets caught up in the novel's eponymous *guaracha,* a song that has "invaded" the Islands and provides the background tune that repeatedly sidetracks the narrative. While she dances, her thoughts emerge in free indirect discourse; she thinks about Iris Chacón—"la oferta suprema de una erótica nacional" (the ultimate promotion of a national erotic), the narrator interjects (18)—about the insipid way el Viejo makes love, about all the testaments to her voluptuousness she suffers on the streets:

> Señal de que lo mío es sacar a los hombres de sus casillas. Señal de que lo mío es lo que es. Señal de que lo mío es caña y azúcar. Señal de que yo estoy buena como la India. Señal de que yo no estoy buena porque yo estoy buenísima. (19)
>
> [A sign that what's mine is the power to get men buck naked. A sign that what's mine is what it is. A sign that what's mine is sugar on the sugar cane. A sign that I'm as tasty-good as La India beer. A sign that I'm not just tasty-good but *finger-lickin'* good.]

All these *señales* (signs or signals), expressed in part with slogans borrowed from Puerto Rican television commercials, indicate that what is hers is hers on the free market, so to speak. And although she panders herself to make some money, she believes that she controls the commodification process of her own flesh. She avers that she chooses to be with el Viejo and tolerates his "not coming" (he's late for their appointment) as well as his sterile speechifying when they finally do have sex. Otherwise without recourse, she recognizes and claims her only sovereignty and possession as that "national erotic" (erótica nacional) embodied, literally, in the weekly televised *Iris Chacón Show,* which is hosted by another woman who has "un salsero entre cuero y carne" (a spicy rhythm between her skin and flesh) (18). In other words, this "sweet young thing" has "got the power," a power not only defined by her sexuality, her self-commodification, and the media, but also by her colonial condition.

That is, if we read Sánchez's novel as the metaphorical representation of the Puerto Rican condition it guardedly offers, this distracted female character may stand (or sit in) for Puerto Rico, her illicit partner being a caricature of corrupt authority, of that body of middle-age parvenus who regularly impose themselves as colonial pimps in a torrid affair between the United States and Puerto Rico euphemistically dubbed a Free Associated State (*Estado Libre Asociado*). His role as a particularly colonial *homo politicus* is suggested by the young woman's contingent contentment with their loveless yet impassioned affair; she believes that she chooses him, just as nominally the Puerto Rican voting populace "democratically" chooses insular elected representatives. Under apparently immutable circumstances, her "choice" is determined by *her* convenience, she asserts, by *her* assessment of "lo mío"—what's mine—and what *she* can get for it from him, namely, part of her income in formal and informal economies designed to make him rich and her poor. These ethically, aesthetically, and economically corrupted roles are also intimated as she surveys the *friquiterías* (naughty remarks) he pronounces during their sex:

> imagina tú, trigueña dulce de la patria mía, que por una casualidad o dictamen del Señor de Belcebú, me sorprenda en estos avatares licenciosos, siendo licenciado como soy, cualesquiera que me supone y quiere en el cumplimiento del deber oficial. (17)

> [imagine, sweet bronze beauty of my fatherland, what would happen if, by some chance or some dictate of the Lord of Beelzebub, someone who thinks I am performing my official duties and wants me to perform my official duties should suddenly discover me, a licensed lawyer, in these licentious incarnations.]

His designation of the woman as the racialized and gendered object "of" (de) *his* "Fatherland" (patria mía) metaphorically implicates the colonial relationship between Puerto Rico (a militarily occupied nation popularly referred to with the feminine pronoun) and its oligarchy, an opportunistic clique that, with few exceptions, has always been an exclusively male group that considers itself innately superior to the Islands' racialized poor majority. In his estimation, having sex with this young woman is a risk to his social position, a titillating act of daring that, if found out, could be disastrous for his political career. But Sánchez suggests that this illicit rendezvous *is* the actual fulfillment of the politician's "official duty" as a legally certified colonial overlord/ pimp of his "Fatherland"; that is, his carnally motivated and aesthetically devoid "duty" is to literally fuck (over) a mulatta (nation)—

Puerto Rico—who is willing to put up with him and all he represents as long as she thinks this relationship is in her best interests, and as long as she gets in exchange some cash that helps her survive.

The affair between "la trigueña dulce" and el Viejo therefore lays out the colonial condition itself. She "chooses" which Viejo fucks her (over)—his identity being just as much el Viejo as *lo viejo* (the same old thing), or over five hundred years of Puerto Rico's colonial history. Yet this process of choosing is also clearly illusory for, ultimately, as the novel intimates, the situation that forces this woman into tolerating one Viejo or another is caused primarily by her material poverty rather than what she considers her conspicuous (and audacious) self-determination.

The opening segment of *La guaracha* leaves the woman waiting, sweating, and distracting herself from the situation as the narrative moves on, re/turning to other scenes of life on the Islands. This co-motion continually shifts as the text progresses, and is orchestrated by a certain *vaivén* that, by underscoring a narration without any direct plot development, becomes a virtual rhythm in the plot's stead.[2] *La guaracha del Macho Camacho* is thus, as Julio Ortega convincingly argues, "a narrative that posits itself as its own demonstration, . . . a story without a plot" (una narrativa que se postulaba como su propia demostración, . . . un relato sin fábula) (1991: 10). In lieu of any plot development, Sánchez molds language into rhythmic expressions that bind what is not actually a story but rather an episodic sequence of lyrical vernacular performances. Almost as if taunting the genre itself, Sanchez's text suggests a way of signifying in the novel that refuses to capitulate to the genre's formal demands. This vaivén recurs with the ubiquitous *guaracha,* the song's lyrics alluding to the rhythm, harmony, and melody that a text can only aspire to re-create for the reader. Isolated on the very first page of the book, the song's refrain, "La vida es una cosa fenomenal / Lo mismo p'al de alante que pal de atrás [*sic*]" (Life is a phenomenal thing / Both in the front and the behind),[3] initiates a soundtrack for the novel, which closes with the full inscription of the song's lyrics on the last page of the book. Like the signals the young woman reads of her "power," the guaracha is a señal that guides the narrative in its *vuelta y vuelta* through colonialism.

Ortega reads the text as a "fictional essay" that analyzes the colonial condition through a species of critical "co-participation" with its readers. As such, "la inteligencia de los hechos, los sujetos y los decires no está en ellos mismos, sino que, lenguaje al fin y al cabo, esos signos nos remiten a otra articulación, a la crítica" (the intelligibility of the action, subjects, and utterances does not exist in or of themselves, but rather, ultimately, in language, as signs that propose another articulation, namely, critique) (12–13). As much as the text diagnoses the colonial condition, Ortega infers, it also affirms the "power of change" by shifting the site of knowledge outside the text and into its readers' reception. Ortega concludes that the novel "es un diagnóstico del malestar pero también un manual de primeros auxilios" (is a diagnosis of the malaise but also a first aid manual) that constitutes a type of "anti-canonical" mode of writing (12). Sánchez's manual/novel therefore provides the possibility of "survival, resistance, and questioning" in colonial Puerto Rican social context (49).

Yet Ortega gives only cursory attention to the specifically Puerto Rican cultural articulation *La guaracha del Macho Camacho* presents as its "spectacle" (12). Among other issues, much more could be said about the counterpoint of sexuality, street wisdom, and racial stratification in the novel's teasing display of a colonial allegory.[4] And most particularly, the role of music as a social cohesive, as the shared vernacular that poses as the novel's only decontextualizable (but ever-contextualizing) utterance, demands closer consideration. Macho Camacho's guaracha gives voice, in an unmistakably Puerto Rican accent, to a collectivizing realization: If "life is phenomenal" (certainly an apt description of Puerto Rico's colonial conditions), then the shared experience of hearing it called such (via the co-motion a guaracha inspires) provides its characters—and its readers—a dynamic moment for making it ontological, for assuming the epi-*fenomenal* posture of "ya deja eso" (13)—enough already—and re/turning to what has been perhaps the only genuinely inclusive national articulation in Puerto Rico's history: popular music.

Luis Rafael Sánchez's *La guaracha del Macho Camacho* may very well function more as an *a cappella* paranational anthem for a colonial territory than as a piece of national literature. Or perhaps, taking the text to an anti-canonical extreme, we might even argue that it is less a novel than a poetically inscribed invitation to dance, the music being everywhere implied but never representable per se.

Accepting this invitation in its most radical connotation entails breaking the literary sound barrier and moving toward a supersonic, epi-*fenomenal* approach that attends to provocative new sounds *and* bodies in the scripting of cultural studies. Dancing this guaracha well means phasing out the motivations of canonical literature—especially all it signifies as a handmaiden to the bourgeois project of cultural nationalism—and privileging the obvious (bodies in motion). This engagement should tune out (or at least tone down) the most problematic assumptions and practices that drone on like the pounding distortion of a cheap bass booster in the soundtrack of both mainstream American and insular Puerto Rican letters. Carefully executed, this epi-*fenomenal* approach could also gear cultural critique for a reexamination of such ideologically induced conventions and categorical concepts as monolingualism, the novel, elite canon formation (always there, despite the "anti-"), the Word (written), the word (spoken), or the ~~*word*~~ (warped into alien form by italics, denoting a non-[English] existence, signifying a violently imposed silence).

La guaracha del Macho Camacho may also provide hints for the diaspora's offshore critique of Puerto Rican colonialism and the specific brand of insular racism-sexism that aids and abets U.S. imperialism on the Islands. For diasporan readers, the novel's co-participational logic opens the possibility of other endings for the young, anonymous mulatta (nation): What would happen if, for example, she decided *not* to tolerate her intimate but loveless and eternally contingent relationship with insular paternalism? What if she decided *not* to participate in the kinds of colonial rituals Sánchez metaphorically exposes, especially the automatic commodification of her flesh and labor for consumption by wealthy but ethically and aesthetically bankrupt middle-aged men? What if she also refused to aspire to the "crabs in a barrel" conditions of the Islands' desperate middle classes and, like Negi's mother in *When I Was Puerto Rican,* or Luisa Capetillo, or even Arturo Schomburg, considered life in New York a better option despite the obvious risks and expense? What if she, like the millions now in economic exile from Puerto Rico, like the working-class diaspora itself, said "enough already" and left the Islands forever? What then would she say? And when she arrived in the States, finding new challenges and other Protean incarnations of colonial paternalism, what movements would her diasporan hermeneutics inspire her to create?

For Boricua critics, charting this metonymic woman's co-motion in the States requires an epi-*fenomenal* approach to cultural studies, colonial diasporan meta/physics, and aesthetic co-participation. It means finding new social texts, new concepts, new ways of reading and writing about her/us, a reviled woman/nation in exile, her/our own (m)Others, whom we are taught to love, hate, and reject as a shameful legacy. Trying to fathom her is always uncanny, since a colonial regime's prime desire is that the colonized forget—forget our own sovereign bodies, our collective will, and whatever lingering memory of self-love we may have smuggled past customs officials. Hence the convenience of the trope of the maligned Black woman, the perfect repository for resentment and self-loathing under colonial paternalism, her arrogant sensuality being our penultimate delusion and her final escape. Being (with) her may also seem uncanny because of prevailing academic traditions created and curated by the colony's *letrados licenciados,* or elite intellectual formations, formations that stalk and prey on her and others who, like her, have been expelled from Puerto Rican national signification—from insular historiography, "high" culture, and other conceptual realms of power—and then incarcerated in the prison house of folklore.

Because the Boricua community is a subaltern colonial diaspora, Boricua critics should attend to this, our dual eviction. Our unique sociohistorical movement emerges in a specific co-motion, an incessant shuttling of radically racialized and gendered bodies—between continents, cities, and neighborhoods, between languages, genres, and identifications—in search of shelter, food, jobs, philosophies, and whatever else we may need. The rhythm of our lives is the rhythm of our diasporan history, back and forth and all over the place, *p'acá y p'allá,* but never quite arriving at or leaving the same stations, ports, people, lives, and forms of expression. We can perform colonial ventriloquism and cite only the metropole's intellectual darlings, but unlearning this ventriloquism, I submit, may bring us closer to home. A Boricua-centered critique helps us find and reclaim our colonial diasporan baggage. Though it is packed quickly, as time and circumstance permit, usually coming apart at the seams, clasps, and zippers, and nearly destroyed en route or sent to the wrong address, who can say this baggage does not maintain its own integrity? A scar, after all, is something that has healed, and the knowledge we carry in this baggage—bruised, disheveled, and uncanny as it all may seem—includes the precious remnants of our very lives and unique legacies.

Popular Music as Social Text: P'acá y p'allá Dialectics

What I have termed *p'acá y p'allá* dialectics may provide one way of accounting for the condition of subaltern, transnational eviction and approximating the epi-*fenomenal*ity of diasporan cultural production. *P'acá y p'allá* means right here, over there, and everywhere in between, among other things, and can imply a crossing or transgression—between places, communities, sounds, and genres—marking a diaspora's interstitially gyrating struggle to survive *in style.* For Boricuas the phrase may further invoke a simultaneous articulation of hope between New York, San Juan, and even Los Angeles, our homespun stopovers in exile, homes away from home away from a colonized island that is, and is more than, a metaphor for our eviction.[5]

Perhaps more so than any other Boricua expressive art, salsa *is* this community in motion and metaphor, abstracted by lyric and made flesh by rhythm, as it glides between the *p'acá*, the whole context of its immediate interaction—the dancing, improvisations, and joy we experience, as well as the racism, exploitation, and sorrow we encounter every day—and the *p'allá*, a geo-philosophical projection of past, present, and future possibilities, an audaciously hopeful realm that is just beyond reach but so close you can feel it coming. This yearning and the work invested in sustaining it are similar to Paul Gilroy's discussion of the moral dimensions of music in the African diaspora; that is, "by posing the world as it is against the world as the racially subordinated would like it to be, this musical culture supplies a great deal of the courage required to go on living in the present" (1993b: 133). And with courage comes strength, conviction, focus, and many other intangible ingredients that can keep the memory of sovereignty and self-love alive.

Ejta música te agita, te llama, it agitates you and invites you to become part of the music, part of its changing meaning in present moments and bodies in co-motion. Moving *p'acá y p'allá,* our music inspires and is inspired by the dialogic flux between the dancer and the dance, between the lyrical production of meaning and everyday experience, between the Boricua subject interpellated by this performative co-motion and her/his collectivized, phenomenal, and epiphenomenological community at large.

This music's interactive modes of storytelling are essential to the *p'acá y p'allá* as a dialectic and diachronic strategy. Since performative trenches can be understood only as they unfold in their infinite variations, compiling an encyclopedic list of clubs, orchestras, and audiences cannot suffice to capture this co-motion for discussion, to make sense of the extratextual experiences that this type of cultural expression conjures. Such conjuring defies any attempt at codification or holistic analysis; this defiance may be precisely why rhythmic literacy has been paramount over formal literacy among Caribbean peoples for at least the past five hundred years.

This Boricua co-motion as we enter the twenty-first century does not imply any sort of ethnic absolutism. Rather, it fuels and is fueled by a certain transnational aesthetic collaboration between members of subaltern Afro/Latin American communities and Afro/Latina/o communities in the United States who share their respective nation-state's habitual rejection of them as normative cultural citizens. Provoked in part by this subjective exile in and from the nation, and grounded in Nuyorican history, salsa at the turn of the twenty-first century has become a shared socio-rhythmic expression of *diageotropic* consciousness for people of color in the United States and Latin America, as well as for those in the Caribbean, Africa, and other places where similar dynamics are at work.[6]

This subaltern aesthetic collaboration *fanning out*, this metaphor in motion and motion in metaphor, renders the corporate appropriation of "salsa" (a convenient misnomer at best) irrelevant. Though it is copyrighted and commodified by corporations (largely in Miami and Los Angeles), the Boricua community presides over salsa as a communicative force just as the African American community in the United States presides over analogous hermeneutic processes intrinsic to rhythm and blues. Though these legacies are both *del pueblo* and *de cartel* (Santa Rosa 1990), or significant both within communally based performance and as a commodity exploited for profit by entertainment conglomerates, ultimately the music's living aesthetic is epi-*fenomenal*, thus impossible to patent and exchange with mere paper currency. It is a living aesthetic whose most innovative artists and audiences hail its epi-*fenomenal*ity in what Jamaica Kincaid (1996) and Leslie Marmon Silko (1991) propose as the only truly sacred time—the present.

Since 1492 sparked this Afromestizo legacy in the Americas, analyzing the production of meaning around the trope of the Quincentennial (1992) helps track the extranarrative significance of salsa as fin-de-siècle Boricua performance art. In a mindfully embodied hermeneutical medley with Sánchez's/Camacho's guaracha, I will spin (for pleasure and meta/physical exegesis) three albums that became huge hits on the Latin Afro-Caribbean circuit around 1992, when I was living in Puerto Rico and, homesick, craving salsa like air: Juan Luis Guerra y 4:40's *Areito* (1992), Willie Colón's *Hecho en Puerto Rico* (Made in Puerto Rico) (1993), and Rubén Blades's *Amor y control* (Love and control) (1992). Critically appreciating this music at this particularly symbolic juncture of the past and present is a method of sampling a living musical culture in conceptual stereo, if you will, one amplifier plugged into an auxiliary receiver catching signals from the past and another plugged into a diasporan tuner scanning localized signals in the here and now. Naturally, this sampling and critique *se vuelven*—re/turn—to how I have experienced this music in present moments unfolding, how it has moved me and those I love in/and/with crowds, and how it has shaped my most intimate impressions of culture and of life itself.

Without Your Love, Woman, I Will Die
(Sin tu amor yo muero, mujer)

Juan Luis Guerra y 4:40's album *Areito* (1992) opens with an incantation, a convergence of voices building a restrained but mounting tension. The lower range voices weave into and between tight percussive sounds, like hands clapping in counterpoint or light sticks being beaten quickly. Deeper tones of drums emerge, moving in and out with syncopated riffs. Above these voices and rhythms the lead vocal elaborates syllables that undulate as in a chant. At moments almost a scream, at moments subdued, the lead vocal is pitted against the rise and fall of cannon fire, an eerie hissing and whining effect, as if the blasts' debris has fallen close by. The piece closes as a faint voice speaks in a strange tongue; as soon as his phrases are uttered, the music abruptly ends, up and out, with a cymbal.

The album's first, brief track leaves the listener pondering the strange music, the strange language, its abrupt ending, and the cymbal, which could be both a musical closure and a sound signifying that the cannon have obliterated the speakers and their drums. But as the rest of the album unfolds, the introductory piece begins to make sense. As the album's title hints, the first sequence dramatizes the opening of an *areito,* a communal get-together of song, dance, discussion, and strategic planning attributed by the earliest Spanish chroniclers to the Taíno peoples who once populated the islands now called Puerto Rico and the Dominican Republic/Haiti. The first victims of the Conquest, the Taínos were decimated by war and disease on contact with Europeans, who otherwise planned to enslave them. The few Taínos who escaped this genocide and enslavement became, along with African maroons, the first post-Columbian Caribbean people. Under extreme duress, this Afro-Taíno social bonding, along with the rape Taínas and African women suffered from the European militia, formed the roots of the contemporary Puerto Rican, Dominican, and Haitian nations. Thus the areito in Guerra's first piece is a war council, a call to action, the cannon representing the onslaught of Columbus and his men, the faint voice speaking in a language few today can recognize.

Alluding to the areito as a living aesthetic legacy of resistance, the second track, "El costo de la vida" (The cost of living), makes this historical reflection clearer by presenting the current scene of Dominican poverty and the island's role in the global political economy. This song is a lively *bachata*, a genre that has been Guerra's biggest success and also a style in the Afro-Caribbean musical repertoire popularly associated with the Dominican Republic. If the album's introduction is a call to war, the next piece is an immediate call to dance, the enjambment of the two calls suggesting their interrelationship. In comparison with the Taíno phrases at the end of the first track, the bachata's opening lyrics, "el costo de la vida sube otra vez"—the cost of living rises again—signal to the listener that here is something that indeed makes perfect sense. These lyrics further imply continuity between both calls in an explicit meditation on (neo)colonialism:

> . . . a nadie le importa que piensa usted.
> ¿Será porque aquí no hablamos Inglés?
> Ah, Ah, es verdad . . .
> Do you understand? Do you! do you!
> Si la gasolina sube otra vez,
> y el peso que baja, ya ni se ve,
> y la democracia no puede crecer,
> si la corrupción juega ajedrez,
> a nadie le importa que piensa usted.
> ¿Será porque aquí no hablamos francés?
> Ah, ah, vous parlez?
> Ah, ah, no monsieur.
>
> [. . . no one cares what you think.
> Could it be because we don't speak English here?

> Aha, that's it . . .
> Do you understand? Do you! do you!
> If the price of gasoline soars again,
> and the peso's value drops out of sight,
> and democracy cannot flourish,
> if corruption is a chess game,
> no one cares what you think.
> Could it be because we don't speak French here?
> Aha, do you speak French?
> Aha, no sir.]

The integral links between language and power, and between Haiti and the Dominican Republic, become crucial in this song, as not speaking "proper" English or French signifies a central cause of both nations' economic and political isolation. If the Taíno language is a temporal projection *p'allá,* then standard French, English, and all they imply in the global political economy are just as distant, while the scene *p'acá* is poverty, "medicine that doesn't cure" (literal as well as figurative), crime, corruption, and underemployment. The music in "El costo de la vida" fuses West African, Afro-Caribbean, and Taíno sounds into both a vibrant political critique and a celebration of life in the dance. The tempo is fast, the sound layered and always shifting between voices and elements of different traditions.

The exploitation of manual workers is also a thematic concern in "El costo de la vida"; the song alludes to the off-shore production zones that define most Caribbean states in the global economy, zones where factories and sweatshops offer extremely low wages and virtually no rights, benefits, or job security for workers, who are often young, female, and faced with few other employment options. The correlation between the Quincentennial and this (neo)colonial predicament is explicitly evoked:

> Somos un agujero en medio del mar y el cielo
> quinientos años después.
> Una raza encendida—
> negra, blanca y Taína.
> ¡Pero, ¿quién descubrió a quién?!
> Umm, es verdad.
> . . . .
> Y ahora el desempleo
> a nadie le importa—

ni a la Mitsubishi
ni a la Chevrolet.

[We're a hole between the sea and the sky
five hundred years later.
A race on fire—
black, white, and Taíno.
But who discovered whom?!
Um, that's it.
. . . .
And now unemployment
is no one's concern—
not Mitsubishi's
nor Chevrolet's.]

Unemployment, the socioeconomic situation's miserable proportions, and the subaltern perspective mean nothing to Mitsubishi and Chevrolet, two corporations among many that, searching for cheap labor and low production costs assured by Caribbean governments and U.S. colonial and neocolonial apparatuses (in the Dominican Republic, Haiti, Puerto Rico, and many other Caribbean locations), reap profits in the billions while the actual communities supplying them with land, infrastructure, and labor continue to languish in some of the Americas' most dire poverty. More important, the song also affirms those dealing with the rising "cost of living" in the fullest sense—the Black, white, and Taíno peoples—who not merely manufacture car parts, assemble stereos, sew designer clothing, and produce other luxuries they may never be able to afford themselves, but who have also invented the musical expression that can kindle voices that dare to question "who discovered whom?!" and thus contest the ubiquitous and uncritical state-sponsored celebrations of the Quincentennial.

The interconnection between the present realities of Caribbean maldevelopment *p'acá* and the historical projection *p'allá*—(back) to the Conquest, (out) toward the trilateral, overdeveloped world, and (up) to a new, critical valorization of an antiracist, antisexist Caribbean subjectivity—simulates the music's sprawling motion back (in history) toward the tradition celebrated in the areito, out (in the present) toward a critical reexamination of global practices of late capitalist human and environmental racism-sexism, and up (as a reconceptualization) toward the hope of reclaiming not only pride in Black/white/Taíno legacies but also the verbal, melodic, rhythmic, and corporal languages that can articulate both a critique of historically grounded, existing relations of power and a celebration of survival in the present.

All the pieces on *Areito* improvise on these reinvigorating and motile notions of multiple sociohistorical locations, languages, musical traditions, and movements, including a frantically paced bachata tribute to motherhood and an exploration of what the Dominican Republic's situation might be if, like Kuwait, it had a wealth of petroleum to exploit.

Yet, if the album has one central, recurring theme, it is love. Not the sappy, sentimental love characteristic of most popular music, but love as loss, yearning, pain—as impassioned *anhelo*. In the song "Señales de humo" communication is on the verge of utter breakdown; the lover attempts to get through to his beloved—to send her señales she can interpret or understand—to no avail, but with the hope that he can contrive a way of signifying that will somehow bridge their distance and mend their misunderstanding:

> Te mando señales de humo
> como un fiel Apache
> pero no comprendes el truco
> y se pierde en el aire.
>
> Te mando la punta de un beso
> que roza la tarde
> y un código morse transmite
> el "te quiero" de un ángel.
> Se pierde en el aire . . .
> Aye, mi amor . . .
>
> [I send you smoke signals
> like a faithful Apache
> but you don't get it
> and it's lost in the air.
>
> I send you the tip of a kiss
> that caresses the afternoon,
> and a Morse code transmits
> the "I love you" of an angel.
> It's lost in the air . . .
> Oh, my love . . .]

Similar to the album's other songs, communication here forms the crux of a dilemma that can be solved only with the imaginative reinvention of language itself and a broad casting-out of this reinvention. This solution demands a more radical shift to a language beyond the usual speech acts, beyond oral or written signification, one that roams; the lover resorts to trying "smoke signals," "Morse code," and then, as a final, desperate attempt, he resolves "inventar un alfabeto en las nubes"—to invent an alphabet in the clouds—that can express the excruciating yearning that threatens to devour him. The music picks up speed as the thwarted lover complains of his plight in a *pregón* (musical pronouncement):

> Mi corazón se me ha dobla'o de tanto querer.
> Ya no quema la luz de mi piel.
> Y si pasa mucho tiempo, mamá,
> sin tu amor yo muero, mujer.
>
> [My heart's been crushed from so much desire.
> The fire no longer burns under my skin.
> And if this goes on much longer, my dear,
> without your love, woman, I will die.]

This love and the anhelo it inspires define the lover's *razón de existencia,* or his very reason for being, a certain emotional quality of life, without which he cannot survive. Although it is common enough to exaggerate the pain of unrequited love in ballads, the extent of this lover's agony, the intense frustration of simply not being able to reach his beloved—whether she be geographically inaccessible, simply out of direct communication with him, or both—forces the anhelo into a credible crisis. This type of anguish is particularly relevant among younger adults who must migrate to find work, often crossing oceans and national borders while traveling thousands of miles from home, which is a common profile in the Puerto Rican, Dominican, and Haitian diasporas in the United States. Although Federal Express, American Airlines, and AT&T rhetorically exist in a global village, it is not so easy for working-class folk on either side of the Caribbean-U.S. divide to communicate, visit, or even exchange things. For young lovers this can mean a tremendously difficult sort of isolation, the anhelo or yearning inspired less by emotional fatigue than by the trauma of such emigration and the insoluble separation it often assures.

Guerra also depicts communicative isolation and anhelo as figurative legacies, and their historical implications are reinscribed in the album's concluding piece, "Naboria daca, mayanimacaná." Here we find a representation of the very first post-Columbian trial of miscommunication in the Caribbean, a moment when language literally attempted to save life from impending death:

> Ahh, naboria daca aé, mayanimacaná.
> Naboria daca guaitiao, mayanimacaná.
> Naboria daca eó.
> . . . .
> Aye, mayanimacaná.
> Mayanimacaná.
> Mayanimacaná.
>
> Ahh, soy un siervo, no me mates.
> Soy un siervo, tu hermano de sangre, no me mates.
> Soy un siervo.
> . . . .
> Aye, no me mates.
> No me mates.
> No me mates.
>
> [Ahh, I am a slave, don't kill me.
> I am a slave, your blood brother, don't kill me.
> I am a slave.
> . . . .
> Aye, don't kill me.
> Don't kill me.
> Don't kill me.]

Again, like the opening moment of the album, that strange language, but loud, clear, beseeching. In this song, however, the liner notes translate the lyrics: "Mayanimacaná, naboria daca"—don't kill me, I am a slave—are the final words of the Taíno genocide's victims as they plead for mercy to no avail. The music here has an eerie, medieval sound, with a boy's choir repeating the refrain while the lead vocal shouts his cry over and over again. Moving *p'allá* back in time once more to the Conquest, the song makes tangible the anguish of a Taíno who, speaking in his own language, could not save himself from his European predators. But the song shifts *p'acá* in its final moment, closing with a Taíno descendant's apostrophe of "Calichi" (a mountain stream—perhaps a deity, or the name of a friend or beloved) to witness his "red, white, and black" heart in anguish:

> Calichi, guarico guakía,
> Calichi, guariquen
> machichi, mayanimacaná,
> machichi yu, peiti, ris.

Naboria daca, mayanimacaná,
Oooooooooooo

Fuente de la montaña alta, ven a nosotros,
Fuente de la montaña alta, ven a ver
mi corazón, no me mates,
mi corazón blanco, negro, rojo.
Soy un siervo, no me mates,
Oooooooooooo

[High mountain stream, come to us,
High mountain stream, come and see
my heart, don't kill me,
my white, black, red heart.
I am a slave, don't kill me,
Ohhhhhhhhhh]

The lyrics do not reveal whether Calichi arrives to bear witness, yet the plea may be answered outside the song, as the listener makes the communication whole again by imagining the connection between herself and the violence of her past. Via an agonized death cry, these imaginary ties are newly bound and broken. The listener's extra-musical response can ultimately become a gesture of love, however, absorbing the song's anhelo by bearing witness to the pain of death and being able to hear (and possibly understand), finally, five hundred years later, in their own language, the vanquished Taínos's testimony.

It is virtually impossible to dance to the concluding moments of *Areito*. The motion is turned inward, the space imagined, the distance severed, rejoined, and severed again. As such, the song offers a type of closure, a momentary resolution of the *p'acá y p'allá,* which, in the spirit of what the Quincentennial signifies for the Spanish- and French-speaking Caribbean, is mournful.

And This Is Why Willie Colón Sings (Y por eso canta Willie Colón)

Another album released in the wake of the Quincentennial, Willie Colón's *Hecho en Puerto Rico* (1993), also incorporates the syncretic Taíno, African, and Spanish musical heritage. On this album Colón deals with issues similar to Guerra's thematic concerns in *Areito*: poverty, crime, corruption, underemployment, and thwarted love, or, in sum, a costo de la vida whose price is emotionally as well as materially dear in the Caribbean and its diaspora.

While the governing metaphor in *Areito* is the exploration of *historia* (history) in the temporal sense, *Hecho en Puerto Rico* is more a collection of *historias,* or stories that explore current scenes of Puerto Rican life. Like short stories, most of these songs develop characters, settings, and plots that are punctuated by refrains that propose that the problems at hand transcend the particularity of the events depicted.

These lyrical stories thus create vehicles for looking at an individual's predicament as emblematic of larger, collective dilemmas. Moving back and forth between the protagonist, his immediate predicament, and the implied connection to a common struggle, Colón's songs empathetically entwine humanized portrayals of common problems with potential communal solutions. Drawn into the dance, the audience is actively engaged in this drama, the lyrics filling a shared imagined space, the antiphonic rhythms creating the co-motion that literally, harmonically, and rhythmically brings it all together.

"Buscando trabajo," for example, elaborates on an all too common problem in contemporary Puerto Rican life—unemployment. The song follows a day in the life of a man who is making the rounds, looking for work and not finding any. The story begins with the sunrise, waking up to the smell of coffee, going downstairs to buy the paper, and embarking on a wage-labor pilgrimage set on a trail of seemingly unending streets, doors, and forms. The first refrain sums up the man's project: "Yo buscando pa' trabajar, voy por las calles de la ciudad" (I go through the city's streets searching for work). Colón enumerates the frustrations of this fruitless endeavor as he describes the crowds of people at the unemployment office. Making it to the front of the line at last, the protagonist finds out that the actual prerequisites for acquiring assistance are *la tarjeta*[7] and a *padrino,* or godfather (in the figurative sense), in a position of institutional power:

> Hoy salí a formar la fila
> en la oficina de empleos
> habían mil sudando el día.
> Cuando dí mis documentos
> me pidieron la tarjeta
> y un padrino en el partido.
> Y así se me escurre el día

tocando de puerta en puerta
tomando lo que aparezca.
Licenciado de papel
voy pateando siete calles
para conseguirme un salve.

[Today I went to get in line
at the employment office
with a thousand people sweating the day away.
When I showed them my documents
they asked for my i.d.
and my godfather in the ruling party.
And so my day goes by
knocking on door after door
taking whatever I can get.
Merely qualified on paper,
I make my way through the streets
just getting lip-service.]

The story narrates a nearly futile struggle, an attempt at dealing with not only the rigors and indignities of looking for whatever day-labor employment he might find on the street but also the very government office supposedly there to help him. Like many Boricuas in the states and Puerto Ricans on the Islands, the narrator finds that the search for work becomes an exercise in humility. Even with the proper documents, looking for work is often an endless cycle of doors' opening only to close, of making do amid an informal economy of scarce and ephemeral odd jobs.

The music builds as the man's journey and patience near their end. Here the refrain is more pronounced, while the protagonist vents his frustrations in a series of pregones that improvise on the way the situation makes him feel:

[*chorus:*] Sigo buscando, buscando trabajo, y sigo buscando, buscando trabajo.
[*lead:*] Me he fajado como un bravo pa' después comerme un clavo.
[*chorus:*] Y sigo buscando, buscando trabajo, y sigo buscando, buscando trabajo.
[*lead:*] Oye, que trabajo da buscar trabajo.
[*chorus:*] Y sigo buscando, buscando trabajo, y sigo buscando, buscando trabajo.
[*lead:*] Y no encontré lo que quería, pero mañana es otro día.

[[*chorus:*] I keep looking, looking for work, and I keep looking, looking for work.
[*lead:*] I've worked so hard for nothing.
[*chorus:*] And I keep looking, looking for work, and I keep looking, looking for work.
[*lead:*] Man, what hard work it is looking for work.
[*chorus:*] And I keep looking, looking for work, and I keep looking, looking for work.
[*lead:*] And I didn't find what I was looking for, but tomorrow's another day.]

The repetition, which in print may seem redundant, serves to emphasize the synchronicity between the pregones and the experiences of others sharing the same frustrations; it also matches the tale's endless cycle of trial and disappointment. But the song is capped with the hopeful possibility of change and a celebration of the mere fact of survival, closing with the line "pero mañana es otro día" (but tomorrow's another day). Along with the upbeat tone and tempo of the story's musical score, the final phrases acknowledge the difficulties of looking for work, the relentless impediments of life *p'acá,* but project *p'allá* to a potentially happy ending or, at the very least (which is quite a lot), the protagonist's inestimable satisfaction in knowing he has made it through another day.

Other songs on the album produce the same sense of story, antiphonic struggle, and hope for a better future, primarily through metaphors of desire and anhelo. In the duet "Idilio de amor" (Idyll of love) a yearning lover finds solace in the extravagantly romantic communion he imagines his beloved sharing with him after years of separation, while the lead in "Desde hoy" (From now on) makes a clean break from his lover in order to end a problematic relationship and start afresh. Throughout *Hecho en Puerto Rico* Colón and his orchestra dramatize the stories and emotions they evoke via melodies, harmonies, lyrics, rhythms, and the imagined possibilities they underscore.

This dramatic evocation is made into an explicit program of action in the song entitled "Por eso canto" (This is why I sing). Here Colón explains his musical project as one of *denunciando* (denouncing) the materially and ideationally oppressive aspects of life in working-class communities. In his words, "hablar al cantar es denunciar y pensar" (speaking in song is to denounce and to consider). The lyrics further provide a metacritical assessment of musical storytelling:

No puedo callar ante lo que me rodea
tampoco ignorar a los que sufren mil penas.
Cantar por cantar no tiene ningún sentido,
Yo quiero cantar porque siento un compromiso.

No puedo callar sabiendo lo que anda mal
cambiar la mirada por temor al que dirán.
Cantar por cantar es repetir mil palabras,
hablar al cantar es conversar con el alma.

[I can't silence myself with what's going on all around me
nor ignore those who suffer miserably.
Singing for singing's sake makes no sense,
I want to sing because I feel a commitment.

I can't silence myself knowing what's going on
nor look away for fear of what folks will say.
Singing for singing's sake is just repeating a bunch of words,
to speak in song is to converse with the soul.]

To sing, for Colón, is to fulfill an obligation to others and to his conscience. Singing solely for the sake of singing, he announces, is an empty gesture, but giving voice to his audience as a collective is to "converse with the soul." As this conversation unfolds, Colón proposes the following: that his message reflects the realities of his communities' challenges, that he is singing for his audience *p'acá*, for their *sentimientos*—their feelings—reaching further *p'allá* to *tantas cosas hermosas,* or the many beautiful things he feels compelled to project. Like the central speaker in the Taíno areito and Afro-Antillean *bomba,* Colón makes music into social critique and a call for action—"echen p'alante"—suggesting a concerted, progressive effort based in subaltern liturgical traditions.

This voice offers ideas for consideration, while the music invites dialogue by opening sonic and physical spaces for response. The success of this communicative co-participation—this shared consideration and denunciation—depends on how the audience responds. Ultimately, when the music builds to an improvisational break that leads to the song's closure, the audience must carry the song's significance into the dance to make this communication whole. Akin to bomba and other genres that evolved in Puerto Rico's coastal slave communities, the drums speak with the dancers, punctuating the dialogue, just as the *clave* (prime rhythm) performs a percussive call and response. Meanwhile the singer, the audience, or the chorus will goad the dancers with interjections specific to music. The interjections Colón uses in his breaks—such as *jele* and *yimboró*—are incorporated improvisational elements of this Afro-Caribbean tradition. Importantly, antiphony is not restricted to the vocals, but underlies the performative logic in its totality.

Conceptualized as a project of resistance, this song and the album overall not only demonstrate a strong connection with the syncretic styles of Puerto Rican oral traditions but also shuttle between the *p'acá y p'allá* of daily life and the hopeful possibilities of collective change in the community's future. Moreover, the meaning of the performative moment depends on the active agency of the audience, whose dialogic and dia-rhythmic responses spur, and are spurred by, the music. In the context of the Quincentennial, Colón's *Hecho en Puerto Rico,* like Guerra's *Areito,* recalls the Caribbean legacy of maldevelopment engendered by the Conquest: underemployment, poverty, and, at times, despair. Nevertheless, the album's title—playing off the label on products made by the Islands' 936 corporations—suggests that it is also a contrapuntal communal affirmation, one that would celebrate creative subversions of colonialism rather than state-sponsored spectacles such as the Gran Regatta Colón.[8]

Stories in Stasis: Amor (bajo) control *(Love [under] control)*

The final musical text in this critical medley, Rubén Blades's *Amor y control* (1992), articulates motifs and motivations concerning the Quincentennial that are far afield from Colón's and Guerra's musical innovations and thematic concerns. I am taking this album to task here because, among other reasons, Blades's aesthetic politics are characteristically progressive, but somehow in the production of this album these politics were relaxed and, arguably, compromised. With no intended disrespect to Mr. Blades, my analysis suggests that this album represents the tensions and tendencies of corporate appropriations of salsa, or the *p'acá y p'allá* as a dissonant socio-rhythmic expression, one that contradicts the aesthetic/ethical substance of the traditions with which Blades improvises as a musician.

Many of the pieces included in *Amor y control* are humorous in the grimmest Latin American mode. In this sense, the album does reflect certain oral and written traditions as well as many current trends in

Latin American fiction. However, as much as Blades attempts to give voice to the Latin American *misère*, his stories and the music under them fail to posit the emergent, hypertextual critique Ortega reads in the work of Luis Rafael Sánchez and other contemporary writers. My argument is that neither the lyrics nor the music on this album open any aperture for communicative co-participation, co-motion, or the projection of possible alternatives that might help effect positive social change. The album overall has a certain abstracted narrative and musical tone that create an unbreachable distance between the musical performance and the audience, and this distance implies a stark contrast with both Willie Colón's and Juan Luis Guerra's dialogic and diarhythmic engagements with living Afro-Caribbean legacies and live audiences. For those who dance, *Amor y control* is less than inspiring; there is no antiphonic motion between voices and drums, no opportunity for physical or sonic dialogue, no improvisation, no explicit elements of Caribbean oral traditions. Rather, the music provides a bed of generic Latin and Luso-American sounds whose sole function is to showcase the lead vocal, hence complementing the narrative stasis maintained by the lyrics.

In *Amor y control* the *p'acá* is explored in gruesome snapshots of death, despair, and hopelessness for the songs' characters and, by extension, the album's audiences. Glowing children die of radiation poisoning after playing with a canister of nuclear waste in the song "El cilindro" (The cylinder), for example, while an unnamed nation of South American Indians performs a ceremony to bid farewell to the Americas' last tree in "Naturaleza muerta" (Dead nature). Unlike the lyrical storytelling of *Areito* and *Hecho en Puerto Rico*, which dramatically critique current social crises while simultaneously celebrating survival and hope, on this album Blades elaborates tales that evoke images of helpless victims caught in a hemispheric web of poverty and apocalyptic degeneration.

One of these tales, "Adán García," like Colón's "Buscando trabajo," narrates a day in the life of a chronically underemployed man. But unlike Colón's and Guerra's antiphonic co-participation with choruses and audiences, this song's only refrain is repeated by the lone lead voice. Furthermore, Adan's refrain leaves no room for hope; in fact, it is a raving rationalization of suicide. Ostensibly because he cannot find enough work to support his family without borrowing some cash from his in-laws, Adán decides to kill himself. He addresses this refrain to his wife (who is voiceless in the song):

> Esto se acabó, vida.
> La ilusión se fue, vieja,
> y el tiempo es mi enemigo.
> En vez de vivir con miedo
> prefiero morir sonriendo
> con el recuerdo vivo.
>
> [It's all over, my dear.
> The illusion is gone, old girl,
> and time is my enemy.
> So rather than live in fear
> I prefer to die smiling
> with the memory alive.]

During the song we also hear that Adán's behavior began to deteriorate as a result of losing his job, but none of the lyrics allude to unemployment specifically as the root of the problems at hand. Instead, an argument with his apparently nagging wife sends Adán out the door of his home, dazed and wandering about town behaving in a deranged way. He gets a pack of cigarettes on credit at a local store, then proceeds to rob a bank with one of his children's water pistols. The police pursue him, but Adán has gone utterly mad:

> Cuentan que al salir Adán corriendo
> del banco, se halló con una patrulla parqueada al frente,
> que no hizo caso al guardia que le dio el "Alto"—
> que iba gritando y sonriendo como un demente.
>
> [They say that when Adán ran out of the bank
> he found a patrol car parked out front,
> that he paid no attention to the officer who shouted "Stop right there"—
> that he went on yelling and smiling like a psycho.]

Psychotic, hysterical, and brandishing his toy gun, Adán is then shot and killed by the police. Alluding to the opening scene of their argument, the song ends with Adán's wife reading the morning paper, whose headlines announce her husband's strange death. This in effect closes the song with the impression that his wife's presence frames Adán's travails and, consequently, his freak suicide as well.

Akin to many of the album's other songs, Adán García's story leaves no room for reconciliation, reconsideration, or any change of circumstances realizable by the co-participational momentum of *Areito, Hecho en Puerto Rico,* or even *La guaracha del Macho Camacho. Amor y control*'s governing metaphor seems to be despair over the dissolution of the patriarchal family and what it implies as a sociohistorical metaphor for national government in Latin America. The patriarch Adán García, no longer able to provide for his family, dies of despair; the peoples of Brazil's first nations, who have always been pushed to the margins of power and have existed in the paternalistic Euro-American imaginary as the embodiment of primitivism and savage naturalism, silently and mysteriously march out of existence along with the last tree; impoverished children, no longer protected by either the patriarchal family or the patriarchal government, die of nuclear contamination. If there is any hope to be derived from the album, it centers on the *yo* of the lead male voice who, in the most banal populist form, exhorts the album's listeners to retain complete and unquestioning faith in him.

This archetypal protagonist assures the audience that he will somehow manage to keep hope alive, and even resembles a Christ figure in "Piensa en mí" (Think of me). This song offers no musical or other metacritical elaboration of the problems at hand, just a series of commentaries on life's difficulties and the saving grace of an omniscient male presence who will make it "all right" in the end. "Piensa en mi" has all the trappings of a love song, but lacks passion, vulnerability, and anguish, elements that could inspire empathy rather than the unconditional submission to the lead voice that "Piensa en mí" implicitly demands. Its corollary piece, "Creo en tí" (I believe in you), would persuade a nameless beloved to believe in his saving grace and thus trust him to resolve some sort of existential crisis. But in a stereotypically masculinist way, "Creo en ti" reaffirms the centrality of the male lead; the relationship between the *yo* and his beloved is reduced to a catalog of its effects on *him*, thus the song's images and ideas orbit around the suffering male lead all over again.

In different poetic modes, other songs on this album also reinscribe a patriarchal presence as the epicenter of *amor* and *control.* Conversely, the feminine presence on the album is relegated to some predictably sexist portrayals: the vain and ignorant beauty contest participants in "El sub-D" (The under-d[eveloped world]), the nagging wife in "Adán García," and the beloved in *Piensa en mí* and *Creo en tí,* who submits her unconditional love for basically nothing but anonymity and domination in return. Sisterhood is nowhere to be found, but as the album closes a mother figure looms large as a site of loss and grief.

Mourning, as in *Areito*, seems to be *Amor y control*'s ultimate gesture, but here the protagonist's personal travails never quite manage to slide *p'allá* to any collectivizing or historicizing realization. In "Canto a la muerte" (Song for death) and "Canto a la madre" (Song for mother), death produces an oddly liberatory emotional anguish not unlike the pathos intrinsic to *Marianismo,* the Catholic cult of the Virgin Mary. The loss of this archetypal mother prompts the *yo*'s grief and, by extension, the album's reflections on the Quincentennial. How secular femininity might fit into the historical panorama is never broached, while the broader thematic of the Quincentennial is only superficially represented on the album's packaging; the cover photo has three Spanish caravels, presumably Columbus's *Niña, Pinta,* and *Santa María,* approaching what seems to be a Caribbean coast line in flames. Yet this motion back in history is merely cosmetic; nowhere do the *yo,* the music, and the audience enter into co-motion with 1492 except by default in its literal imposition as a cover.

Blades's musical and narrative disengagements are most clearly expressed in the album's final song, "Conmemorando" (Commemorating), which is a catchword for his project of recuperating the good, the bad, and the ugly in his reevaluation of Latin America's post-Columbian history. In this song Blades is critical of the exaggerated celebrations and public spectacles that marked the Día de la Raza (Columbus Day in the United States) all over Latin America in 1992. Yet unlike Colón's and Guerra's antiphonic strategies, Blades's critique is basically downloaded onto the music, with few improvisational breaks, no space for interlocution, and, with the exception of the somber repetition of a medieval-sounding chorus, no engagement between voices. Like Guerra's "Naboria daca mayanimacaná," which uses a boys' choir, "Conmemorando" employs sounds associated with early Western music, but in Blades's piece the appropriation lacks the grating friction between content and form executed so gorgeously in Guerra's composition. Furthermore, the message, like the music, is remote, offering a functionalist reading of unequal relations of power in the Americas' history:

> Negativo y positivo se confunden
> en la herencia del 1492.
> Hoy, sin ánimo de ofensa
> hacia él que distinto piensa,
> conmemoro, pero sin celebración.

[The negative and positive issues get confused
in the legacy of 1492.
Today, hoping not to offend
those who disagree,
I commemorate, but won't celebrate.]

The reconciliatory spirit of the lyrics here is contradictory, not only in light of the rest of the album's histrionic pessimism but, arguably, considering this specific song's lyrical content as well. Throughout, "Conmemorando" refers to the atrocities concomitant with 1492 (most notably the genocide of the Indian peoples of the Americas), yet the lyrics also sketch into the historical panorama a portrait of Cristóbal Colón (Christopher Columbus) as a man "made omnipotent by his faith" and rationalizes what is termed Castile and Aragon's "imperialism" with the mixed intentions of New World mercenaries and colonists. The strategy of *con-memorando,* of remembering *with*—as opposed to *against*—the grain of conventional historical discourse, not only lacks the urgency of Colón's *denunciando* strategy and Guerra's invocation of the areito, but, again, seems a large step to the right of Blades's own earlier albums.

The portrait of Cristóbal Colón in "Conmemorando" alludes to the figure of a lonely, misunderstood, and essentially alienated Renaissance man, whose overflowing creative powers are checked by a world more concerned with military domination than poetry. Altogether, I find the album's narrative voice or *yo* a likely metonym for Cristóbal Colón, his anhelo functioning more to evoke sympathy, pity, or even adoration than to inspire empathy. Again the epicentral male authority, Colón would represent a sort of metanarrative presence that is always already there as the patriarchal authority in absentia. Reanimating a Columbus figure to conclude *Amor y control* suggests that the album can be read as a picaresque exploration of the prototypical Euro-American male psyche, a realm that, despite the musical tradition the album borrows as a soundtrack, revolves around the pathetic, alienated, and definitively solipsistic *yo,* simultaneously and categorically excluding any collectivizing co-motion in the exposition of his Christ-like passion.

Enough Already! . . . ¿Vamoh a bailal? *(Wanna dance?)*

In collaboration with other African American and Caribbean musicians and audiences, the Boricua community has offered the world a precious gift of love and hope in music, which has been both graciously accepted by those who use it elegantly and rudely abused by corporate interests that reduce it to just another convenient or profitable diversion. And whether it is a Dominican, Panamanian, Japanese, or Senegalese improvisation, Boricua music has become part of an epi-*fenomenal*ity that, at the dawn of the twenty-first century, seems to be capable of simultaneously transcending and reaffirming a particular subaltern aesthetic contribution that, in its fullest expression, provokes artists and audiences to defy essentialist identity politics, ineffective racial or ethnic divisions, and the policing of geo-philosophical borders.

Hailing salsa in the context of Boricua literary history (and vice versa) represents not merely an effort to study the co-motion of this music in prose analysis but also a recuperation of aesthetic forms whose nondiscursive dimensions are usually considered irrelevant to cultural criticism. Literally breaking this critical silence with song and dance, we face the formidable challenge of analyzing self-representational expressive strategies that undermine their own authoritative prerogative to define, delimit, and objectify, strategies entangled in an antiphonic, supersonic, and epi-*fenomenal* co-motion that requires a certain *shuttling-between and -beyond* for the generation of knowledge, a groove that fans out to absorb and be absorbed by others. At its best, this kind of knowledge does not pretend to establish philosophical truths, populist mantras, or any other positivist theorems; rather, its significance is molded by a definitively interactive performativity. And this circumspect co-motion, this untamable hermeneutical movement *p'acá y p'allá,* compels us to acknowledge that there are simply some quintessential human experiences that formal literacies and the fetishes they imply cannot ever hope to arrest and detain.

With this *shuttling-between and -beyond* in mind I have tried to apprehend the historical continuity and human contiguity intrinsic to extraliterary signification performed collectively in the Puerto Rican (and other) working-class diaspora, here specifically in reference to a heavily laden historical juncture—the five hundredth anniversary of the European invasion of the Americas. Taking my lead from Luis Rafael Sánchez, I have aimed to capture the nuances of cultural expression without getting strapped into the generic categories, impotent conventions, and sterile platitudes that such a project usually implies, yet always and ever *pegá* (stuck) perforce to literary criticism and cultural studies, which are themselves inescapably affianced to brutal institutional partners. Perhaps this exemplifies *p'acá y p'allá* dialectics in theoretical praxis, or the ways that a woman of color can appropriate the technologies of academic discourse while simultaneously renegotiating the "Word" and all it signifies *con cada vuelta* (with each re/turn). Perhaps too, having been reduced to dark meat, wombs, and working hands by colonial paternalistic orders for the past five hundred years, women of color in the Americas may even be best prepared to lead as a consciously embodied avant-garde, one entitled to preside over the categorical imperative *to move* (beautifully).

Could this kind of re/turning point toward the possibility of a unique diasporan and womanist *escritura* that audaciously crosses the generic and gendered boundaries of "textuality/sexuality," "criticism/fiction," "Word/word/~~word~~," "I/you/we," and "past/present/future"? In many ways, reading a musical culture as social text may itself be read as an experimental endeavor to speak to and from both folklorized peripheries and official intellectual centers. At the very least, if there is any absolute conclusion I have reached as a literary historian, it is that published texts alone do not suffice to make sense of the experience of the Puerto Rican diaspora, which perhaps signals how obsolete notions of the written word as the exclusive repository and reflection of history and culture actually are. This may be a signal that any self-conscious and self-critical attempt to create a narrative history of a multiply marginalized colonial community will necessarily erupt in complications that even the most sophisticated theoretical maneuvers cannot resolve.

Rather than providing a tidy reconciliation between text and context, between narrative and analysis, analytical tactics that propose a dynamic interplay between what various social texts say and what they may or may not mean could be an option for cultural critics interested in deactivating some of the more toxic bases of knowledge always hidden in the folds of academic discourses. *P'acá y p'allá* dialectics is a hermeneutical concoction I employ in this pursuit, which helps introduce a certain discursive field that connotes its own nondiscursive dimensions. Ultimately, this device might be a way of reanimating Saussure's linguistic sign (via Volosinov) by demonstrating how the apparently arbitrary relationship between signifier and signified may be approximated with rhythmic metaphors that catch the vaivén of this relationship *as presence,* that is, without relegating it to some perpetually deferring linguistic formula. In simpler terms, *p'acá y p'allá* dialectics suggests a set of tools for exploring how the dancer and the dance are inextricably and immediately meshed by motion, rhythm, and sound. Here, the dancer might pose as the signifier, the dance as her signified, the succession of movements their chain of signification, and the rhythms they embody their discursive field. But this of course suggests that print articulation alone cannot fully represent the co-motion of culture; it reminds us, again, that existence should never be reduced to language alone,[9] that cultural literacy should never be exclusively based in literature per se and, consequently, that cultural critics—and their critiques—should get out and dance a bit more often.

Notes

NOTES TO THE INTRODUCTION

1. Faythe Turner's (1978) dissertation thesis is the first explicit thematic study of mainland Boricua literature. For sociological studies of Puerto Rican identity, with references to Boricua literature, see Flores (1993) and Mohr (1982). For readings of selected Boricua authors in comparison and contrast with insular Puerto Rican writers, see Barradas (1998) and Fernández Olmos (1989). For a preliminary introduction to early Hispanic theater in the United States, see Kanellos (1984). There is a collection of interviews with Boricua authors compiled by Hernández (1997). Kanellos's (1989) bio-bibliography of Hispanic writers is an important research tool as well.

Anthologies of Boricua literature abound, and most include critical introductions by the editors. Multigenre anthologies of Puerto Rican writing in English include Santiago (1995), Turner (1991), and De Jesús (1997). The major anthologies of or including Boricua poetry are Marzán (1980), López-Adorno (1991), Barradas and Rodríguez (1980), Algarín and Piñero (1975), and Algarín and Holman (1994). Anthologies of Boricua theater include Algarín and Griffith (1997), Kanellos and Huerta (1989), and Antush (1991, 1994).

2. On the effects of slavery for people of color in Puerto Rico, see Kinsbruner (1996), who argues that during the plantation era in Puerto Rico the free *gente de color* population (people of color, which included various castes) outnumbered the enslaved African population; however, historians of the Black community in Puerto Rico have contended that structural inequalities on the Islands have always been organized by race (Sued and López 1986), and that nineteenth-century slavery exacerbated racial biases for all African descendants on the Islands. Throughout the late nineteenth and twentieth centuries, these biases became a crucial catalyst for migration to the United States.

3. Puerto Rico's international boundaries encompass a main island as well as a number of smaller islands, many of which are inhabited by residents and/or militarily occupied by the U.S. government. Here and throughout this study I use the term "Islands" (capitalized to clarify its function as a proper noun) as a synonym for Puerto Rico's complete territory and population.

4. For a fuller discussion of discourse and power, see Foucault (1972–77). On writing cultural intellectual history, see Dirlik, Bahl, and Gran (2000).

5. On subaltern studies, see Guha and Spivak (1988).

NOTES TO CHAPTER 1

1. The most notable exceptions to this rule are Piñeiro de Rivera's (1989) anthology of Schomburg's essays and Ramos's (1992) anthology of selections from Capetillo's major work.

2. Both are fleetingly mentioned in Bernardo Vega's text (1988: 120, 111–12, 88–89, 134–35).

3. See, for example, Eugene Mohr's (1982: 3–23) reading of Vega's *Memorias* (1988) as a heroic epic.

4. Unless otherwise noted, all English translations are mine.

5. Capetillo's only biography is Norma Valle Ferrer, *Luisa Capetillo: Historia de una mujer proscrita* (1990). Most of the biographical information here relies on this text and Julio Ramos's (1992: 65–66) chronology.

6. For a detailed discussion of the practice of *lectores* in workshops, see Ramos (1992: 11–58).

7. Here and throughout my citations of Capetillo's work, I have corrected a few minor typographical errors, but I have deliberately refrained from standardizing her grammar.

8. For a full discussion, see García and Quintero Rivera (1982: 33–41).

9. Iglesias de Pagán (1973: 28) suggests that the FLT leadership and its membership had been critical of the Autonomist movement as early as 1897.

10. Anarchist organizations in New York's Spanish-speaking community were an integral part of the city's political scene during the final decades of the nineteenth century. However, Bernardo Vega (1988: 107–9) recollects that a group called La Resistencia was one of only a few of these organizations still intact after 1899, when the end of the Spanish American War resulted in confusion and political disintegration among expatriate groups. Vega also mentions that a major controversy of the period was provoked by a speech given by the FLT leader Santiago Iglesias in Rochester, New York, which Arturo Schomburg and others attacked for its explicitly racist comparison of Puerto Rican and African American workers (1988: 111–12).

11. *Qué dirán* literally means "what will people say?"

12. Detailed in "Apuntes biográficos" of the 1992 reissue of Zeno Gandía's *La charca* (v). This edition is part of an Instituto de Cultura Puertorriqueña popular library series.

NOTES TO CHAPTER 2

1. Schomburg's birth certificate indicates that his mother was Puerto Rican. "Schumburg" was entered on this document as both his mother's and his maternal grandmother's surname; since Arturo Alfonso was born out of wedlock, he thus legally retained his *grandmother's* surname. Since Schomburg, or Schumburg, was a German immigrant family name in Puerto Rico, it is also likely that in fact his maternal grandmother was either born in Puerto Rico or married a Puerto Rican of German descent. Therefore it is also probable that the relative he claimed as his maternal grandfather in St. Croix was actually his great-uncle, or another elder male relative in his extended family. Furthermore, since his mother was Puerto Rican, it is likely that his father (whom he apparently never met) was also Puerto Rican.

Although his biographers have tried to dismiss his Puerto Rican family history, the documentary evidence is as yet irrefutable. I have discussed at length the possible motives behind the myth of his family history, including the sexist subtext of his anxieties of paternity (Sánchez González 2001). For a look at the perpetuation of this myth in contemporary scholarship, see Gates (1999), Sinnette (1989), and James (1998).

2. On a biographical note, spiritual possession was not an alien concept to Williams, as the recollections he wrote of certain episodes in his mother's house suggest. More could be said of how Williams was inspired in his poetic theories—the grasping of an intangible, immediate "thing"—by the epiphanic moments his mother experienced. See *Yes, Mrs. Williams* (1959) and *Autobiography* (1951: 15–17).

3. This issue surfaced in Williams's friendship with Wallace Gould as well. In his autobiography, Williams recounts, with characteristic nonchalance, Gould's taunt that his sons needed to be sent to the South to become real "white men" (1951: 259). Gould's remark apparently infuriated Williams's wife.

4. For a closer discussion of racist discourse, primitivism, and U.S.-UK modernist poetics in more specific readings of Lawrence's and Stein's work, see Nielson (1988).

5. Many of Williams's Spanish-language passages in *Yes, Mrs. Williams* indicate that he had some difficulties writing standard Spanish, but this kind of limited formal literacy despite functional oral proficiency is common in the Boricua community.

6. In his biography of his mother, Williams notes her family's downward social mobility during Elena's adolescence, explaining that, given the family's financial circumstances, her sojourn in Paris was intended to provide her with some sort of professional training in the arts. In an interesting though subtle allusion, he also narrates how he found Elena in bed one night earnestly practicing her pronunciation of *s* in Spanish (apparently made more difficult by her

false teeth), capturing what could be read as an indication of his mother's class and racial anxieties (1959: 118–19). Pronouncing the final *s* as an aspirant commonly signifies the accent of the racialized poor in Puerto Rico. Evidently Williams was aware of the sociolinguistic suggestion of this kind of pronunciation, since he included his mother's joke on the subject soon afterwards in his text (121).

7. Williams's acquaintance with racism-sexism in Caribbean context is illustrated in the following passage from *Yes, Mrs. Williams* (1959: 10):

> When Georgie, our colored girl, who could peg a stone left-handed over the top of the chestnut tree next door, which neither of us boys [Williams and his brother] could do, when this Georgie climbed over the top of the grape arbor back of us to get into her room at two A.M. Pop knew about it, as he always did. Next morning at breakfast table with sleepy-eyed Georgie stumbling over him, he let her have it. That word out of my father's mouth surprised me; it hurt, but it was meant to—straight from the West Indies.

8. In my research, I have found evidence of only one organization, La Resistencia, that appears to have continued its activities in the wake of 1898 (see chapter 1, note 10). This organization was an anarchist group, and thus clearly outside Schomburg's political perspective.

9. Schomburg's organizational affiliations tended to revolve around his scholarly interests. He was a member of the American Negro Academy, and president of this organization from 1920 to 1929 (Ortiz 1986: 63). For most of his adult life, Schomburg was affiliated with liberal organizations such as the NAACP, the Urban League, and a number of other local and national civil rights organizations.

10. As I have discussed at length elsewhere (Sánchez González 2001).

11. Schomburg took offense when he received such xenophobic insults. This is evident in his private and published correspondence. An example is a letter he drafted to Wendell Phillips Dabney, editor of the Cincinnati paper *The Union*. Apparently, a Cincinnati minister publicly told Schomburg to "go home" to Puerto Rico. The remark riled Schomburg, who responded in his letter to the editor by elaborating his service to the cause of Puerto Rican independence.

12. The general public in the United States apparently has very negative perceptions of both the Romani and Boricuas. Polling results published in a *New York Times* article ("Study Points to Increase in Tolerance of Ethnicity") indicate that, of all ethnic and racial groups, "Gypsies" and (mainland) "Puerto Ricans" scored the lowest and second lowest, respectively, in terms of ethnic prestige (January 8, 1992: A10).

13. A reading based in correspondence with the documentary's director,

Frances Negrón-Muntaner, who explained that Bambara's remarks were expressed with joking sarcasm.

14. My translation and emphases. Standardizing Schomburg's letter here would entail extensive revisions of the document. I have refrained from overhauling Schomburg's grammar and syntax, though I have modified some of his spelling and punctuation.

15. On the disappearance of the Puerto Rican archive, see Salgado's (1999) discussion of the history and major sources, including Gómez Cañedo (1964), Dávila (1976), and Castro Arroyo (1986–87).

NOTES TO CHAPTER 3

1. Latimer is the reference librarian included in the Schomburg hiring controversy of 1932. See chapter 2.

2. For an excellent biographical overview of Belpré's career, see Hernández-Delgado (1992).

3. *Perez and Martina* established Belpré's long professional relationship with a small New York publisher, F. Warne. Belpré wrote on the frontispiece of the text that the "story has never been published," which, given her acumen as a researcher and librarian, was most likely true.

4. This text is not paginated.

5. Belpré's husband wrote a musical score for the story's puppet show, entitled "Dance of Señor Cat" (dated September 1953). A copy of this composition is in her collected papers. The black cat's theme indicates a slinky dance interspersed with jerks (triplets punctuated by half-steps) in the intro, which could add a physically performative layer to his intimidating personification.

6. According to her collected papers, these sources include *The Popular Poetry in Puerto Rico* (n.p., 1933), *Cuentos y tradiciones de mi tierra* (n.p., 1938), *Canciones y juegos de Puerto Rico* (n.p., 1940), and *Raices de mi tierra* (n.p., 1941).

7. These and subsequent lyrics are the English translations that Belpré provides in the text.

8. Belpré coedited the first of these titles with Marta Arnoldson, Christine Behrman, and Mary K. Conwell. I could not find a copy of the second title, which may not be extant.

9. The romantic trappings of literary genres that explore national formation have been analyzed in countless articles and monographs. In British imperial studies, Edward Said's *Orientalism* (1978) has spawned an entire generation of criticism dealing with the political subtexts of colonial-era British literature. More recently, Doris Sommer (1991) has analyzed similar subtexts in Latin American literatures.

10. Interestingly, I found occasional affirmation of this myth in Arturo Schomburg's archival papers as well.

11. For biographical sketches of Yuisa and Pedro Mexias based on archival documents of the period, see Sued Badillo and López Campos (1986). According to the historical documents López and Sued analyze, Yuisa and Pedro were not the romantic couple this legend suggests.

NOTES TO CHAPTER 4

1. Thomas's other recordings include *No Mo' Barrio Blues* (1996), *Sounds of the Street* (1994), and another publication is *Stories from El Barrio* (1978). Mohr's other publications include *All for the Better: A Story of El Barrio* (1993), *El Bronx Remembered: A Novella and Stories* (1975), *La canción del coquí y otros cuentos* (1995a), *Felita* (1979), *Going Home* (1986), *Growing Up Inside the Sanctuary of My Imagination* (1994), *In Nueva York* (1977), *The Magic Shell* (1995b), *A Matter of Pride and Other Stories* (1997), *Old Letivia and the Mountain of Sorrows* (1996), and *Rituals of Survival: A Woman's Portfolio* (1985).

2. For information about Boricua political mobilization and platform during the civil rights movement, see Young Lords Party (1971).

3. Truman's 1947 Civil Rights Act was intended to be the first step in this public relations makeover, as the Committee on Civil Rights explained early in 1946:

> Our position in the post-war world is so vital to the future that our smallest actions have far-reaching effects. . . . We cannot escape the fact that our civil rights record has been an issue in world politics. The world's press and radio are full of it. . . . Those with competing philosophies have stressed—and are shamelessly distorting—our shortcomings. . . . They have tried to prove our democracy an empty fraud, and our nation a consistent oppressor of underprivileged people. . . . The United States is not so strong, the final triumph of the democratic ideal is not so inevitable that we can ignore what the world thinks of us on our record. (Cited in Zinn 1980: 440)

Civil rights activists considered this "democratic ideal" a euphemism for U.S. political, military, and economic advantage in the postwar scrimmage for power and influence, which included the founding of the U.S.-led International Monetary Fund (IMF) in 1944, the United Nations (UN) in 1945, the Rio Pact in 1947, the subsequent Organization of American States (OAS) in 1948, the National Security Act of 1949, as well as the establishment of colonial home rule in Puerto Rico in 1947.

4. The connections between the Cold War and the civil rights movement are

important to point out, since most of the country's covert intelligence agencies (such as the CIA) were born out of the National Security Act (1949), and many of the practices used in the international operations mentioned above were ultimately turned into the modus operandi for dealing with domestic insurgents. That is, the same tactics used by U.S. agents for committing espionage and provoking political upheaval in Greece, Turkey, Iran, Guatemala, and elsewhere were employed against the base community organizations (primarily but not exclusively among Blacks) in the States that, in the federal government's view, threatened to instigate insurgency among the nation's minority populations.

Under the auspices of the Federal Bureau of Investigation (FBI), the domestic Counterintelligence Program (COINTELPRO) conducted surveillance on hundreds of grassroots community organizations and used a number of covert methods to dismantle them, including the deployment of agents provocateurs as well as government-trained assassins. See Merrill Ramirez (1990) and Churchill and Vander Wall (1988).

5. For a reading of Nicholasa Mohr's fiction as a failed feminist revision of the bildungsroman, see Fernández Olmos (1989–90).

6. For a discussion of class "commitment" and "alignment" in literature, see Raymond Williams (1977: 199–205).

7. Marta Sánchez (1998: 7) argues that Piri here "redirects the racial logic of white supremacy (black/white) into a nationalist logic of U.S. continental expansion and conquest of Puerto Ricans, which in turn gets redirected once again into the unambiguous gender hierarchy of male over female. He moves the site of tension to a space that affords him mobility. This is Piri's bottom line. Woman is the bottom of the barrel."

NOTES TO CHAPTER 5

1. On the West Coast, "Latina" became a common moniker for progressive Boricua and Chicana women who, in the wake of the civil rights movement, adopted the term to express collaboration between politicized "Hispanic" feminists in the United States. Today the term is so widely used that it is losing this specific connotation.

2. Playing off Deleuze and Guattari's (1986) discussion of Kafka as a minority writer.

3. "Culture of poverty" refers to a specific theory in ethnography—a subfield of cultural anthropology—that blames transgenerational poverty in U.S. communities of color on the culture of the communities themselves. The foundational fiction for this theory is Lewis (1965).

4. In fact, I think that if Santiago would have edited out the last section of the text (its epilogue), the conclusion would have been more consistent with the rest of the text. Perhaps she (or her editors) preferred a tidy, happy ending.

However, her subsequent publication (an explicit novel), *América's Dream* (1996), would suggest otherwise. Furthermore, her most recent autobiographical novel, *Almost a Woman* (1998), does nothing to revise the material and perspective already presented in *When I Was Puerto Rican*.

5. Factory labor in Puerto Rico was promoted to North American investors as a female workforce, hence many of the jobs made available at that time targeted women workers. For a feminist critique of this development debacle, see Cardona Gerena (1995).

6. In my experiences presenting earlier versions of this essay at conferences both in Puerto Rico and the States, progressive Boricua feminists vehemently expressed their outrage about Santiago's published work. Publicly, a number of these feminists voiced their concern that my analysis here was not nearly as polemical as it should be.

NOTES TO CHAPTER 6

1. In English: "If you/they re/turn right now, with circumspect motion and a circumspect gaze, you/they will see her sitting." In Spanish the verb *volverse* suggests, among other things, to return, to turn, to become, and to twirl (as in dancing), which is impossible to capture with the English verb "to turn." Since Sánchez's narrative is highly wrought poetic language based in Puerto Rico's lingua franca, many shades of meaning are lost in the translation of this and subsequent passages.

2. *Vaivén* is a word derived from *va y viene,* literally a coming and going or any back and forth motion. Vaivén is commonly used as well in music to express a dynamic rhythmic motion or well-executed improvisation.

3. In Puerto Rican context, this phrase has a number of sexual connotations.

4. As one critic asserts, the novel might also be read as a "burlesque drag show" (Cruz-Malavé 1995: 153).

5. Alluding to Martin Espada's (1987) poetical play on literal and figurative eviction in the Boricua community.

6. *Diageotropism* is the tendency of rhizomes and other plants to fan out as they grow horizontal to the earth. *Diageotropic* in this context helps describe the diasporan spread of subaltern peoples, aesthetic processes, and cultural forms across the globe.

7. *La tarjeta* means literally "the card." In this context it could mean an unemployment identification card or a voter's registration card (which in Puerto Rico is a common proof of residency, indicating how and whether a person voted in the last election).

8. Until 1996, article 936 of the U.S. Internal Revenue Code exempted U.S. corporations in Puerto Rico from paying federal taxes and tariffs on any commodity *hecho en Puerto Rico* (made in Puerto Rico).

9. As Volosinov rather dryly argued: "Everything ideological possesses semiotic value," thus a "sign is not only a reflection, a shadow, of reality, but is also itself a material segment of that very reality"—a materiality that, like popular music in concrete performance, can only take shape in the process of social interaction (1973: 10–11). Or, as Deleuze and Guattari assert: "A semiotic chain is like a tuber agglomerating very diverse acts, not only linguistic, but also perceptive, mimetic, gestural, and cognitive: there is no language in itself, nor are there any linguistic universals" (1972–80: 7).

Bibliography

ARCHIVAL COLLECTIONS

Pura Belpré Papers. Centro de Estudios Puertorriqueños, Hunter College, New York.

Collección Puertorriqueña. Biblioteca Lázaro, Universidad de Puerto Rico, Río Piedras.

Schomburg Papers. Schomburg Center for Research in Black Culture, New York Public Library.

BOOKS AND ARTICLES

Acosta-Belén, Edna and Christine E. Bose (1990) "From Structural Subordination to Empowerment: Women and Development in Third World Contexts." *Gender & Society* 4, no. 3 (September): 299–320.

Ahearn, Barry (1994) *William Carlos Williams and Alterity: The Early Poetry.* New York: Cambridge University Press.

Ahmad, Aijaz (1992) *In Theory: Classes, Nations, Literatures.* New York: Verso.

Alarcón, Norma (1989) "Traddutora, Traditora: A Paradigmatic Figure of Chicana Feminism." *Cultural Critique* 13 (Fall): 57–87.

Algarín, Miguel and Lois Griffith, eds. (1997) *Action: The Nuyorican Poets Café Theater Festival.* New York: Simon and Schuster.

Algarín, Miguel and Bob Holman, eds. (1994) *Aloud: Voices from the Nuyorican Poets Café.* New York: Henry Holt.

Algarín, Miguel and Miguel Piñero, eds. (1975) *Nuyorican Poetry: An Anthology of Puerto Rican Words and Feelings.* New York: William Morrow.

Allen, Paula Gunn (1986) *The Sacred Hoop: Recovering the Feminine in American Indian Traditions.* Boston: Beacon Press.

Althusser, Louis (1971) *Lenin and Philosophy and Other Essays.* Trans. Ben Brewster. New York: Monthly Review Press.

Antush, John V., ed. (1991) *Recent Puerto Rican Theater: Five Plays from New York.* Houston: Arte Público Press.

——— (1994) *Nuestro New York: An Anthology of Puerto Rican Plays.* New York: Mentor.

Anzaldúa, Gloria (1987) *Borderlands/La Frontera: The New Mestiza*. San Francisco: Spinsters/Aunt Lute.

———, ed. (1990) *Making Face, Making Soul: Haciendo caras*. San Francisco: Aunt Lute.

Aparicio, Frances (1998) *Listening to Salsa: Gender, Latin Popular Music, and Puerto Rican Cultures*. Hanover: University Press of New England.

Azize Vargas, Yamila, ed. (1987) *La mujer en Puerto Rico: Ensayos de investigación*. Río Piedras: Ediciones Huracán.

Baker, Houston A., Jr. ed. (1982) *Three American Literatures: Essays in Chicano, Native American, and Asian American Literature for Teachers of American Literature*. New York: Modern Language Association of America.

——— (1987) *Modernism and the Harlem Renaissance*. Chicago: University of Chicago Press.

——— (1995) "Critical Memory and the Black Public Sphere." In *The Black Public Sphere: A Public Culture Book*, ed. Black Public Sphere Collective, 5–37. Chicago: University of Chicago Press.

Bakhtin, M. M. (1986) *Speech Genres and Other Essays*. Trans. Vern W. McGee. Ed. Caryl Emerson and Michael Holquist. Austin: University of Texas Press.

Barradas, Efraín (1998) *Partes de un todo: Ensayos y notas sobre literatura puertorriqueña en los Estados Unidos*. San Juan: Editorial de la Universidad de Puerto Rico.

Barradas, Efraín and Rafael Rodríguez, eds. (1980) *Herejes y mitificadores: Muestra de poesía puertorriqueña en los Estados Unidos*. Trans. Carmen Lilianne Marín. Río Piedras: Ediciones Huracán.

Belpré, Pura (1932/rpt. 1960) *Perez and Martina*. 2d ed. New York: F. Warne.

——— (1946) *The Tiger and the Rabbit and Other Tales*. Boston: Houghton Mifflin. Rpt. (1977) New York: Eliseo Torres and Sons.

——— (1962) *Juan Bobo and the Queen's Necklace: A Puerto Rican Folk Tale*. New York: F. Warne.

——— (1969a) *Oté: A Puerto Rican Folk Tale*. New York: Pantheon.

——— (1969b) *Santiago*. New York: F. Warne.

——— (1972) *Dance of the Animals: A Puerto Rican Folk Tale*. New York: F. Warne.

——— (1973) *Once in Puerto Rico*. New York: F. Warne.

——— (1978) *The Rainbow-Colored Horse*. New York: F. Warne.

——— (1996) *Firefly Summer*. Houston: Arte Público Press.

Benmayor, Rina, Rosa Torruellas, and Ana L. Juarbe (1992) *Responses to Poverty among Puerto Rican Women: Identity, Community and Cultural Citizenship*. New York: Centro de Estudios Puertorriqueños.

Bremen, Brian (1993) *William Carlos Williams and the Diagnosis of Culture*. New York: Oxford University Press.

Cadilla, Ulisis (n.d.) *Rememorando el pasado histórico*. N.p.
Capetillo Perón, Luisa (1904–7) *Ensayos libertarios*. Arecibo, PR: Imprenta Unión Obrera.
——— (1910) *La humanidad en el futuro*. San Juan: Tipografía Real Hermanos.
——— (1911) *Mi opinión: Sobre las libertades, derechos y deberes de la mujer como compañera, madre y ser independiente*. San Juan: Biblioteca Roja/Times Publishing Company.
——— (1916) *Influencias de las ideas modernas*. San Juan: Tipografía Negrón Flores.
Cardona Gerena, Israel (1995) "Development Policies and the Politics of Gender: Puerto Rico, 1946–1960." Ph.D. diss., Fordham University.
Castañeda, Antonia (1990) "The Political Economy of Nineteenth Century Stereotypes of Californianas." In *Between Borders: Essays on Mexicana/Chicana History,* ed. Adelaida R. del Castillo, 213–36. Encino, CA: Floricanto.
——— (1993) "Memory, Language and Voice of Mestiza Women on the Northern Frontier: Historical Documents as Literary Text." In *Recovering the U.S. Hispanic Literary Heritage,* vol. 1, ed. Ramón Gutiérrez and Genaro Padilla, 265–77. Houston: Arte Público Press.
Castro Arroyo, María de los Angeles (1986–7) "El Centro de Investigaciones Históricas: Breve historia de un proceso (1946–1986)." *Boletín del Centro de Investigaciones Históricas* 2: 9–26.
Césaire, Aimé (1955/trans. 1972) *Discourse on Colonialism*. Trans. Joan Pinkham. New York: Monthly Review Press.
Chabram, Angie (1990) "Chicana/o Studies as Oppositional Ethography." *Cultural Studies* 4, no. 3 (October): 228–47.
Churchill, Ward and Jim Vander Wall (1988) *Agents of Repression: The FBI's Secret Wars against the Black Panther Party and the American Indian Movement*. Boston: South End Press.
Cintrón, Humberto (1972) *Frankie Cristo*. New York: Taino Publishing Company and Vantage Press.
Clifford, James (1988) *The Predicament of Culture: Twentieth-Century Ethnography, Literature and Art*. Cambridge: Harvard University Press.
——— (1994) "Diasporas." *Cultural Anthropology* 9, no. 3: 302–38.
Colón, Alice and Ana M. Fabián, eds. (1995) *Mujeres en el Caribe: Desarollo, paz y movimientos comunitarios*. Río Piedras: IEC, CERES, CIS, UPR.
Colón, Jesús (1961/rpt. 1982) *A Puerto Rican in New York and Other Sketches*. 2d ed. New York: International Publishers.
Cooney, Rosemary Santana and Alice Colón (1996) "Work and Family: The Recent Struggles of Puerto Rican Females." In *Historical Perspectives on Puerto Rican Survival in the United States,* 2d ed., ed. Clara E. Rodríguez and Virginia Sánchez Korrol, 69–85. Princeton, NJ: Marcus Wiener.
Cruz, Nicky (1968) *Run, Baby, Run*. Plainfield, NJ: Logos International.

Cruz-Malavé, Arnaldo (1995) "Toward an Art of Transvestism: Colonialism and Homosexuality in Puerto Rican Literature." In *¿Entiendes? Queer Readings, Hispanic Writings*, ed. Emilie L. Bergmann and Paul Julian Smith, 137–67. Durham: Duke University Press.

Danticat, Edwidge (1998) *The Farming of Bones*. New York: Soho Press.

Dávila, Carmen Alicia (1976) "El Archivo General de Puerto Rico, trayectoria institucional." *Boletín del Archivo General de Puerto Rico* 1:1.

De Jesús, Joy L., ed. (1997) *Growing Up Puerto Rican: An Anthology*. New York: Morrow.

Deleuze, Gilles, and Félix Guattari (1972–80/trans. 1987) *A Thousand Plateaus: Capitalism and Schizophrenia*. Trans. Brian Massumi. Minneapolis: University of Minnesota Press.

——— (1986) *Kafka: Toward a Minor Literature*. Trans. Dana Polan. Minneapolis: University of Minnesota Press.

Deloria, Vine (1969/rpt. 1988) *Custer Died for Your Sins: An Indian Manifesto*. New York: Macmillan.

Derrida, Jacques (1994) *Spectres of Marx: The State of the Debt, the Work of Mourning, and the New International*. Trans. Peggy Kamuf. New York: Routledge.

Dirlik, Arif, Vinay Bahl, and Peter Gran, eds. (2000) *History after the Three Worlds: Post-Eurocentric Historiographies*. Lanham, MD: Rowman and Littlefield.

Espada, Martín (1987) *Trumpets from the Islands of Their Eviction*. Tempe, AZ: Bilingual Press/Editorial Bilingüe.

Esteves, Sandra María (1980) *Yerba buena: Dibujos y poemas*. Greenfield Center, NY: Greenfield Review Chapbook (47).

Fanon, Frantz (1961/trans. 1963) *The Wretched of the Earth*. Trans. Constance Farrington. New York: Grove Press.

Fernández Olmos, Margarite (1989) *Sobre la literatura puertorriqueña de aquí y de allá: Approximaciones feministas*. Santo Domingo: Editora Alfa y Omega.

——— (1989–90) "Growing Up Puertorriqueña: The Feminist Bildungsroman and the Novels of Nicholasa Mohr and Magali García Ramis." *Centro* 2, no. 7: 56–73.

Flores, Juan (1985) "Puerto Rican Literature in the United States: Stages and Perspectives." *ADE Bulletin* 91 (winter): 39–44.

——— (1993) *Divided Borders: Essays on Puerto Rican Identity*. Houston: Arte Público Press.

——— (2000) *From Bomba to Hip-Hop: Puerto Rican Culture and Latino Identity*. New York: Columbia University Press.

Foucault, Michel (1972–77/trans. 1980) *Power/Knowledge: Selected Interviews and Other Writings, 1972–1977*. Ed. and trans. Colin Gordon et al. New York: Pantheon.

García, Gervasio L. and A. G. Quintero Rivera (1982) *Desafío y solidaridad: Breve historia del movimiento obrero puertorriqueño.* Río Piedras: Ediciones Huracán/CEREP.

García, Jesús (Chucho) (1995) *La Diaspora de los kongos en las Américas y los Caribes.* Caracas: Dirección de Desarrollo Regional de la Fundación Afroamericana, Editorial APICUM, UNESCO.

Gates, Jr. Henry Louis (1988) *The Signifying Monkey: A Theory of African-American Literary Criticism.* New York: Oxford University Press.

——— (1992) *Loose Canons.* New York: Oxford University Press.

——— (1999) *Africana: The Encyclopedia of the African and African American Experience.* New York: Basic Civitas Books.

Gilroy, Paul (1993a) *The Black Atlantic: Modernity and Double Consciousness.* Cambridge: Harvard University Press.

——— (1993b) *Small Acts: Thoughts on the Politics of Black Cultures.* London: Serpent's Tail.

Glasser, Ruth (1995) *My Music Is My Flag: Puerto Rican Musicians and Their New York Communities, 1917–1940.* Berkeley: University of California Press.

Glissant, Eduoard (1981/trans. 1989) *Caribbean Discourse: Selected Essays.* Trans. J. Michael Dash. Charlottesville: University Press of Virginia.

Gómez, Alma, Cherrie Moraga, and Mariana Romo-Carmona, eds. (1983) *Cuentos: Stories by Latinas.* New York: Kitchen Table/Women of Color Press.

Gómez Cañedo, Lino (1964) *Los archivos históricos de Puerto Rico.* San Juan: Instituto de Cultura Puertorriqueña.

Gordils, Yanis (1985) "Island and Continental Puerto Rican Literature: Cross-Cultural and Intertextual Considerations." *ADE Bulletin* 91 (winter): 52–55.

Guha, Ranajit and Gayatri Chakravorty Spivak (1988) *Selected Subaltern Studies.* New York: Oxford University Press.

Hancock, Ian (1987) *The Pariah Syndrome: An Account of Gypsy Slavery and Persecution.* Ann Arbor: Karoma.

Harjo, Joy and Gloria Bird, eds. (1997) *Reinventing the Enemy's Language: Contemporary Native Women's Writings of North America.* New York: Norton.

Harlow, Barbara (1987) *Resistance Literature.* New York: Methuen.

Harris, Joseph E., ed. (1982) *Global Dimensions of the African Diaspora.* Washington, DC: Howard University Press.

Hernández Aquino, Luis (1993) *Diccionario de voces indígenas de Puerto Rico.* Río Piedras: Editorial Cultural.

Hernández, Carmen Dolores (1997) *Puerto Rican Voices in English: Interviews with Writers.* Westport, CT: Praeger.

Hernández-Delgado, Julio (1992) "Pura Teresa Belpré, Storyteller and Pioneer Puerto Rican Librarian." *Library Quarterly* 62, no. 4: 425–40.

Hutchinson, George (1995) *The Harlem Renaissance in Black and White.* Cambridge: Belknap/Harvard University Press.

Iglesias de Pagán, Igualdad (1973) *El obrerismo en Puerto Rico: Época de Santiago Iglesias (1896–1905)*. Palencia de Castilla, España: Ediciones Juan Ponce de León.

Jaimes, M. Annette, ed. (1992) *The State of Native America: Genocide, Colonization, and Resistance*. Boston: South End Press.

James, Winston (1998) *Holding Aloft the Banner of Ethiopia: Caribbean Radicalism in Early Twentieth-Century America*. London: Verso.

Jameson, Fredric (1986) "Third World Literature in the Era of Multinational Capitalism." *Social Text* (fall): 65–88.

——— (1992) *Postmodernism, or The Cultural Logic of Late Capitalism*. Durham: Duke University Press.

Jones, Leroi and Larry Neal, eds. (1968) *Black Fire: An Anthology of Afro-American Writing*. New York: William Morrow.

Kanellos, Nicolás, ed. (1984) *Hispanic Theatre in the United States*. Houston: Arte Público Press.

——— (1989) *Biographical Dictionary of Hispanic Literature in the United States: The Literature of Puerto Ricans, Cuban Americans and Other Hispanic Writers*. New York: Greenwood.

Kanellos, Nicolás and Jorge A. Huerta, eds. (1989) *Nuevos pasos: Chicano and Puerto Rican Drama*. Houston: Arte Público Press.

Kim, Elaine H. (1982) *Asian American Literature: An Introduction to the Writings and Their Social Context*. Philadelphia: Temple University Press.

Kincaid, Jamaica (1996) *The Autobiography of My Mother*. New York: Farrar, Straus, and Giroux.

Kinsbruner, Jay (1996) *Not of Pure Blood: The Free People of Color and Racial Prejudice in Nineteenth-Century Puerto Rico*. Durham: Duke University Press.

Kropotkin, Peter (1912/rpt. 1993) *Fields, Factories and Workshops*. New Brunswick, NJ: Transaction.

Kutzinski, Vera (1987) *Against the American Grain: Myth and History in William Carlos Williams, Jay Wright and Nicolás Guillén*. Baltimore: Johns Hopkins University Press.

Lacan, Jacques (1966/trans. 1977) *Écrits: A Selection*. Trans. Alan Sheridan. New York: Norton.

Laviera, Tato (1979) *La Carreta Made a U-Turn*. Gary, IN: Arte Público Press.

——— (1985) *AmeRícan*. Houston: Arte Público Press.

Lemelle, Sidney J. and Robin D. G. Kelley, eds. (1994) *Imagining Home: Class, Culture, and Nationalism in the African Diaspora*. London: Verso.

Lewis, Gordon K. (1963) *Puerto Rico: Freedom and Power in the Caribbean*. New York: Monthly Review Press.

Lewis, Oscar (1965) *La Vida: A Puerto Rican Family in the Culture of Poverty, San Juan and New York*. New York: Random House.

Lomas, Clara (1993) "The Articulation of Gender in the Mexican Borderlands, 1900–1915." In *Recovering the U.S. Hispanic Literary Heritage,* vol. 1, ed. Ramón Gutiérrez and Genaro Padilla, 293–308. Houston: Arte Público Press.

——— (1994) Preface and introduction to *The Rebel,* by Leonor Villegas de Magnon, vii-lvi. Houston: Arte Público Press.

López, Iris (1994) "The Social Construction of Reproductive 'Choice': An Ethnographic Study of Puerto Rican Women and Sterilization in New York City." In *Género y mujeres puertorriqueñas/Gender and Puerto Rican Women,* ed. Alice Colón, 105–26. Río Piedras: Centro de Investigaciones Sociales.

López, Lillian and Pura Belpré (1974) "Reminiscences of Two Turned-On Puerto Rican Librarians." In *Puerto Rican Perspectives,* ed. Edward Mapp, 83–96. Metuchen, NJ: Scarecrow Press.

López-Adorno, Pedro (1991) *Papiros de Babel: Antología de la poesía puertorriqueña en Nueva York: Selección, estudio preliminar y viñetas críticas.* Río Piedras: Editorial de la Universidad de Puerto Rico.

Lukács, Georg (1971) *The Theory of the Novel: A Historico-Philosophical Essay on the Forms of Great Epic Literature.* Trans. Anna Bostock. Cambridge: Massachusetts Institute of Technology Press.

Maldonado-Denis, Manuel (1988) *Puerto Rico: Una interpretación históricisocial.* 12th ed. Mexico City: Siglo Veintiuno Editores.

Manrique, Manuel (1966) *Island in Harlem.* New York: Day.

Marable, Manning (1991) *Race, Reform and Rebellion: The Second Reconstruction in Black America, 1945–1990.* Jackson: University Press of Mississippi.

Marzán, Julio (1994) *The Spanish American Roots of William Carlos Williams.* Austin: University of Texas Press.

———, ed. (1980) *Inventing a Word: An Anthology of Twentieth-Century Puerto Rican Poetry.* New York: Columbia University Press

McKay, Claude (1940) *Harlem: Negro Metropolis.* New York: Dutton.

Memmi, Albert (1957/trans. 1965) *The Colonizer and the Colonized.* Trans. Howard Greenfield. New York: Orion Press.

Merrill Ramirez, Marie Antoinette (1990) "The Other Side of Colonialism: COINTELPRO Activities in Puerto Rico in the 1960's." Ph.D. diss., University of Texas at Austin.

Mohr, Eugene (1982) *The Nuyorican Experience: Literature of the Puerto Rican Minority.* Westport, CT: Greenwood.

Mohr, Nicholasa (1973) *Nilda.* New York: Bantam. Rpt. (1986) Houston: Arte Público Press.

——— (1975) *El Bronx Remembered: A Novella and Stories.* New York: Harper and Row.

——— (1977) *In Nueva York.* New York: Dial.

——— (1979) *Felita.* New York: Dial.

Mohr, Nicholasa (1985) *Rituals of Survival: A Woman's Portfolio*. Houston: Arte Público Press.

——— (1986) *Going Home*. New York: Dial.

——— (1993) *All for the Better: A Story of El Barrio*. New York: Steck Vaughn.

——— (1994) *Growing Up Inside the Sanctuary of My Imagination*. New York: J. Messner.

——— (1995a) *La canción del coquí y otros cuentos*. New York: Viking.

——— (1995b) *The Magic Shell*. New York: Scholastic.

——— (1996) *Old Letivia and the Mountain of Sorrows*. New York: Viking.

——— (1997) *A Matter of Pride and Other Stories*. Houston: Arte Público Press.

Monteflores, Carmen de (1989) *Cantando bajito/Singing Softly*. San Francisco: Spinsters/Aunt Lute.

Moraga, Cherrie and Gloria Anzaldúa, eds. (1983) *This Bridge Called My Back: Writings by Radical Women of Color*. 2d ed. New York: Kitchen Table/Women of Color Press.

Moran, Rachel F. (1996) "Unrepresented." *Representations* 55 (summer): 139–54.

Morris, Aldon D. (1984) *The Origins of the Civil Rights Movement: Black Communities Organizing for Change*. New York: Free Press.

Morrison, Toni (1987) *Beloved*. New York: Knopf.

——— (1992) *Playing in the Dark: Whiteness and the Literary Imagination*. Cambridge: Harvard University Press.

Navarro, Mireya (2000) "Puerto Rican Presence Wanes in New York: Falling Back: A Special Report." *New York Times,* 28 February, A1, A20. Census Bureau Source Analysis, Susan Weber.

Nielson, Aldon Lynn (1988) *Reading Race: White American Poets and the Racial Discourse in the Twentieth Century*. Athens: University of Georgia Press.

Nieto Gómez, Anna (1974) "La feminista." *Encuentro Femenil* 1, no. 2: 34–47.

Oliphant, Dave (1995) Review of *The Spanish American Roots of William Carlos Williams,* by Julio Marzán. *William Carlos Williams Review* 21, no. 1 (spring): 69–73.

Ortega, Julio (1991) *Reapropriaciones: Cultura y nueva escritura en Puerto Rico*. Río Piedras: Editorial de la Universidad de Puerto Rico.

Ortiz, Victoria (1986) "Arthur A. Schomburg: A Biographical Essay." In *The Legacy of Arthur A. Schomburg: A Celebration of the Past, a Vision for the Future,* comp. Schomburg Center for Research in Black Culture, exhibit catalog. New York: New York Public Library.

Ortiz Cofer, Judith (1989) *The Line of the Sun*. Athens: University of Georgia Press.

——— (1990) *Silent Dancing: A Partial Remembrance of a Puerto Rican Childhood*. Houston: Arte Público Press.

——— (1993) *The Latin Deli*. Athens, GA and London: University of Georgia Press.

——— (1995) *An Island Like You*. New York: Orchard.

——— (1998) *The Year of Our Revolution*. Houston: Arte Público Press.

Ostolazo Bey, Margarita (1989) *Política sexual en Puerto Rico*. Río Piedras: Ediciones Huracán.

Pérez, Emma (1991) "Sexuality and Discourse: Notes from a Chicana Survivor." In *Chicana Lesbians: The Girls Our Mothers Warned Us About*, ed. Carla Trujillo, 159–84. Berkeley: Third Woman Press.

Picó, Fernando (1988) *Historia general de Puerto Rico*. Río Piedras: Ediciones Huracán.

Pietri, Pedro (1973) *Puerto Rican Obituary*. New York: Monthly Review Press.

Piñeiro de Rivera, Flor, ed. (1989) *Arthur Alfonso Schomburg: A Puerto Rican's Quest for His Black Heritage*. San Juan: Centro de Estudios Avanzados de Puerto Rico y el Caribe.

Quintero Rivera, A. G. (1998) *Salsa, sabor y control: Sociología de la música tropical*. Mexico: Siglo Ventiuno Editores.

Ramos, Julio, ed. (1992) *Amor y anarquía: Los escritos de Luisa Capetillo*. Río Piedras: Ediciones Huracán.

Rhys, Jean. (1966/rpt. 1982) *Wide Sargasso Sea*. New York: Norton.

Ridge, Lola (1926) "American Sagas." *New Republic* 48 (March 24): 148–49.

Rodó, José Enrique (1900/rpt. 1983) *Ariel: Liberalismo y Jacobinismo*. Montevideo: Imprenta de Dornaleche y Reyes.

Romero-Cesareo, Ivette (1994) "Whose Legacy? Voicing Women's Rights from the 1870's to the 1930's." *Callaloo* 17, no. 3: 770–89.

Said, Edward (1978/rpt. 1979) *Orientalism*. New York: Random House.

Saldívar, Ramón (1990) *Chicano Narrative: The Dialectics of Difference*. Madison: University of Wisconsin Press.

Saldívar-Hull, Sonia (1991) "Feminism on the Border: From Gender Politics to Geopolitics." In *Criticism in the Borderlands: Studies in Chicano Literature, Culture and Ideology*, ed. Héctor Calderón and José David Saldívar, 203–20. Durham: Duke University Press.

Salgado, César A. (1999) "Archivos encontrados: Edgardo Rodríguez Juliá o los diablejos de la historiografía criolla." *Cuadernos Americanos* 73: 153–203.

Sánchez, Luis Rafael (1976/rpt. 1989) *La guaracha del Macho Camacho*. Buenos Aires: Ediciones de la Flor.

Sánchez, Marta E. (1985) *Contemporary Chicana Poetry: A Critical Approach to an Emerging Literature*. Berkeley: University of California Press.

——— (1998) "More Than Black and White: Interethnic Connections in U.S. Latino and African American Culture." Paper presented at the conference "Bastards of Imperialism: Identity, Nation, and Citizenship in the Wake of

Spanish and U.S. Expansions," Stanford University, Palo Alto, CA, April 30–May 2.

Sánchez, Rosaura (1993) "Nineteenth Century Californio Narratives: The Hubert H. Bancroft Collection." In *Recovering the U.S. Hispanic Literary Heritage,* vol. 1, ed. Ramón Gutiérrez and Genaro Padilla, 279–92. Houston: Arte Público Press.

Sánchez, Rosaura and Beatrice Pita (1992) Introduction to *The Squatter and the Don,* by María Amparo Ruiz de Burton, 5–51. Houston: Arte Público Press.

Sánchez González, Lisa (1993–94) "Can the Elite Dance? (Y Otras desgracias)." *Emergences* 5–6: 122–36.

——— (2001) "Arturo Schomburg: A Transamerican Intellectual." In *African Roots/American Cultures: Africa in the Creation of the Americas,* ed. Sheila Walker. Lanham, MD: Rowman and Littlefield.

Sánchez Korrol, Virginia (1994) *From Colonia to Community: The History of Puerto Ricans in New York City*. 2d ed. Berkeley, Los Angeles: University of California Press.

Sandoval, Chela (1991) "U.S. Third World Feminism: The Theory and Method of Oppositional Consciousness in the Postmodern World." *Genders* 10 (spring): 1–24.

Santiago, Esmeralda (1993) *When I Was Puerto Rican*. New York: Addison-Wesley.

——— (1996) *América's Dream*. New York: Harper Collins.

——— (1998) *Almost a Woman*. Reading, MA: Perseus.

Santiago, Roberto (1995) *Boricuas: Influential Puerto Rican Writings*. New York: One World.

Schomburg, Arturo A. (1927a) "Creole-criollo." *Light* IV, no. i (November 26): n.p.

——— (1927b) "In Quest of Juan de Pareja." *The Crisis* XXXIV (July): 153–54, 174.

Silko, Leslie Marmon (1991) *Almanac of the Dead*. New York: Simon and Schuster.

Sinnette, Elinor Des Verney (1989) *Arthur Alfonso Schomburg: Black Bibliophile and Collector: A Biography*. Detroit: New York Public Library and Wayne State University Press.

Sommer, Doris (1991) *Foundational Fictions: The National Romances of Latin America*. Berkeley: University of California Press.

South Bronx Library Project (1977) *Libros en español: An Annotated List of Children's Books in Spanish*. New York: New York Public Library.

Stein, Gertrude (1909) *Three Lives: Stories of Good Anna, Melanchtha, and the Gentle Lena*. New York: The Grafton Press.

Sued Badillo, Jalil and Angel López Campos (1986) *Puerto Rico negro*. Río Piedras: Editorial Cultural.

Thomas, Piri (1967/rpt. 1974) *Down These Mean Streets*. New York: Knopf.
——— (1972) *Savior, Savior Hold My Hand*. Garden City, NY: Doubleday.
——— (1974) *Seven Long Times*. New York: Praeger Publishers.
——— (1978) *Stories from El Barrio*. New York: Alfred A. Knopf.
Tölölyan, Khachig (1996) "Rethinking *Diaspora*(s): Stateless Power in the Transitional Moment," *Diaspora* 5, no. 1: 3–36.
Torres, Edwin (1975) *Carlito's Way*. New York: Saturday Review Press.
Turner, Faythe (1978) "Puerto Rican Writers on the Mainland, the Neoricans: A Thematic Study." Ph.D. diss., University of Massachusetts.
———, ed. (1991) *Puerto Rican Writers at Home in the USA: An Anthology*. Seattle: Open Hand Publishers.
United Nations Development Programme (1993) *Human Development Report*. New York: Oxford University Press.
Valle Ferrer, Norma (1990) *Luisa Capetillo: Historia de una mujer proscrita*. San Juan: Editorial Cultural.
Vega, Bernardo (1988) *Memorias de Bernardo Vega*. 4th ed. Ed. César Andreu Iglesias. Río Piedras: Ediciones Huracán.
Volosinov, V. N. (1973) *Marxism and the Philosophy of Language*. Trans. Ladislav Matejka and I. R. Titunik. Cambridge: Harvard University Press.
Wallace, Michelle (1992) "Negative Images: Towards a Black Feminist Cultural Criticism." In *Cultural Studies*, ed. Lawrence Grossberg et al., 654–64. New York: Routledge.
Warrior, Robert Allen (1995) *Tribal Secrets: Recovering American Indian Intellectual Traditions*. Minneapolis: University of Minnesota Press.
White, Hayden (1973) *Metahistory: The Historical Imagination in Nineteenth-Century Europe*. Baltimore: Johns Hopkins University Press.
Whitman, Walt (1855/rpt. 1968) *Leaves of Grass*. New York: New York Public Library.
Williams, Raymond (1977) *Marxism and Literature*. New York: Oxford University Press.
Williams, William Carlos (1923) *The Great American Novel*. Paris: Three Mountains Press.
——— (1925) *In the American Grain*. Norfolk, CT: New Directions. Rpt. (1956) New York: New Directions.
——— (1946–58) *Paterson*. New York: New Directions.
——— (1951) *Autobiography*. New York: Random House.
——— (1959) *Yes, Mrs. Williams*. New York: McDowell, Obolensky. Rpt. (1982) New York: New Directions.
——— (1974) *The Embodiment of Knowledge*. New York: New Directions.
Young Lords Party (1971) *Palante: Young Lords Party*. New York: McGraw-Hill.
Zamudio-Taylor, Victor (1993) "Demystifying Marginality: Identity, Tradition

and Resistance." In *In/Out of the Cold,* comp. Center for the Arts Yerba Buena Gardens, exhibit catalogue, 18–21. San Francisco: Center for the Arts Yerba Buena Gardens.

Zavala, Iris M. (1992) *Colonialism and Culture: Hispanic Modernisms and the Social Imaginary*. Bloomington: Indiana University Press.

Zeno Gandía, Manuel (1894/rpt. 1992) *La charca*. San Juan: Instituto de Cultura Puertorriqueña.

Zinn, Howard (1980/rpt. 1990) *A People's History of the United States*. New York: Harper Collins.

COMPACT DISCS AND VIDEOCASSETTES

Blades, Rubén (1992) *Amor y control*. With Son del Solar. Sony Discos Internacional, CDZ-80839, 471643-2.

Colón, Willie (1993) *Hecho en Puerto Rico*. Sony Discos Internacional, DCC-881040, 4-469580.

Colón, Willie and Rubén Blades (1995) *Tras la tormenta*. Sony Tropical, CDT-81498/478354-2.

Guerra, Juan Luis (1992) *Areito*. With 4:40. BMG Music, 3456-2RL.

Negrón-Muntaner, Frances, dir. (1994) *Brincando el charco: Portrait of a Puerto Rican*. New York: Women Make Movies, videocassette.

Santa Rosa, Gilberto (1990) *El caballero de la salsa*. Combo Records, RCSC 2069, 00898.

Thomas, Piri (1994) *Sounds of the Street*. Cheverote Productions, CD 793937-9260-23.

——— (1996) *No Mo' Barrio Blues*. Cheverote Productions, CD 793937-2177-25.

Index

Alarcón, Norma, 140
Albizu Campos, Pedro, 104
Algarín, Miguel, 103
Allen, Paula Gunn, 16
Almanza, Susana, 139
Althusser, Louis, 26
American Federation of Labor (AFL), 32
anarchism, 22–23; and feminism, 29; La Resistencia, 192n. 10. *See also* Federación Libre de Trabajadores
archives, 4–5, 7–8, 14, 71–74; archival rememory, 6; Centro de Estudios Puertorriqueños, 5, 71–73; Colección Puertorriqueña, 5, 71; Schomburg Center, 5, 55, 63, 65–66, 70. *See also* New York Public Library, 135th Street branch
areito, 170–74
Ateneo Puertorriqueño, 39

Baker, Houston, Jr., 16–17, 48–49
Bakhtin, M. M., 10, 106
Bakunin, Mikhail, 33
Balzac, Honoré de, 33
Bambara, Toni Cade, 60–61
Becerril, Joaquín, 64–66
Belpré, Pura Teresa, 9–10, 13, 14, 69–70, 102, 120, 121, 140; biography, 74–84; *Dance of the Animals,* 101; "Iviahoca," 100; *Juan Bobo and the Queen's Necklace,* 100; *Libros en Español,* 97; *Once in Puerto Rico,* 10, 91–92, 97–100; *Oté,* 100; *Perez and Martina,* 10, 84–91; *Puerto Rico in Children's Books,* 97; *The Rainbow-Colored Horse,* 101; *Santiago,* 100–101; and Arturo Schomburg, 55; *The Tiger and the Rabbit and Other Tales,* 10, 85, 91–96; "Yuisa and Pedro Mexias," 98–100
Betances, Ramón Emeterio, 20
Black Panther Party, 119
Blades, Rubén, 13, 170; *Amor y Control,* 182–87
Boricua: definition, 1; literary anthologies, 191n. 1
Brau, Salvador, 65
Bremen, Brian, 47–48
Brontë, Charlotte, 38
Burgos, Julia de, 14. *See also* Esteves, Sandra María

Cabral, Amilcar, 104
Cadilla Martínez, María, 99
Campeche, José, 65
Capetillo, Luis, 23–24
Capetillo, Luisa, 6, 7, 13, 14, 70, 71, 72, 78, 81, 84, 101, 102, 120, 132, 140, 143, 146, 166; biography, 21–25; *Ensayos libertarios,* 25–27; *La humanidad en el futuro,* 24; *Influencias de las ideas modernas,* 25, 34–40; *Mi opinión,* 27–31
Carrión, Tomás, 65–66
Casas, Bartolomé de las, 1
Casita María, 80
Césaire, Aimé, 104
Chacón, Iris, 162
Chernyshevsky, N. G., 33
Cintrón, Humberto, 134
Civil Rights Movement, 4, 10–11, 104–6; and the "Cold War," 104–5
Clifford, James, 62
COINTELPRO, 196–97n. 4
Colón, Hernando, 1
Colón, Jesús, 14, 21
Colón, Willie, 13; *Hecho en Puerto Rico,* 170, 177–83, 186
Committee on Civil Rights, 196n. 3

Cordero, Rafael, 65
Cortés, Hernán, 99
Cruz, Nicky, 134
Cruzada del Ideal, 32–33. *See also* Federación Libre de Trabajadores
"Culture of Poverty," 141, 197n. 3

Dabney, Wendell Phillips, 194n. 11
Deleuze, Gilles, 199n. 9
Deloria, Vine, 67, 138
Derkes, Eleuterio, 65
Derrida, Jacques, 49
diageotropism, 169, 198n. 6
Dickens, Charles, 38
Diderot, Denis, 33
Du Bois, W. E. B., 55, 62–64
Dunbar, Paul Lawrence, 55

Educational Alliance, 79
Escalante, Hildamar, 82
Espada, Martín, 14
Esteves, Sandra María, 14, 103; "A Julia de Burgos," 18

Fanon, Frantz, 104
Federación Libre de Trabajadores, 24, 30–33, 192n. 10
Figueroa, Sotero, 65–66
Flores, Juan, 18–20
Foucault, Michel, 44
Freud, Sigmund, 48

Gates, Henry Louis, Jr., 67
Gilroy, Paul, 168
Glissant, Eduoard, 6–7, 56
Gompers, Samuel, 32
González, Juan, 103
Gordils, Yanis, 18–20
Gordon, John Crosby, 58
Gould, Wallace, 193n. 3
Gramsci, Antonio, 35
Guattari, Félix, 199n. 9
Guerra, Juan Luis, 13; *Areito,* 170–77, 182, 183, 186
Guillén, Nicolás, 46
Guzmán, Pablo, 103, 118–19

Harlem Renaissance, 7–8, 40–41, 43, 56
Henna, Julio, 55
Henry Street Settlement, 79
Herrera, Sylvia, 139
Hostos, Eugenio María de, 20
Hugo, Victor, 24
Hurston, Zora Neale, 39

Iglesias, Santiago, 31, 192n. 10
Iglesias de Pagán, Igualdad, 192n. 9

Jameson, Fredric, 34, 48

Kim, Elaine, 16
Kincaid, Jamaica, 169
Kinsbruner, Jay, 191n. 2
Kropotkin, Peter, 24
Kutzinski, Vera, 46–47

Lacan, Jacques, 48
La Liga Puertorriqueña e Hispánica, 80
La Milagrosa, 79
Latimer, Catherine Allen, 62–64, 74–75
Latina feminism, 11, 135–41
Laviera, Tato, 14, 103; *La Carreta Made a U-Turn,* 18–20
Lawrence, D. H., 52
literary history, genres, and movements 4–6; anticolonialism, 104–5; autobiographical novel, 11–12, 107; *bildungsroman,* 105, 149, 154; canon formation, 4, 8, 16–21, 40, 68–69; modernism, 7–8, 40–41, 43–47, 56, 66–69; novel of emergence, 10, 106, 131–33; social realism, 106
Lomas, Clara, 16
Lowe, Lisa, 16

Maceo, Antonio, 59
Madison House, 79
Manrique, Manuel, 134
Marín, Gonzalo, 65
McKay, Claude, 55, 60
Memmi, Albert, 104
Mesa-Baines, Amalia, 139
Mill, John Stuart, 24
Mohr, Nicholasa, 10, 13, 19–20, 77, 103, 105–7, 137, 140, 143, 146, 158; *Nilda,* 120–33
Monteflores, Carmen de, 11, 134; *Cantando bajito/Singing Softly,* 141–49, 153, 154, 158–60
Morales, Iris, 103, 120–21, 127

Morrison, Toni, 16
Museo del Barrio, 72

New York Public Library (NYPL), 72, 76, 79, 97, 101; Aguilar branch, 79–80, 91; 135th Street branch, 9, 73–75, 79; Seward Park branch, 79. *See also* archives
Nuyorican: definition, 1; Nuyorican Renaissance, 103–5

Operation Bootstrap, 11, 107, 156
Ortega, Julio, 164–65, 183
Ortiz Cofer, Judith, 11, 134; *The Line of the Sun,* 141–42, 148–54, 156–60
Otero, Anita, 59

Pareja, Juan de, 59
Pérez, Emma, 137
Perón, Margarita, 23–24
Pietri, Pedro, 103; *Puerto Rican Obituary,* 135
Piñero, Miguel, 14, 103
Pound, Ezra, 52
publishers, industry, 11–12, 134–37; Arte Público Press, 135; Bilingual Press/Edición Bilingüe, 135; F. Warne, 195n. 3

Ramos, Julio, 22–23
Rhys, Jean, 87
Ridge, Lola, 54
Rivera, Edward, 134
Rivera, Oswald, 134
Rodó, José Enrique, 50
Rodríguez, Abraham, 134
Rodríguez de Tío, Lola, 35
Rose, Ernestine, 75

Saldívar, Ramón, 16
Sánchez, Luis Rafael, 161–66, 188
Sánchez, Marta, 197n. 7
Sánchez Korrol, Virginia, 17
Santiago, Esmeralda, 11, 134; *When I Was Puerto Rican,* 141–42, 153–60
Santiago, Soledad, 134
Saussure, Ferdinand de, 189
Schomburg, Arturo Alfonso, 7–8, 13, 21, 40–41, 55–67, 70, 72, 84, 101–2, 132, 166; biography, 42–46. *See also* archives
Shelter, the, 80
Silko, Leslie Marmon, 169

Sommer, Doris, 49
South Bronx Library Project, 97
Stein, Gertrude, 52

Tenepal, Malintzin, 99
Thomas, Piri, 10, 13, 103, 143; *Down These Mean Streets,* 105–19, 131–33; *Savior, Savior, Hold My Hand,* 118, 135; *Seven Long Times,* 118
Timothee, P. C., 65–66
Tolstoy, Leo, 24, 33, 39
Torres, Edwin, 134
Turgenev, I. S., 24

Unión Obrera, 34
Union Settlement, 79
United States: 1898 invasion, 1, 59–60, 192; Imperialism, 50–51; IRS article 936, 198n. 8; propaganda, 11, 197n. 5

Valle Ferrer, Norma, 192n. 5
Vega, Bernardo, 14, 21, 31, 192n. 3, 192n.10
Vega, Ed, 134
Vernet, Madeleine, 28
Viramontes, Helena María, 137
Volosinov, V. N., 199n. 9

Wallace, Michelle, 44
Wheatley, Phillis, 39
White, Clarence Cameron, 83–84
Whitman, Walt, 51, 82
Williams, Elena Hoheb, 42, 61–62, 193n. 2, 193–94n. 6
Williams, William Carlos, 7–8, 13, 40–41, 66–67, 70–72, 102–3; *Autobiography,* 42, 62; biography, 42–46, 54–55, 61–62; *The Great American Novel,* 40; *In the American Grain,* 46–55, 62, 67; *Paterson,* 47; *Yes, Mrs. Williams,* 42, 54–55, 62
Wright, Jay, 46

xanthagunephagia, 140

Young Lords Party, 118–20

Zavala, Iris, 47
Zeno Gandía, Manuel, 19–20, 31, 39
Zola, Émile, 24, 33, 38

About the Author

Lisa Sánchez González studied Classics and Comparative Literature at UCLA, where she received her Ph.D. in 1995. She has taught at universities in the United States, Puerto Rico, and Brazil. Her essays have appeared in a number of scholarly journals and anthologies, including *American Literary History, Cultural Studies, Recovering the U.S. Hispanic Literary History,* and *African Roots/American Cultures. Boricua Literature* is her first book.

Professor Sánchez González lives in Austin, where she teaches American and world literature at the University of Texas.